Family Circle®

ANNUAL
recipes
2008

Walnut Brownies page 26
Cocoa-Oatmeal Jumbos page 27

Meredith® Books
Des Moines, Iowa

Chocolate-Cherry Loaf
(Recipe page 46)

WELCOME TO THE FIRST FAMILY CIRCLE®
ANNUAL RECIPES COOKBOOK!

This has been a very exciting year at Family Circle®, full of fresh ideas, inspiring stories and—of course—great food. And with everyone keeping a close watch on their budget—which means less eating out— we filled the book with delicious, affordable, easy-to-prepare meals.

But cooking for families and friends isn't just about putting food on the table. It's about being together around the table. And when done right, entertaining at home is often more fun and satisfying than dining at a restaurant. So no matter what you're looking for—a quick but impressive dinner, a wow-'em dessert or a sizzling grill-out menu— you're sure to find recipes that add just the right amount of flair to fit the occasion.

We know all too well that weeknight cooking can be the biggest challenge in the kitchen. (Who doesn't sometimes dread being asked the inevitable, "Mom, what's for dinner?") That's why we've focused on quick, simple and affordable ways to help you bring tasty and nutritious food to your table every night of the week. And if your household is anything like mine, variety is important—especially when you're feeding kids. With this book, you're sure to keep new dinner ideas flowing. In addition to plenty of kid-friendly dinner options, we feature seasonal entrées, so dinner stays fresh and exciting all year long.

Gathering around the dinner table with family and friends is a time to catch up, build connections, laugh and enjoy life. So let's get cooking!

Linda

Linda Fears, Editor in Chief
Family Circle® magazine

Family Circle® Annual Recipes 2008

Editor: Jan Miller
Contributing Editors: Annie Krumhardt, Shelli McConnell
Contributing Designer: Jill Budden
Editorial Assistant: Sheri Cord
Book Production Manager: Mark Weaver
Imaging Center Operator: Tony Jungweber
Contributing Proofreaders: Jeanette Astor, Brenna Eldeen, Judy Friedman
Contributing Indexer: Elizabeth T. Parsons

Meredith® Books

Editorial Director: John Riha
Managing Editor: Kathleen Armentrout
Executive Editor: Jennifer Darling
Group Editor: Jan Miller
Copy Chief: Doug Kouma
Senior Copy Editors: Kevin Cox, Jennifer Speer Ramundt, Elizabeth Keest Sedrel
Assistant Copy Editor: Metta Cederdahl

Executive Director, Sales: Ken Zagor
Director, Operations: George A. Susral
Director, Production: Douglas M. Johnston
Business Director: Janice Croat

Vice President and General Manager, SIP: Jeff Myers

Family Circle® Magazine

Editor in Chief: Linda Fears
Creative Director: Karmen Lizzul
Food Director: Regina Ragone
Senior Food Editor: Julie Miltenberger
Associate Food Editor: Michael Tyrrell
Assistant Food Editor: Cindy Heller
Editorial Assistant: Katie Kemple
Test Kitchen Associate: Althea Needham

Meredith Publishing Group

President: Jack Griffin
Executive Vice President: Doug Olson
Vice President, Manufacturing: Bruce Heston
Vice President, Consumer Marketing: David Ball
Vice President, Corporate Sales: Michael Brownstein
Consumer Product Marketing Director: Steve Swanson
Consumer Product Marketing Manager: Wendy Merical
Business Manager: Darren Tollefson

Meredith Corporation

Chairman of the Board: William T. Kerr
President and Chief Executive Officer: Stephen M. Lacy

In Memoriam: E.T. Meredith III (1933–2003)

Pictured on the front cover:
Double Chocolate Cake
(recipe page 24)
Photography by James Baigrie

Copyright © 2008 by
Meredith Corporation.
Des Moines, Iowa.
First Edition.
Printed in the United States of America.
ISSN: 1942-7646
ISBN: 978-0-696-24188-8

All of us at Meredith® Books are
dedicated to providing you with
information and ideas to enhance your
home. We welcome your comments and
suggestions. Write to us at: Meredith
Special Interest Media, 1716 Locust St.,
Des Moines, IA 50309-3023.

DINNER IS SERVED! After a busy day, there's nothing like a fresh, flavorful, home-cooked meal enjoyed at your own table. With this collection of *Family Circle* recipes from 2008, we've made it easier than ever to serve up delicious food you cook yourself—whether it's for a quick weeknight dinner or for a special evening with friends. You'll see the recipes are organized month-by-month, so it's simple to find the perfect dish for any occasion. In addition to hundreds of healthful, great-tasting recipes, you'll find dozens of helpful how-to photographs and tips throughout the book. Plus, be sure to check out Reader Recipes, starting on page 312, for a collection of our favorite recipes submitted to us from readers like you.

Along with feature food stories from *Family Circle* in 2008, look for these regular installments:

▸ Healthy Family Dinners Look here to find a week's worth of easy-to-make, family-friendly meals.

▸ Quick and Easy Here are no-fuss recipes featuring a specific ingredient or cooking method.

▸ Slow-Cooker Solutions Learn to use your slow-cooker to make effortless meals (and even desserts!).

▸ Cooking School Expand your cooking repertoire using step-by-step instructions to classic dishes.

Chipotle Mini Burgers
page 145

Whipped-Potato Casserole
page 282

contents

Sparkling Sangria page 195

Ratatouille page 38

Shrimp Stir-Fry page 17

Classic Apple Pie page 227

Vanilla Pots de Crème page 65

Salad Pizza page 87

Grilled Pork Chops and Peach-Plum Salsa page 207

january

Chicken and Corn Chili
(Recipe page 14)

WHEN THERE'S A CHILL IN THE AIR,
WARM UP WITH THESE FAMILY-FRIENDLY
FAVORITES—FROM GOOD-FOR-YOU
ENTRÉES TO MOUTHWATERING
CINNAMON BUNS.

Classic Cinnamon Buns
page 11

Plum-Glazed Pork Loin
page 17

Chicken Cordon Bleu
page 19

EVERYONE WILL LOVE THESE EASY, SCRUMPTIOUS TREATS.
BY KAREN TACK

classic cinnamon buns

MAKES: 14 buns. **PREP:** 20 minutes. **RISE:** 2¼ hours. **BAKE:** at 350° for 40 minutes.

1 **cup whole milk**
1 **envelope (¼ ounce) active dry yeast**
¼ **cup warm water (100° to 110°)**
3 **tablespoons granulated sugar**
2 **eggs**
¼ **cup (½ stick) unsalted butter, melted**
4½ **to 5 cups all-purpose flour**
½ **teaspoon salt**
Filling:
½ **cup (1 stick) unsalted butter, softened**
¼ **cup granulated sugar**
1 **cup packed light brown sugar**
1 **tablespoon cinnamon**
1 **cup coarsely chopped pecans**
1 **cup raisins**
Glaze:
2 **cups confectioners' sugar**
1 **to 3 tablespoons milk**

1. Heat the milk in a small saucepan over medium heat until it just begins to boil. Remove from heat and let stand until cooled to room temperature.
2. Meanwhile, sprinkle the yeast over the warm water in a large bowl. Add 1 tablespoon of the sugar and let stand until foamy, about 5 minutes. Beat in the remaining 2 tablespoons sugar, eggs and butter. Beat in cooled milk.
3. Gradually add the flour and salt, scraping down side of bowl, until a soft dough forms. Turn dough onto a floured work surface and knead the remaining flour into the dough, adding more flour if too sticky. Knead for about 10 minutes until smooth. The dough will be soft.
4. Grease a large bowl. Place the dough in the bowl. Cover with plastic wrap and place in a warm spot until doubled in size, about 1½ hours.
5. Coat two 9-inch round baking pans with nonstick cooking spray. Line bottoms with waxed paper; coat paper with spray. Prepare **Filling:** Mix butter, both kinds of sugar and cinnamon together in a medium-size bowl.

6. Punch down dough. Roll out dough on a lightly floured surface to an 18 x 12-inch rectangle. Spread the butter-sugar mixture over the dough. Sprinkle with nuts and raisins. Starting on one long side, roll up jelly roll fashion and pinch seam to close.
7. Cut crosswise into 14 generous 1-inch pieces. Arrange 7 pieces, cut-side down, in each prepared pan. Cover with plastic wrap and let sit in a warm spot until buns double in size, about 30 to 45 minutes. Or cover tightly with plastic wrap and refrigerate until the following morning.
8. Heat oven to 350°. Uncover pans and bake buns until they are golden-brown and bubbly, 30 to 40 minutes. Transfer to a wire rack and let cool 10 minutes.
9. Prepare **Glaze:** Mix confectioners' sugar and 1 tablespoon of the milk, adding more milk as necessary, to make a smooth glaze. Invert buns to a serving platter. Drizzle glaze on top of buns (about ⅓ cup per pan). Serve warm.

PER BUN: 496 calories; 18 g fat (7 g sat.); 7 g protein; 79 g carbohydrate; 3 g fiber; 114 mg sodium; 60 mg cholesterol.

PHOTOGRAPHY BY RITA MAAS

slim-down SUPPERS

SLOW COOKERS ARE TIME-SAVING SUPERSTARS—
AND EASY WAYS TO CUT FAT AND CALORIES. THESE
SIX MEALS WILL PUT YOUR FAMILY ON THE FAST
TRACK TO GOOD NUTRITION. **BY CINDY HELLER**

This veggie-
packed dish is a
great source of
vitamins A and C.
(Recipe page 17)

PHOTOGRAPHY BY JAMES BAIGRIE

Fruit and spices infuse this roast with plenty of flavor while keeping the meat moist and tender. (Recipe page 17)

This filling, low-cal chili is the perfect antidote to overindulgent holiday eating.

turkey lasagna

MAKES: 8 servings. **PREP:** 10 minutes.
COOK: 10 minutes. **SLOW-COOK:** 4 hours on HIGH; 5 hours on LOW.

- 1 medium-size onion, chopped
- 2 cloves garlic, minced
- 1¼ pounds ground turkey
- 1 teaspoon dried oregano
- ½ teaspoon salt
- ¼ teaspoon black pepper
- 1 container (15 ounces) low-fat ricotta
- 1 cup Italian-blend shredded cheese
- 12 lasagna noodles (12 ounces) broken in half
- 1 package (10 ounces) frozen chopped broccoli, thawed and squeezed dry
- 1 jar (26 ounces) chunky tomato sauce

1. In a large nonstick skillet, cook onions and garlic over medium-high heat for 4 minutes or until softened. Add turkey to skillet and cook, breaking up large chunks, for about 6 minutes or until no longer pink; drain fat. Season turkey with oregano, salt and pepper. Set aside.
2. In a small bowl, combine ricotta and ½ cup of the Italian shredded cheese.
3. In a 5- to 6-quart slow cooker, layer half the uncooked noodles, overlapping as necessary. Spread half of both the meat mixture and broccoli over noodles, then top with about half of the tomato sauce and **¼ cup water.** Gently spread ricotta mixture on top, and continue layering with remaining noodles, meat, broccoli, sauce and an additional **¼ cup water.**
4. Cover and cook on HIGH for 4 hours or LOW for 5 hours. Sprinkle remaining ½ cup of Italian cheese on top for last 15 minutes of cooking or until melted.

PER SERVING: 333 calories; 14 g fat (6 g sat.);
27 g protein; 24 g carbohydrate; 3 g fiber;
826 mg sodium; 85 mg cholesterol.

chicken and corn chili

MAKES: 6 servings. **PREP:** 10 minutes.
SLOW-COOK: 4 hours on HIGH; 6 hours on LOW.

- 1 large onion, chopped
- 1 pound boneless, skinless chicken breasts
- 2 cups low-sodium chicken broth
- 1 green pepper, seeded and chopped
- 1 jalapeño chile, seeded and chopped
- 1¾ teaspoons ground cumin
- ½ teaspoon cayenne pepper
- ¾ teaspoon salt
- 1 can (14.5 ounces) diced tomatoes with jalapeños, drained
- 1½ cups frozen corn, thawed
- 2 cans (15 ounces each) cannellini beans, drained and rinsed
- 2 tablespoons stone-ground cornmeal
  Shredded Monterey Jack cheese

1. In a 5- to 6-quart slow cooker, combine onion, chicken, low-sodium broth, green pepper, jalapeño, 1½ teaspoons of the cumin, ¼ teaspoon of the cayenne and ¼ teaspoon of the salt. Cover and cook on HIGH for 4 hours or LOW for 6 hours.
2. Remove the chicken to a cutting board and allow to cool slightly. Shred the chicken and return it to the slow cooker with remaining ¼ teaspoon *each* of the cumin and cayenne, and the tomatoes, corn and beans. Gently mash some of the beans against the side of the bowl to thicken the chili. Stir in the cornmeal and the remaining ½ teaspoon salt. Let sit a few minutes to soften the cornmeal. Serve sprinkled with a little of the Monterey Jack cheese.

PER SERVING: 287 calories; 3 g fat (1 g sat.);
27 g protein; 38 g carbohydrate; 9 g fiber;
736 mg sodium; 45 mg cholesterol.

Go ahead, it's okay to count tomato sauce as a serving of veggies.

Pairing whole-grain buns with peppers and onions boosts the fiber on these heros.

sausage and peppers

MAKES: 6 servings. **PREP:** 10 minutes.
SLOW-COOK: 3 hours on HIGH; 6 hours on LOW. **COOK:** 1 minute. **BROIL:** 2 minutes.

- 4 large sweet peppers of assorted colors, seeded and sliced
- 1 large onion, cut into wedges
- 1 package (20 ounces) hot or sweet Italian turkey sausages
- ¼ cup red wine vinegar
- ½ teaspoon dried thyme
- ½ teaspoon black pepper
- 1½ tablespoons cornstarch mixed with 2 tablespoons water
- 1 tablespoon grainy mustard
- 6 multigrain submarine or hoagie rolls (about 3 ounces each)

1. Combine peppers, onion, sausages, vinegar, thyme and black pepper in a 5- to 6-quart slow cooker.

2. Cook on HIGH for 3 hours or LOW for 6 hours. Use a slotted spoon to remove peppers and sausages from slow cooker; set aside and keep warm.

3. Heat broiler. Pour liquid from slow cooker into a small saucepan. Whisk in cornstarch mixture and mustard. Bring to a boil; boil 1 minute or until thickened.

4. Meanwhile, slice rolls almost all the way through lengthwise. Place on a baking sheet, cut-side up, on top rack under broiler for 1 to 2 minutes or until toasted. Cut sausages diagonally into ½-inch-thick slices and stir back into pepper mixture. Place a scant 1 cup sausage mixture on each roll. Drizzle each sandwich with a generous 2 tablespoons sauce, reserving remaining sauce for dipping. Serve immediately.

PER SERVING: 470 calories; 15 g fat (6 g sat.); 28 g protein; 55 g carbohydrate; 6 g fiber; 1,063 mg sodium; 56 mg cholesterol.

This Asian-accented salmon is a simple way to add beneficial omega-3s to your diet.

easy salmon and bok choy

MAKES: 4 servings. **PREP:** 10 minutes.
SLOW-COOK: 1 hour on HIGH; 2 hours on LOW.

- 1½ pounds salmon, patted dry
- 3 tablespoons minced fresh ginger
- 2 cloves garlic, minced
- ½ cup low-sodium chicken broth
- 3 tablespoons rice vinegar
- 2 tablespoons sugar
- 2 tablespoons low-sodium soy sauce
- 1 medium-size head bok choy, trimmed and cut into 1-inch pieces, stems and leaves separated (4 cups each)
- 1 teaspoon hoisin sauce
- ¼ cup thinly sliced scallions

1. Coat a 5- to 6-quart slow-cooker bowl with nonstick cooking spray and arrange salmon in it, tucking the thin end of fillets underneath. Sprinkle ginger and garlic over salmon.
2. In a medium-size saucepan, bring broth, vinegar, sugar and soy sauce to a boil over high heat. Pour liquid around salmon, not over, and cook on HIGH for 1 hour or LOW for 2 hours.
3. Stir the bok choy stems into slow cooker for last 30 minutes of cooking time on HIGH or the last hour of cooking time on LOW. Add leaves to the slow cooker for final 10 minutes of cooking time on HIGH or final 30 minutes of cooking time on LOW.*
4. Carefully remove salmon from slow cooker with a wide spatula; set aside and keep warm. Stir hoisin into liquid. Sprinkle salmon with scallions and serve with bok choy and liquid.
***Note:** While this dish can be cooked on HIGH, the color will be more vibrant and the flavor more delicate if cooked on LOW.

PER SERVING: 312 calories; 12 g fat (2 g sat.); 38 g protein; 14 g carbohydrate; 3 g fiber; 515 mg sodium; 94 mg cholesterol.

plum-glazed pork loin

MAKES: 4 servings. **PREP:** 15 minutes.
SLOW-COOK: 4 hours on HIGH; 6 hours on LOW. **COOK:** 1 minute.

- 3 ripe red plums, pitted and coarsely chopped
- ¼ cup golden raisins
- 2 teaspoons minced fresh ginger
- 1 small onion, chopped
- ⅓ cup sugar
- 2 tablespoons cider vinegar
- ¼ teaspoon cinnamon
- ¼ teaspoon curry powder
- ½ teaspoon salt
- ½ teaspoon black pepper
- 1 boneless pork loin roast (about 2¼ pounds), trimmed
- ¾ pound green beans, trimmed
- 1 teaspoon Dijon mustard
- 1 tablespoon cornstarch mixed with 1 tablespoon water

1. In a 5- to 6-quart slow cooker, combine plums, raisins, ginger, onion, sugar, vinegar, cinnamon, curry powder and ¼ teaspoon *each* of the salt and pepper. Stir until evenly distributed.
2. Sprinkle pork with remaining ¼ teaspoon *each* salt and pepper and place it into the plum mixture in the slow cooker. Cook for 4 hours on HIGH or 6 hours on LOW.
3. Stir in green beans for last 25 minutes of cook time on HIGH or last hour of cook time on LOW. Remove pork and green beans from slow cooker. Pour sauce into a saucepan; stir in mustard. Over high heat (on stovetop), whisk in cornstarch mixture; cook for 1 minute or until thickened. Slice pork and drizzle with plum sauce.

PER SERVING: 534 calories; 15 g fat (5 g sat.); 57 g protein; 42 g carbohydrate; 5 g fiber; 463 mg sodium; 151 mg cholesterol.

shrimp stir-fry

MAKES: 6 servings. **PREP:** 10 minutes.
SLOW-COOK: 1¾ hours on HIGH; 3½ hours on LOW.

- 1 pound carrots, peeled and cut diagonally into ½-inch slices
- 1 medium-size sweet red pepper, seeded and cut into ½-inch slices
- ¾ cup low-sodium chicken broth
- ¼ cup low-sodium teriyaki sauce
- 2 tablespoons cornstarch
- 1 tablespoon oyster sauce
- 2 teaspoons sugar
- 1 pound shrimp, peeled and deveined
- 8 ounces snow peas, trimmed
- 1 can (8 ounces) bamboo shoots Sliced scallions (optional)
- 3 cups cooked brown rice

1. Place carrots and red pepper slices in a 5- to 6-quart slow cooker. In a small bowl, blend broth, teriyaki, cornstarch, oyster sauce and sugar. Pour into slow cooker and cook on HIGH for 1¾ hours or LOW for 3½ hours.
2. Stir shrimp, snow peas and bamboo shoots (drained) into the slow cooker for the final 20 minutes of cook time. Sprinkle with scallions and serve with brown rice.

PER SERVING: 277 calories; 3 g fat (1 g sat.); 21 g protein; 42 g carbohydrate; 6 g fiber; 349 mg sodium; 115 mg cholesterol.

cooking **school**

THIS CLASSIC STUFFED CHICKEN DISH IS SURE PLEASE EVERYONE AT YOUR FAMILY'S TABLE. FOLLOW OUR STEP-BY-STEP INSTRUCTIONS FOR DELECTABLE CHICKEN CORDON BLEU. **BY JULIE MILTENBERGER**

Keep your eye on the chicken while cooking—reduce heat if browning too quickly.

chicken cordon bleu

MAKES: 4 servings. **PREP:** 20 minutes. **COOK:** 6 minutes. **BAKE:** at 350° for 15 minutes.

- 4 boneless, skinless chicken breast halves (about 1½ pounds total)
- 4 slices thinly sliced Black Forest ham
- 1 cup shredded Gruyère or Swiss cheese (3 to 4 ounces)
- 8 teaspoons Dijon or honey mustard
- ¼ cup all-purpose flour
- 2 large eggs, lightly beaten
- 1 cup seasoned dry bread crumbs
- ¼ cup vegetable oil

1. Heat oven to 350°. Place one breast half between two sheets of waxed paper on a cutting board. Pound to an even thickness of ¼ inch with the flat side of a meat mallet, a rolling pin or cast iron pan **(photo 1).** Repeat with remaining chicken breasts.

2. Spread out one piece of ham; pile ¼ cup of the cheese in the middle, then tightly fold up burrito-style to enclose **(photo 2).** Spread one pounded chicken breast with 2 teaspoons of mustard. Place ham bundle on chicken; slide to one narrow end. Roll chicken breast, enclosing bundle **(photo 3).**

Secure with a toothpick or two; tuck in any loose ends. Repeat for a total of four stuffed chicken breasts.

3. Spread flour onto a dinner plate, and pour eggs into a pie dish and bread crumbs onto a second dinner plate. Coat one stuffed breast with flour, dip in egg completely **(photo 4),** then coat with bread crumbs, adhering with fingers if needed. Repeat with all chicken pieces.

4. Heat oil in a 12-inch skillet with a tight-fitting lid over medium-high heat. Add chicken pieces and brown, covered, 3 minutes. Flip chicken over, and continue to cook, covered, an additional 2 to 3 minutes. Transfer to a shallow baking dish and bake at 350° for 12 to 15 minutes or until temperature registers 160° on an instant-read thermometer.

PER SERVING: 515 calories; 22 g fat (7 g sat.); 57 g protein; 20 g carbohydrate; 1 g fiber; 1,165 mg sodium; 241 mg cholesterol.

Pound chicken with a smooth mallet or rolling pin to an even thickness.

Place ¼ cup of the cheese in the middle of one ham slice. Fold up like a burrito.

Spread mustard on chicken, add cheese-ham bundle, and roll tightly to enclose.

Once chicken is secured with toothpicks and coated with flour, dip in egg to coat.

Food styling: Toni Brogan. Prop styling: Lynda White.

february

Tropical Tart
(Recipe page 24)

AS THE COOL TEMPERATURES OF WINTER
LINGER, COZY UP TO SIMPLE, HEALTHY
MAIN DISHES AND TREAT-YOURSELF
CHOCOLATE DESSERTS.

chocolate heaven

FROM DEVILISH TO DIVINE, THE MOST IRRESISTIBLE VERSIONS OF OUR BEST-LOVED SWEET TREATS.

BY JULIE MILTENBERGER

Our brownies are loaded with walnuts and our jumbo cookies are chock-full of raisins and oats. (Recipes pages 26 and 27)

PHOTOGRAPHY BY JAMES BAIGRIE

A double hit of chocolate—
in the layers and in the
frosting—makes this cake
a truly decadent dessert.
(Recipe page 24)

Food styling: Sara Neumeier. Prop styling: Loren Simons.

double chocolate cake

MAKES: 16 servings. **PREP:** 30 minutes.
MICROWAVE: 2 minutes, 45 seconds.
BAKE: at 350° for 35 minutes.

Cake:

4 ounces bittersweet chocolate
1 teaspoon vegetable oil
2¼ cups all-purpose flour
½ cup unsweetened cocoa powder
1½ teaspoons baking soda
½ teaspoon salt
¾ cup (1½ sticks) unsalted butter, softened
1½ cups sugar
4 eggs
2 teaspoons vanilla extract
2 tablespoons white vinegar
1⅓ cups milk

Frosting:

1 bag (12 ounces) white chocolate chips
1 container (8 ounces) sour cream
½ cup (1 stick) unsalted butter, softened
3 cups confectioners' sugar
Chocolate curls, to garnish (optional)

1. Prepare **Cake:** Coat two 9 x 2-inch round baking pans with nonstick cooking spray. Line bottoms with waxed paper; spray paper.
2. Break up chocolate into a small microwave-safe bowl; add oil. Microwave on HIGH power for 1 minute; stir until smooth. Cool slightly.
3. In medium-size bowl, mix flour, cocoa, baking soda and salt. In large bowl, with mixer on medium speed, beat butter and sugar until fluffy, about 3 minutes. Add eggs, one at a time, beating after each. Beat in chocolate mixture and vanilla.
4. Place vinegar in a 2-cup capacity measuring cup. Add milk and stir until blended. On low speed, beat flour mixture into butter mixture, alternating with milk, beginning and ending with flour; beat 1 minute. Spread into pans.
5. Bake at 350° for 35 minutes or until toothpick inserted in centers tests clean. Cool cakes in pans on wire racks 15 minutes. Turn cakes out onto racks; cool layers completely (about 2 hours).
6. Prepare **Frosting:** In large glass bowl, microwave white chocolate on 50% power for 1 minute; stir. Microwave another 30 seconds until melted and smooth. Let cool slightly.
7. With mixer, beat in sour cream and butter until smooth. Refrigerate

10 minutes. On low speed, beat in sugar until blended; continue to beat until fluffy. If too soft, refrigerate 10 minutes. Spread 1 cup frosting on top of one layer. Stack with second cake layer. Spread thin coating of frosting around side of cake. Refrigerate or freeze 15 minutes, until firm. Frost side and top with remaining frosting; garnish with curls, if desired. Refrigerate until set, 20 minutes.

PER SERVING: 567 calories; 30 g fat (18 g sat.); 7 g protein; 71 g carbohydrate; 2 g fiber; 251 mg sodium; 107 mg cholesterol.

tropical tart

MAKES: 16 servings. **PREP:** 25 minutes.
MICROWAVE: 45 seconds. **COOK:** 3 minutes.
REFRIGERATE: 1½ hours.

Crust:

1 bag (7.25 ounces; 24 cookies) square chocolate cookies (such as Pepperidge Farms Chessmen)
6 tablespoons unsalted butter, melted
1 tablespoon sugar

Filling:

⅔ cup dried pineapple, chopped
⅓ cup coconut-flavored rum (such as Malibu) or pineapple juice
¾ cup heavy cream
1 cup (6 ounces) semisweet chocolate chips
½ cup macadamia nuts, chopped
½ cup plus 2 tablespoons sweetened flake coconut
1 envelope (from a 2.6-ounce package) powdered dairy topping mix
½ cup milk
1 teaspoon vanilla extract

1. Prepare **Crust:** Set aside one cookie. In food processor, crush remaining cookies until crumbs are even in size. Add butter and sugar; pulse to blend. Press into a 9-inch tart pan. Refrigerate while making filling.
2. Prepare **Filling:** Combine pineapple and rum or juice in a small microwave-safe bowl. Microwave on HIGH power for 45 seconds. Let stand 5 minutes.
3. Meanwhile, heat cream in a small saucepan over medium-high heat just until bubbly around the edges, about 3 minutes. Place chocolate in a bowl and pour hot cream over chocolate. Let stand 1 minute, then stir or whisk until smooth.
4. Drain pineapple (discarding liquid) and stir into chocolate mixture, along with nuts and ½ cup of the coconut. Spread into crust. Refrigerate 1½ hours.
5. Combine topping mix, milk and vanilla in a medium-size bowl. Beat on low speed until blended, then on high for 4 minutes. Spread over chocolate mixture. Toast remaining 2 tablespoons coconut; sprinkle over tart. Crush remaining cookie; sprinkle over coconut and serve.

PER SERVING: 275 calories; 19 g fat (10 g sat.); 2 g protein; 26 g carbohydrate; 2 g fiber; 72 mg sodium; 37 mg cholesterol.

bittersweet chocolate pudding

MAKES: 6 servings. **PREP:** 5 minutes.
COOK: 12 minutes.
REFRIGERATE: at least 2 hours.

- ¾ cup sugar
- ¼ cup cornstarch
- 2 tablespoons unsweetened cocoa powder (plus more for dusting)
  Pinch ground nutmeg
- 3½ cups milk
- 4 ounces bittersweet chocolate, chopped
- 1 teaspoon vanilla extract
  Whipped cream or whipped topping, for serving (optional)

1. In a medium-size heavy-bottomed saucepan, whisk together the sugar, cornstarch, cocoa powder and nutmeg. Gradually add milk, whisking constantly to keep mixture from getting lumpy.
2. Transfer saucepan to stovetop, and heat over medium heat, stirring constantly with a wooden spoon. Bring to a boil (about 10 minutes), then boil 2 minutes.
3. Remove from heat and add chopped chocolate. Stir until all pieces are melted. Stir in vanilla. Strain into a large bowl, then either cover surface with plastic wrap or divide into individual cups and cover. Refrigerate until cold, about 2 hours. Serve with whipped cream or whipped topping, dusted with cocoa, if desired.

PER SERVING: 328 calories; 12 g fat (8 g sat.); 6 g protein; 49 g carbohydrate; 2 g fiber; 72 mg sodium; 20 mg cholesterol.

Try Dutch-processed cocoa in this pudding; it will give a richer, more luxurious flavor.

No peeking! If you open the oven while the meringues are baking, they may collapse.

cocoa meringues

MAKES: about 42 cookies.
PREP: 20 minutes.
BAKE: at 250° for 1 hour, 15 minutes.
MICROWAVE: 1 minute.

- ⅔ cup sugar
- 3 tablespoons unsweetened cocoa powder
  Pinch ground cinnamon
- 4 egg whites, at room temperature
- ¼ teaspoon cream of tartar
- 2 squares (1 ounce each) semisweet chocolate, chopped

1. Heat oven to 250°. Line two large baking sheets with nonstick foil.
2. In a small bowl, whisk together the sugar, cocoa powder and ground cinnamon. Place egg whites into the bowl of a standing mixer, or a large bowl. Add the cream of tartar.
3. Begin beating egg whites on low speed, using the whip attachment, until foamy. Increase the speed to medium, and add sugar mixture, one tablespoon at a time, until medium-stiff peaks form.
4. Transfer mixture to a large pastry bag fitted with a large star tip (go to confectioneryhouse.com to purchase). Pipe onto prepared baking sheets. Bake at 250° for 1 hour, 15 minutes—do not open oven door or meringues may collapse. Turn off oven; let meringues sit in oven at least ½ hour, then remove baking sheets from oven. Carefully remove cookies directly to cooling racks. Cool completely.
5. Place semisweet chocolate in a small microwave-safe bowl. Microwave 1 minute, then stir until smooth. Transfer to a small plastic bag. Snip off a corner. Transfer meringues to a sheet of waxed paper. Drizzle with melted chocolate. Let dry completely. Store in airtight container at room temperature.

PER MERINGUE: 20 calories; 0 g fat (0 g sat.); 0 g protein; 4 g carbohydrate; 0 g fiber; 5 mg sodium; 0 mg cholesterol.

walnut brownies

MAKES: 16 brownies.
PREP: 10 minutes. **COOK:** 4 minutes.
BAKE: at 350° for 35 minutes.

- 4 ounces unsweetened chocolate, chopped
- ½ cup (1 stick) unsalted butter
- 1½ cups sugar
- 1 cup walnuts, chopped
- ½ teaspoon salt
- 4 eggs
- ¾ cup mini semisweet chocolate chips
- 1 cup all-purpose flour
- 2 teaspoons vanilla extract
  Confectioners' sugar, for dusting

1. Heat oven to 350°. Line a 13 x 9 x 2-inch baking pan with nonstick foil.
2. Combine chocolate and butter in a medium-size saucepan. Heat over medium heat, stirring, until chocolate is melted and mixture is smooth, about 4 minutes. Let cool slightly.
3. Stir in sugar, walnuts and salt. Stir in eggs, one at a time. Stir in ½ cup of the mini chips, the flour and the vanilla. Pour into prepared pan. Sprinkle top with the remaining ¼ cup mini chips.
4. Bake at 350° for 35 minutes or until brownie is dry on top. Cool in pan on wire rack for 10 minutes, then use foil to lift brownie from pan. Cool, then dust with confectioners' sugar, if desired.

PER BROWNIE: 299 calories; 18 g fat (8 g sat.); 4 g protein; 33 g carbohydrate; 2 g fiber; 91 mg sodium; 69 mg cholesterol.

cocoa-oatmeal jumbos

MAKES: 16 to 20 jumbo cookies.
PREP: 20 minutes.
BAKE: at 350° for 17 minutes.

- ¾ cup all-purpose flour
- ½ cup cocoa powder
- 1 teaspoon baking soda
- ½ teaspoon salt
- 2 sticks (1 cup) unsalted butter, softened
- ¾ cup packed light-brown sugar
- ¾ cup granulated sugar
- 2 eggs
- 1 teaspoon vanilla extract
- 2¼ cups old-fashioned oats
- 1 cup raisins
- 1 cup semisweet chocolate chips

1. Heat oven to 350°. Have two large nonstick baking sheets ready.
2. Combine flour, cocoa, baking soda and salt in a bowl. In a large bowl, beat butter and both kinds of sugar until creamy, about 3 minutes. Beat in eggs and vanilla. On low speed, beat in flour mixture, then stir in oats, raisins and chocolate chips.
3. Dollop ¼-cupfuls of batter onto baking sheets. Bake cookies at 350° for 17 minutes. Let cool on baking sheets for 5 minutes, then transfer cookies to wire racks to cool completely.

PER COOKIE: 296 calories; 15 g fat (9 g sat.); 4 g protein; 42 g carbohydrate; 3 g fiber; 151 mg sodium; 51 mg cholesterol.

health benefits
THE FLAVANOL FACTOR

▶ Chocolate's natural flavanols help keep the blood vessels smooth and pliable, and naturally thin the blood, making it less likely to clot.
▶ Preliminary studies show that cocoa flavanols can help blood flow throughout the body, resulting in improved skin quality and even a boost in your brain power.

▶ You don't need to overindulge. In a recent study published in the *Journal of the American Medical Association,* eating about 30 calories a day—that's less than half an ounce of dark chocolate (try one square of Dove dark chocolate)—was associated with a lowering of blood pressure without weight gain or other adverse effects.

chicken dinners
WITH A TWIST

Scarpiella, cooked with peppers, onions and potatoes, is a lean one-dish supper. (Recipe page 35)

FROM BUFFALO-STYLE PIZZA TO APPLE CIDER DRUMSTICKS, THESE INSPIRED DISHES ARE SURE TO BECOME FAMILY FAVORITES.
BY MICHAEL TYRRELL

We use chicken thighs in our Caribbean curry; they're moist and flavorful—not to mention inexpensive. (Recipe page 35)

PHOTOGRAPHY BY ALISON MIKSCH

Is it done? Insert a thermometer in the thickest part of the thigh (away from bone) to make sure.

roast chicken and barley pilaf

MAKES: 4 servings. **PREP:** 20 minutes. **ROAST:** at 450° for 60 minutes. **COOK:** 25 minutes.

Chicken:
- 1 whole chicken, skin on, about 3½ to 4 pounds
- ¼ teaspoon salt
- ¼ teaspoon black pepper
- 4 cloves garlic, peeled and sliced
- 12 sprigs fresh herbs, such as rosemary, sage, and/or oregano
- 1 cup chicken broth

Barley Pilaf:
- 1 tablespoon olive oil
- ½ cup diced onion (about ½ medium onion)
- ½ cup diced carrot (about 1 large carrot)
- 4 ounces mixed sliced mushrooms
- 2 cups chicken broth
- 1 cup barley
- ¼ teaspoon salt
- ¼ teaspoon pepper
- ¼ teaspoon ground nutmeg

1. Roast Chicken: Heat oven to 450°.
2. Gently lift skin from breasts and legs and season with the salt and pepper. Place some of the garlic slices and fresh herbs under the skin. Place remaining garlic and herbs in the cavity of the chicken.
3. Place chicken on a rack in a large roasting pan. Pour the chicken broth into the bottom of the pan. Roast for 50 to 60 minutes or until the internal temperature reaches 170° on an instant-read thermometer. Tent with foil halfway through cooking.

4. Make **Barley Pilaf:** Meanwhile, in a medium-size saucepan, heat oil over medium-high heat. Add onion, carrot and mushrooms and cook, stirring occasionally for 5 minutes. Add broth, barley, salt, pepper and nutmeg. Reduce heat to medium, cover and simmer for 15 to 20 minutes or until tender, stirring occasionally. Add a few tablespoons water if mixture becomes too dry.
5. Allow chicken to rest 10 minutes. Remove skin, slice and serve with pilaf.

PER SERVING: 497 calories; 18 g fat (4 g sat.); 48 g protein; 36 g carbohydrate; 5 g fiber; 925 mg sodium; 128 mg cholesterol.

chicken scaloppine marsala

MAKES: 4 servings. **PREP:** 20 minutes.
COOK: 20 minutes.

Potatoes:
- 1½ pounds yukon gold potatoes, scrubbed and cut into 1½-inch pieces
- 1 cup chicken broth
- ½ teaspoon salt
- ⅛ teaspoon black pepper
  Pinch ground nutmeg and cayenne
- 1 tablespoon chopped parsley

Chicken:
- 1¼ pounds chicken cutlets
- ⅛ teaspoon salt
- ⅛ teaspoon black pepper
- 1 cup beef broth
- 1 tablespoon all-purpose flour
- ½ cup marsala wine
- 1 can (4 ounces) sliced mushrooms, drained
- 2 tablespoons unsalted butter
- 1 tablespoon chopped parsley

1. Prepare **Potatoes:** Place potatoes in a medium-size pot and cover with lightly salted cold water. Bring to a boil. Lower heat to medium and simmer for 15 to 20 minutes until fork tender.
2. Drain potatoes. Mash until desired consistency, gradually adding chicken broth. Stir in salt, pepper, nutmeg, cayenne and parsley.
3. Prepare **Chicken:** While potatoes are cooking, heat a nonstick skillet over medium-high heat. Spray with nonstick cooking spray. Season chicken with the salt and pepper. Cook for 2 minutes per side. Remove to a plate.
4. Let skillet cool slightly and wipe clean. Whisk together beef broth and flour. Add to skillet and bring to a simmer. Stir in marsala and drained mushrooms. Add chicken and any accumulated juices. Simmer gently, covered, for 15 minutes.
5. Turn off heat; whisk in butter. Sprinkle with parsley and serve with potatoes.

PER SERVING: 398 calories; 9 g fat (4 g sat.); 39 g protein; 34 g carbohydrate; 4 g fiber; 844 mg sodium; 99 mg cholesterol.

buffalo chicken pizza

MAKES: 12 slices. **PREP:** 10 minutes. **COOK:** 8 minutes. **BAKE:** at 450° for 10 minutes.

- 2 **pounds chicken tenders**
- ⅓ **cup Frank's hot sauce**
- ¼ **cup chicken broth**
- 2 **thin crust Boboli (10 ounces each)**
- ⅔ **cup reduced-fat blue cheese dressing (such as Wishbone Light)**
- 1 **cup shredded part-skim mozzarella**
- 4 **celery ribs, cut into 2-inch pieces**

1. Heat oven to 450°.
2. Place chicken in a large skillet; add cold water to cover. Cover; bring to a boil. Reduce heat to medium-low and simmer for 8 minutes or until internal temperature of chicken reaches 160° on an instant-read thermometer. Remove from skillet; slice into strips.
3. In a large bowl, mix together the hot sauce and broth. Add the chicken strips and toss to coat with the broth mixture.

4. Place a pizza crust on a baking sheet and spread with ⅓ cup of the dressing. Scatter half of the chicken over the dressing and half of the shredded mozzarella cheese. Drizzle some of the broth mixture over top. Repeat with remaining pizza crust, dressing, chicken and mozzarella.
5. Bake pizzas at 450° for 10 minutes or until crusts are lightly browned and the cheese is bubbly. Remove from oven and scatter celery over pizzas. Serve with a tossed salad and extra hot sauce on the side, if desired.

PER SLICE: 285 calories; 9 g fat (2 g sat.); 25 g protein; 24 g carbohydrate; 1 g fiber; 722 mg sodium; 49 mg cholesterol.

Add fiber and whole grain to this pizza by opting for a whole-wheat crust.

apple cider drumsticks

MAKES: 4 servings. **PREP:** 10 minutes.
MARINATE: 1 hour.
ROAST: at 375° for 60 minutes.
COOK: 8 minutes.

- 1 **can (6 ounces) thawed apple juice concentrate**
- ¼ **cup cider vinegar**
- 1 **teaspoon pumpkin pie spice**
- ½ **teaspoon salt**
- ¼ **teaspoon black pepper**
- 8 **chicken drumsticks, skin removed**
- 2 **Gala apples, cored and cut into ½-inch slices**
- ¾ **cup fat-free half-and-half**
- 1 **tablespoon all-purpose flour**
- 1 **tablespoon Dijon mustard**
- 2 **cups cooked brown rice**

1. In a large resealable plastic bag, combine apple juice concentrate, cider vinegar, pumpkin pie spice and ¼ teaspoon of salt. Add chicken; shake to coat. Refrigerate for at least 1 hour.
2. Heat oven to 375°. Place a rack in a roasting pan and spray with nonstick cooking spray. Remove the chicken from the marinade and reserve the marinade. Place the chicken in the roasting pan and season with the remaining ¼ teaspoon salt and the pepper. Roast for 50 to 60 minutes or until the internal temperature reads 170° on an instant-read thermometer. Baste with marinade twice during cooking.
3. Heat a large nonstick skillet over medium-high heat. Spray with nonstick cooking spray. Add apples; sauté for 6 minutes, turning apples halfway through cooking. Remove apples to a plate and keep warm.
4. Wipe out the skillet and add the marinade. Bring to a simmer. In a medium bowl, whisk together the half-and-half, flour and Dijon mustard. Gradually whisk in the heated apple juice concentrate mixture. Return mixture to the skillet and simmer for an additional minute.
5. Serve the chicken with the apples, brown rice and sauce.

PER SERVING: 433 calories; 7 g fat (2 g sat.); 31 g protein; 61 g carbohydrate; 3 g fiber; 534 mg sodium; 87 mg cholesterol.

For easy prep, marinate drumsticks overnight in the refrigerator.

This sauce also makes a great dip for raw vegetables.

thai peanut chicken

MAKES: 4 servings. **PREP:** 15 minutes. **COOK:** 2 minutes. **BROIL:** 6 minutes.

Sauce:
- 2 tablespoons reduced-sodium soy sauce
- 1 tablespoon lemon juice
- 1 teaspoon cornstarch
- ½ teaspoon garlic powder
- ¼ to ½ teaspoon red pepper flakes
- ¼ cup smooth peanut butter

Chicken:
- 2 large boneless, skinless chicken breasts, about 10 ounces each, cut in half lengthwise (see photo)
- ⅛ teaspoon salt
- ⅛ teaspoon black pepper
- 2 cups cooked white rice
- 1 small red sweet pepper, cored, seeded and thinly sliced
- 2 scallions, trimmed and thinly sliced
- ½ pound steamed snow peas

1. Make **Sauce:** In small bowl, whisk together soy sauce, lemon juice, cornstarch, garlic powder and red pepper flakes. In small saucepan, whisk together peanut butter with **½ cup hot water**. Stir in soy sauce mixture and bring to a simmer over medium heat until mixture thickens, about 2 minutes. Reserve.

2. Make **Chicken:** Heat broiler and spray boiler pan with nonstick cooking spray. Season chicken with salt and pepper. Broil for 3 minutes per side or until internal temperature reaches 160° on an instant-read thermometer.

3. Slice chicken and serve with rice and peanut sauce. Garnish with red pepper and scallions. Serve with snow peas.

PER SERVING: 415 calories; 10 g fat (2 g sat.); 42 g protein; 38 g carbohydrate; 4 g fiber; 547 mg sodium; 82 mg cholesterol.

safe slicing

Hold chicken in place with fingers on flat surface. Start at nontapered end and cut horizontally into two equal pieces.

caribbean chicken curry

MAKES: 4 servings. **PREP:** 15 minutes.
COOK: 38 minutes.

- 1 tablespoon vegetable oil
- 1 pound boneless, skinless chicken thighs, cut into 1-inch pieces
- ½ teaspoon salt
- ¼ teaspoon black pepper
- 1 medium onion, thinly sliced
- 1 clove garlic, peeled and chopped
- 2 teaspoons hot curry powder
- 1 can (10¾ ounces) reduced-fat, low-sodium condensed cream of chicken soup (such as Campbell's Healthy Request)
- 1⅓ cups skim milk
- 1 medium tomato, seeds squeezed out and chopped
- 1 mango, peeled, pitted and thinly sliced
- ¼ cup dark raisins
- 1 cup couscous prepared with 1 cup chicken broth

1. Add oil to a large pot and heat over medium-high heat. Season chicken with ¼ teaspoon salt and the black pepper. Add to pot and cook for 7 minutes. Remove to a plate.
2. Add onion and garlic and cook, stirring, 5 minutes, until lightly browned. Add the curry and cook for 1 minute. In a medium-size bowl, whisk together the condensed soup and milk, and stir into pot.
3. Add remaining ¼ teaspoon salt, tomato, mango, raisins, chicken and any juices from plate to the pot. Bring to a boil. Lower heat and simmer with the lid slightly ajar for 25 minutes, stirring occasionally. Serve with cooked couscous.

PER SERVING: 516 calories; 13 g fat (3 g sat.); 34 g protein; 68 g carbohydrate; 5 g fiber; 997 mg sodium; 120 mg cholesterol.

chicken scarpiella

MAKES: 4 servings. **PREP:** 20 minutes.
BAKE: at 400° for 50 minutes.

- 4 fully cooked Italian- or sun-dried-tomato-flavor chicken sausage (such as Al Fresco), about 12 ounces, cut into 1-inch pieces
- 1 large sweet onion, peeled, halved and cut into ½-inch rings
- 2 green bell peppers, about 1 pound, cored, seeded and cut into 1-inch pieces
- 1 pound small red-skinned potatoes, cut into ¾-inch pieces
- 4 hot cherry peppers, trimmed, seeds removed and thinly sliced
- 3 cloves garlic, peeled and smashed
- 1 tablespoon olive oil
- ¾ teaspoon dried Italian seasoning
- ½ teaspoon salt
- ¼ plus ⅛ teaspoon black pepper
- 2 skinless chicken breast halves, bone in, cut in half crosswise, about 1½ pounds total
- ½ cup chicken broth
  Steamed broccoli (optional)

1. Heat oven to 400°. In a large roasting pan, combine sausage, onion, green pepper, potatoes, cherry peppers and garlic. Add olive oil and toss together. Season with ½ teaspoon of Italian seasoning, ¼ teaspoon of salt and ¼ teaspoon of pepper. Place on lower rack of oven. Bake at 400° for 10 minutes.
2. Meanwhile, spray a baking dish with nonstick cooking spray. Place chicken in dish and season with remaining ¼ teaspoon Italian seasoning, ¼ teaspoon salt and ⅛ teaspoon pepper. Pour broth into bottom of dish. Once sausage mixture has baked 10 minutes, add chicken to oven on top rack. Bake both dishes at 400° for 30 minutes or until the internal temperature of chicken reads 160° on an instant-read thermometer and potatoes are fork tender. Stir vegetables twice during baking.
3. Add chicken to vegetables; cook an additional 5 to 10 minutes or until internal temperature of chicken registers 170°.
4. Transfer chicken and vegetables to a large platter and serve.

PER SERVING: 403 calories; 12 g fat (3 g sat.); 42 g protein; 32 g carbohydrate; 5 g fiber; 920 mg sodium; 159 mg cholesterol.

healthier kid-friendly
ALTERNATIVES TO FAST FOOD

oven-baked chicken nuggets

Cut **1½ pounds boneless, skinless chicken breasts** into 1½-inch pieces. Mix together **¾ cup seasoned bread crumbs** and **¼ cup grated Parmesan cheese.** Dip chicken in **3 beaten egg whites**; coat in bread-crumb mixture. Bake at 450° for 10 minutes or until internal temperature reaches 160° on an instant-read thermometer. Turn once during baking. Serve with **barbecue sauce** or a mixture of equal parts **honey mustard** and **light mayonnaise.**

chicken mozzarella sandwiches

Broil **4 thin chicken cutlets** for 2 minutes per side. Turn off broiler and top each cutlet with **2 tablespoons heated Marinara sauce** and 3 tablespoons **shredded part-skim mozzarella cheese.** Heat until cheese melts. Serve on **whole-grain soft rolls or crusty French bread.**

crunchy chicken fingers with curry ketchup

Dip **2 pounds chicken tenders** in 2 beaten eggs. Coat with **1½ cups cornflake crumbs.** Sprinkle with **garlic salt** (optional). Bake at 450° for 20 to 25 minutes, turning once, until internal temperature reaches 160° on an instant-read thermometer. Serve with Curry Ketchup: Blend **1 cup ketchup, 1 teaspoon mild curry powder** and **1 finely chopped scallion** until smooth.

slow-cooker solutions

WITH A LITTLE PLANNING AHEAD—AND THESE GREAT-TASTING RECIPES—
YOUR SLOW-COOKER PROVIDES THE PERFECT TOOL FOR EFFORTLESS MEALS.
BY CINDY HELLER

A toss in fresh parsley at the last minute gives the potatoes a fresh accent. (Recipe page 38)

PHOTOGRAPHY BY ALEXANDRA GRABLEWSKI

sour cherry rice pudding

MAKES: 4 servings. **PREP:** 5 minutes.
SLOW-COOK: 4 hours, 50 minutes on LOW.

- 1 **cup water**
- ¾ **cup arborio rice, rinsed and drained**
- 1 **can (12 ounces) evaporated milk**
- ⅔ **cup sugar**
- ½ **cup milk**
  Pinch salt
- ½ **cup cherry juice**
- 1 **cup dried cherries**
- ⅛ **teaspoon ground cinnamon**
  Pinch ground nutmeg

1. Combine water, rice and evaporated milk in a 2- to 3-quart round slow cooker.
2. In a small saucepan, cook the sugar and milk over medium-high heat for 1 minute or until bubbles appear around the edges and the sugar has dissolved. Stir into slow cooker with salt. Cover and cook on LOW for 4½ hours.
3. While rice is cooking, bring cherry juice to a boil and pour over cherries in a small bowl; let stand 10 minutes. Drain, reserving juice.
4. Stir in the cherries, 3 tablespoons juice, cinnamon and nutmeg into slow cooker; cover and cook on LOW for 20 minutes more.
5. Turn cooker off and allow pudding to cool, partially covered, for 30 minutes.

PER SERVING: 506 calories; 1 g fat (1 g sat.); 13 g protein; 109 g carbohydrate; 8 g fiber; 205 mg sodium; 8 mg cholesterol.

As it cooks, arborio rice releases starch, giving the pudding a decadent, creamy texture.

The heating elements of a slow cooker are around the sides so for the most evenly cooked food, fill the cooker only half to three-quarters full.

honey barbecue ham with roasted potatoes

MAKES: 12 servings. **PREP:** 10 minutes. **COOK:** 5 minutes. **SLOW-COOK:** 2 hours on HIGH or 5 hours on LOW.

- ½ cup ketchup
- 2 tablespoons cider vinegar
- 2 tablespoons dark-brown sugar
- 1 teaspoon Worcestershire sauce
- 1 teaspoon plus 1 tablespoon vegetable oil
- ¼ teaspoon dry mustard
- 3½ pounds fully cooked boneless ham
- 3 pounds potatoes, cut into 1-inch pieces
- 1 tablespoon chopped fresh parsley
- ½ teaspoon salt
- ½ teaspoon black pepper

1. In a small saucepan, stir together ketchup, vinegar, sugar, Worcestershire, 1 teaspoon oil and mustard. Bring to a simmer and cook for 5 minutes.

2. Score surface of ham, making diamond shapes ½-inch deep. Place ham in a 4- to 5-quart slow cooker and brush generously with the barbecue sauce.

3. In a large bowl, stir together potatoes and remaining tablespoon of vegetable oil. Place potatoes around ham in slow cooker. Cook for 2 hours on HIGH or 5 hours on LOW, brushing ham generously with sauce once every hour.

4. Remove ham from slow cooker and set aside. Stir parsley, salt and pepper into potatoes and serve with ham and remaining sauce.

PER SERVING: 273 calories; 9 g fat (3 g sat.); 24 g protein; 26 g carbohydrate; 2 g fiber; 1,139 mg sodium; 55 mg cholesterol.

ratatouille

MAKES: 6 servings. **PREP:** 15 minutes. **STAND:** 20 minutes. **SLOW-COOK:** 3 hours on HIGH or 5 hours on LOW.

- 1 small eggplant (about 1 pound), peeled and cut into ½-inch cubes
- ⅛ teaspoon plus ¼ teaspoon salt
- 1 medium-size red onion, chopped
- 2 medium-size sweet bell peppers, seeded and cut into ¾-inch pieces
- 1 package (10 ounces) mushrooms, cleaned and quartered
- 1 can (14.5 ounces) diced tomatoes
- 1 can (8 ounces) tomato sauce
- ¾ teaspoon black pepper
- ½ teaspoon Italian seasoning
- 1 medium-size yellow squash, quartered and cut into ¾-inch pieces
- 1 tablespoon fresh chopped basil
  Olive oil, for drizzling (optional)

1. Place eggplant in a strainer and sprinkle with ⅛ teaspoon salt; let stand for 20 minutes and press out as much liquid as possible.

2. In a 4- to 5-quart slow cooker, combine eggplant, onion, bell peppers and mushrooms. Drain diced tomatoes and stir in along with tomato sauce, black pepper and Italian seasoning. Cook on HIGH for 3 hours or LOW for 5 hours.

3. Add squash into slow cooker for last 45 minutes of cooking time. Before serving, stir in basil and remaining ¼ teaspoon salt and drizzle with olive oil, if desired.

PER SERVING: 82 calories; 0 g fat (0 g sat.); 5 g protein; 18 g carbohydrate; 6 g fiber; 446 mg sodium; 0 mg cholesterol.

A stint in the slow cooker gives this classic Provencal stew its unbeatable flavor.

cooking school

THIS CLASSIC FRENCH POTATO DISH IS A WINNER AT ANY FAMILY TABLE.
FOLLOW OUR STEP-BY-STEP INSTRUCTIONS FOR NO-FAIL AU GRATIN POTATOES.

BY JULIE MILTENBERGER

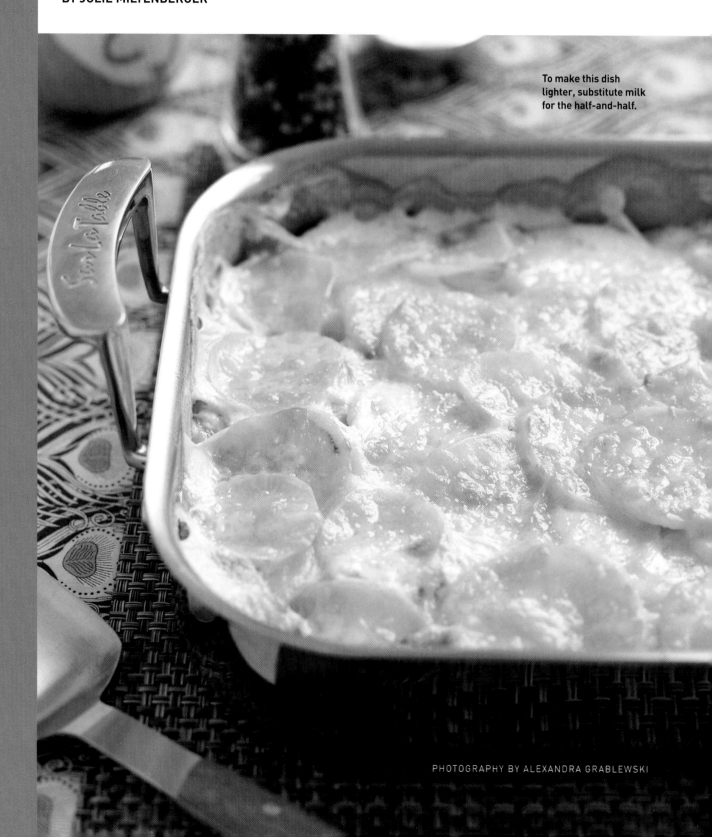

To make this dish lighter, substitute milk for the half-and-half.

au gratin potatoes

MAKES: 6 servings. **PREP:** 20 minutes. **BAKE:** at 375° for 55 minutes.

- 2 pounds all-purpose potatoes, peeled
- 3 tablespoons all-purpose flour
- 1 teaspoon salt
- 2 scallions, trimmed and sliced
- 4 ounces Gruyère or Emmentaler cheese, shredded (about 1½ cups)
- 2 cups half-and-half
  Pinch ground nutmeg
- 2 tablespoons grated Asiago or Parmesan cheese

1. Heat oven to 375°. Coat a 1½-quart baking pan with nonstick cooking spray.
2. Place a handheld mandoline (available at oxo.com or at kitchen accessory stores) over a large bowl. Place one potato on the slicer, and secure with guard. Using back-and-forth motion, carefully slice potato into ⅛-inch-thick slices **(photo 1).** Alternatively, thinly slice potatoes with knife on a cutting board. Repeat with all potatoes.
3. Sprinkle flour and salt over potato slices, and toss with your hands to coat potatoes **(photo 2).**

4. Begin layering: Spread ⅓ of the potato slices over bottom of prepared pan, then sprinkle with half the scallions. Top with ⅓ of the shredded Gruyère cheese, about ½ cup **(photo 3).** Repeat with more potato slices, the remaining scallions and ½ cup shredded cheese. Top with remaining potato slices.
5. In a small saucepan, combine the half-and-half and the nutmeg. Bring to a simmer and remove from heat. Carefully pour over potatoes, then cover pan with foil. Bake at 375° for 30 minutes. Carefully remove foil, sprinkle with remaining ½ cup shredded cheese and the Asiago or Parmesan. Return to oven and bake for 25 minutes, until top is lightly browned and potatoes are tender. Let stand 15 minutes before serving.

PER SERVING: 312 calories; 15 g fat (9 g sat.); 14 g protein; 33 g carbohydrate; 3 g fiber; 498 mg sodium; 63 mg cholesterol.

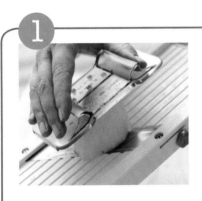

Carefully slice potatoes with mandoline, using guard to avoid scraping your knuckles.

Sprinkle flour and salt over potato slices, then toss with your hands to coat slices completely.

Layer potatoes, then scallions and cheese. Repeat; add the warm half-and-half mixture.

Food styling: A.J. Battifarano. Prop styling: Lynda White.

march

Glazed Carrots
with Ginger
(Recipe page 63)

AS WINTER DRAWS TO AN END, SET THE
MOOD FOR SPRING WITH FRESHLY
BAKED BREAKFAST TREATS, TASTIER-
THAN-EVER VEGGIES AND LIGHT
PASTA DINNERS.

Chocolate-Cherry Loaf
page 46

Cuban Sandwiches
page 59

Vanilla Pots de Crème
page 65

rise and shine

MAKE YOUR MORNING BRIGHTER WITH A BATCH OF MINI MUFFINS OR A BANANA-CRUNCH LOAF—START TO FINISH, EACH TAKES LESS THAN AN HOUR.

BY JULIE MILTENBERGER

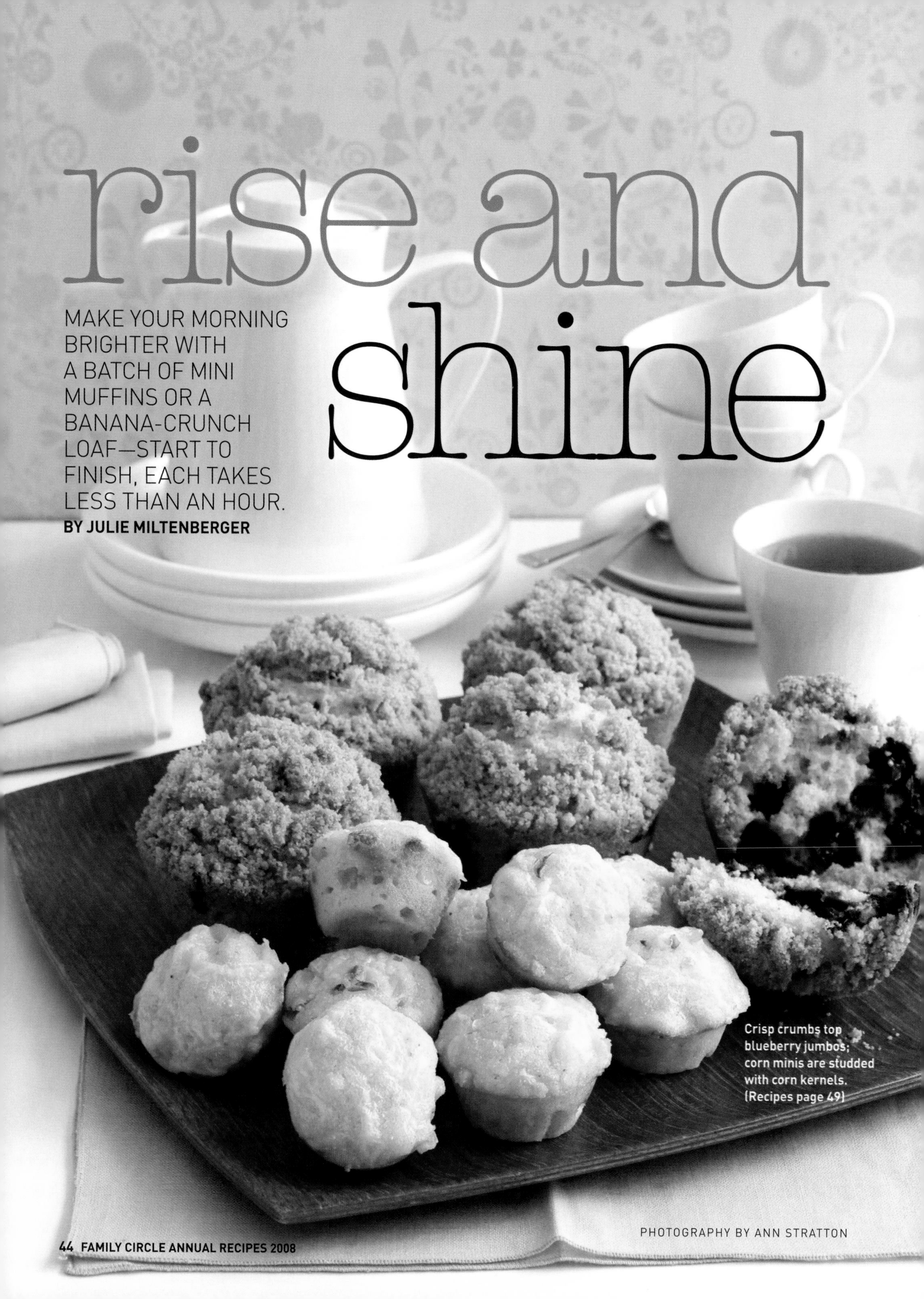

Crisp crumbs top blueberry jumbos; corn minis are studded with corn kernels. (Recipes page 49)

PHOTOGRAPHY BY ANN STRATTON

To keep this loaf
fresh and moist,
store up to one week
in a tightly sealed
plastic bag.
(Recipe page 46)

Food styling: Michael Pederson. Prop styling: Denise Canter.

chocolate-cherry loaf

MAKES: 3 mini loaves (8 slices each) or one standard-size loaf.
PREP: 20 minutes. **BAKE:** at 350° for 35 minutes.

⅓ cup cocoa powder
⅓ plus ¾ cup sugar
2¼ cups all-purpose flour
1 teaspoon baking powder
½ teaspoon baking soda
¼ teaspoon salt
2 eggs
⅓ cup oil
½ teaspoon almond extract
1 cup sour cream
½ cup dried cherries, chopped
3 tablespoons mini chocolate chips

1. Heat oven to 350°. Coat three 5¾ x 3 x 2⅛-inch loaf pans with nonstick cooking spray.
2. In small bowl, whisk cocoa powder, ⅓ cup of the sugar and **⅓ cup water** until smooth. Set aside.
3. In a large bowl, whisk flour, baking powder, baking soda and salt. In a medium-size bowl, whisk together remaining ¾ cup sugar, the eggs, oil and almond extract. Whisk in sour cream.
4. Stir sour cream mixture into flour mixture until blended. Stir 1½ cups of the batter into the cocoa mixture, along with the chopped cherries, until no white streaks remain. Dollop alternating spoonfuls of batter into prepared pans. Swirl batters together with a butter knife until marbled in appearance. Top each loaf with 1 tablespoon mini chips.
5. Bake at 350° for 35 minutes, until toothpick inserted in center of loaves comes out clean. Cool loaves in pans on wire rack for 10 minutes, then remove directly to rack to cool completely.
Note: Batter may be baked as one 9 x 5 x 3-inch loaf; increase baking time to 45 to 50 minutes; test center of loaf with a toothpick before removing.

PER SLICE: 201 calories; 8 g fat (3 g sat.); 3 g protein; 29 g carbohydrate; 1 g fiber; 103 mg sodium; 29 mg cholesterol.

zucchini-carrot muffins

MAKES: 12 mini bundt cakes.
PREP: 15 minutes.
BAKE: at 350° for 25 minutes.

2 cups all-purpose flour
¾ teaspoon baking soda
¾ teaspoon baking powder
½ teaspoon salt
½ teaspoon ground ginger
½ teaspoon ground cinnamon
Pinch ground cloves
2 eggs
½ cup vegetable oil
¾ cup sugar
1 small zucchini, shredded (¾ cup)
1 small carrot, grated (½ cup)
½ cup sunflower seeds

1. Heat oven to 350°. Coat the 12 wells of a mini bundt or standard-size muffin pan with nonstick cooking spray.
2. Whisk together flour, baking soda, baking powder, salt, ginger, cinnamon and cloves in a large bowl.
3. Mix eggs, oil and sugar in medium-size bowl. Whisk for 30 seconds to dissolve sugar. Stir in shredded zucchini and carrot.
4. Stir egg mixture into flour mixture. Stir in sunflower seeds. Divide batter equally among wells, a slightly heaping ¼ cup in each.
5. Bake at 350° for 23 to 25 minutes or until crowned and lightly browned. Remove from pan to wire racks to cool.

PER MINI BUNDT: 252 calories; 13 g fat (1 g sat.); 4 g protein; 31 g carbohydrate; 1 g fiber; 256 mg sodium; 35 mg cholesterol.

Mini bundt pans are an easy way to make muffins look fancy.

To ensure a tender loaf or muffin, be careful not to overmix the batter.

banana-crunch loaf

MAKES: 3 loaves, 6 slices per loaf.
PREP: 10 minutes.
BAKE: at 350° for 33 minutes.

    2 cups all-purpose flour
    2 teaspoons baking powder
   ½ teaspoon ground cinnamon
   ½ teaspoon salt
    2 eggs
   ¾ cup light-brown sugar
   ½ cup (1 stick) unsalted butter, melted
    2 large ripe bananas, mashed (1 cup)
    1 teaspoon vanilla extract
   ½ cup chopped walnuts
   ¾ cup low-fat granola (without raisins),
       lightly crushed

1. Heat oven to 350°. Coat three
5¾ x 3 x 2⅛-inch loaf pans with nonstick
cooking spray.*
2. In a large bowl, whisk together the
flour, baking powder, cinnamon and salt.
Make a well in the center of the dry
ingredients; set aside. In a medium-size
bowl, combine the eggs, light-brown
sugar and melted butter. Whisk until
smooth. Add mashed banana and vanilla.
Pour banana mixture into well in dry
ingredients; stir just until moist. Stir in
chopped walnuts.
3. Divide batter evenly among the
prepared pans. Sprinkle crushed granola
over all pans, dividing evenly.
4. Bake the loaves at 350° for 30 to
33 minutes or until set and golden
around the edges. Let the loaves cool in
the pan on a wire rack for 5 minutes.
Transfer directly to rack; serve warm,
if desired.
***Note:** This batter may also be prepared
as 12 standard-size muffins. Reduce
baking time to 25 minutes.

PER SLICE: 188 calories; 8 g fat (4 g sat.);
3 g protein; 26 g carbohydrate; 1 g fiber;
158 mg sodium; 37 mg cholesterol.

corn muffins

MAKES: 24 mini muffins.
PREP: 15 minutes.
BAKE: at 425° for 17 minutes.

  1¼ cups cornmeal
    1 cup all-purpose flour
   ¼ cup sugar
  1¼ teaspoons salt
    2 teaspoons baking powder
    2 eggs, lightly beaten
   ¼ cup vegetable oil
   ¼ teaspoon hot-pepper sauce
    1 cup milk
    1 cup shredded pepper-Jack cheese
       (about 4 ounces)
    1 cup fresh corn kernels

1. Heat oven to 425°. Coat two mini
muffin pans with nonstick cooking spray.
2. Blend cornmeal, flour, sugar, salt
and baking powder in a large bowl.
3. Stir together eggs, oil, hot pepper
sauce, milk, ½ cup of the cheese and
the corn in a small bowl. Stir into
cornmeal mixture just until dry
ingredients are moistened. Divide
evenly among prepared muffin cups,
⅓ cup per indentation. Sprinkle muffins
evenly with remaining cheese.
4. Bake at 425° for 15 to 17 minutes or
until a wooden toothpick inserted in
center comes out slightly moist with
crumbs attached. Run a thin knife around
edge of muffins and remove to a wire
rack to cool. Serve slightly warm.

PER MUFFIN: 116 calories; 5 g fat (1 g sat.);
3 g protein; 15 g carbohydrate; 1 g fiber;
40 mg sodium; 24 mg cholesterol.

blueberry-crumb muffins

MAKES: 6 jumbo muffins.
PREP: 20 minutes.
BAKE: at 350° for 35 minutes.

Crumb Topping:
   ⅔ cup all-purpose flour
   ⅓ cup light-brown sugar
   ¼ teaspoon ground cinnamon
   ⅛ teaspoon ground nutmeg
   ⅛ teaspoon salt
   ¼ cup (½ stick) cold butter, cut up
Muffins:
    2 cups all-purpose flour
   ⅔ cup granulated sugar
   ¾ teaspoon baking powder
   ½ teaspoon baking soda
   ¼ teaspoon salt
    2 eggs
   ⅔ cup vegetable oil
   ½ pint (1 cup) fresh blueberries
       Confectioners' sugar (optional)

1. Heat oven to 350°. Coat the
six wells of a jumbo muffin pan
with nonstick cooking spray.
Prepare **Crumb Topping:** In a medium-
size bowl, whisk together flour, light-
brown sugar, cinnamon, nutmeg and
salt. Work in butter with your fingertips
until crumbs are formed. Set aside until
batter is mixed and in the muffin pan.
2. Prepare **Muffins:** In a small bowl,
whisk together flour, granulated sugar,
baking powder, baking soda and salt.
Set aside. In a large bowl, whisk
together **¼ cup water,** the eggs and oil.
Stir flour mixture into oil mixture just
until moistened. Gently fold in berries.
3. Divide batter among prepared wells,
about ⅔ cup in each. Top batter with
crumb topping, dividing equally (about
¼ cup on each).
4. Bake at 350° for 33 to 35 minutes.
Cool in pans for 10 minutes, then
transfer directly to wire rack and
continue to cool. Before serving, dust
with confectioners' sugar, if desired.

PER MUFFIN: 651 calories; 34 g fat (7 g sat.);
8 g protein; 80 g carbohydrate; 2 g fiber;
327 mg sodium; 92 mg cholesterol.

HEALTHY FAMILY DINNERS™

light pasta DELIGHTS

SURPRISE YOUR FAMILY WITH OUR MENU OF DELICIOUS, NUTRITIOUS RECIPES THAT SKIMP ON CALORIES WITHOUT SACRIFICING FLAVOR.

BY CINDY HELLER

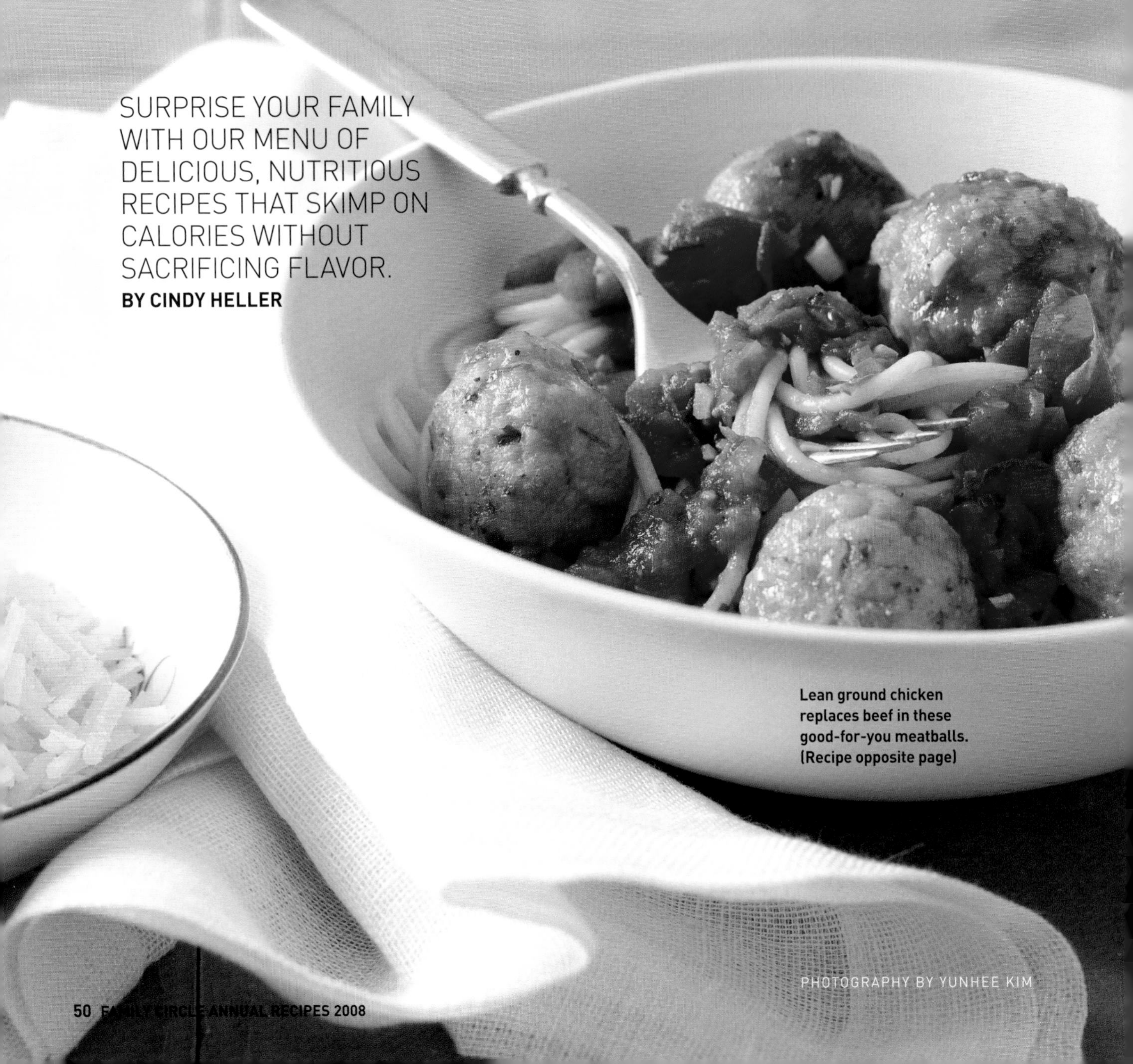

Lean ground chicken replaces beef in these good-for-you meatballs. (Recipe opposite page)

PHOTOGRAPHY BY YUNHEE KIM

rigatoni with creamy tomato sauce

MAKES: 4 servings.
PREP: 10 minutes. **COOK:** 6 minutes.

- 12 ounces rigatoni
- 1 teaspoon canola oil
- 3 cups sliced mushrooms
- ½ teaspoon salt
- ⅓ cup red wine
- 1½ cups light tomato sauce (such as Ragú)
- ¼ teaspoon black pepper
- ½ cup part-skim ricotta
- ¼ cup chopped fresh basil, plus more to garnish

1. Bring a large pot of salted water to a boil. Cook rigatoni according to package directions. Drain and return to pot.
2. While pasta is cooking, heat oil in a medium-size saucepan over medium-high heat. Add mushrooms and salt to saucepan; cook 3 minutes. Add wine to saucepan and cook for 3 minutes. Stir tomato sauce, black pepper, ricotta and basil into pan until well blended.
3. Pour sauce over pasta and stir to combine. Serve immediately, garnished with additional fresh basil, if desired.

PER SERVING: 420 calories; 5 g fat (2 g sat.); 18 g protein; 75 g carbohydrate; 5 g fiber; 607 mg sodium; 9 mg cholesterol.

Fresh basil adds the perfect finishing touch this simple pasta dish.

spaghetti with chicken meatballs

MAKES: 6 servings. **PREP:** 15 minutes. **BAKE:** at 375° for 24 minutes. **COOK:** 14 minutes.

- 2 slices whole-grain white bread, torn into pieces
- ¼ cup skim milk
- 1 pound ground chicken
- 2 tablespoons grated Parmesan cheese
- 4 tablespoons chopped parsley
- ½ teaspoon plus ⅛ teaspoon salt
- 1 tablespoon canola oil
- 2 garlic cloves, minced
- 2 pounds plum tomatoes, cored, seeded and cut into ½-inch pieces
- 2 tablespoons balsamic vinegar
- ½ teaspoon Italian seasoning
- ⅛ teaspoon black pepper
- 1 box (14.5 ounces) fiber- and calcium-enriched spaghetti (such as Ronzoni Smart Taste)

1. Heat oven to 375°. Line a rimmed baking sheet with foil and place a baking rack over it; coat rack with nonstick cooking spray and set aside.
2. In a large bowl, combine bread pieces and milk and let stand for 5 minutes or until bread softens. Mash with fork until a paste forms. Add chicken, Parmesan, 2 tablespoons of the parsley and ½ teaspoon salt, and stir until mixed.
3. With clean hands kept wet with water, shape mixture into thirty 1½-inch meatballs. Place meatballs on prepared rack and bake at 375° for 24 minutes.
4. While meatballs are cooking, make sauce. Heat oil in a nonstick medium-size skillet over medium heat. Add garlic and cook for 1 minute. Add tomatoes, balsamic vinegar, Italian seasoning and black pepper and increase heat to medium-high. Cook for about 13 minutes. Stir in remaining ⅛ teaspoon salt and 2 tablespoons parsley.
5. Cook pasta according to package directions. Drain and reserve ½ cup pasta water. Transfer pasta to a large serving bowl and top with meatballs. Stir pasta water into sauce and spoon sauce on top of pasta and meatballs.

PER SERVING: 432 calories; 13 g fat (3 g sat.); 24 g protein; 65 g carbohydrate; 10 g fiber; 394 mg sodium; 93 mg cholesterol.

Subbing broccoli for some of the oil in this homemade pesto adds flavor and body while slashing fat.

ravioli with pesto

MAKES: 6 servings. **PREP:** 15 minutes. **COOK:** 8 minutes.

- 1 teaspoon canola oil
- 2 cups sliced mushrooms
- 1 small sweet red pepper, cut into 2-inch-long strips
- 4 cups broccoli flowerets
- 1 cup packed baby spinach leaves
- ¼ cup pine nuts
- ⅓ cup grated Parmesan cheese
- ⅓ cup olive oil
- ¼ teaspoon salt
- ⅛ teaspoon black pepper
- 2 packages (9 ounces each) light four-cheese ravioli

1. Heat oil in a large skillet over medium-high heat. Add mushrooms and cook 3 minutes. Add red pepper, broccoli and **⅓ cup water**; cover and cook 4 minutes or until broccoli is crisp-tender. Remove lid; cook another 1 minute or until water has evaporated. Using tongs, remove 1 cup of broccoli from skillet and set aside. Remove skillet from heat; cover.

2. In a food processor, combine reserved broccoli, spinach, pine nuts, Parmesan, olive oil, salt and black pepper. Pulse until blended and smooth; set aside.

3. Meanwhile, cook pasta according to package directions. Drain, reserving ½ cup water, and return the pasta to the pot. Stir the mushroom mixture into the pasta pot with ½ cup pesto, adding the reserved pasta water if necessary to thin the sauce. Refrigerate unused sauce for up to 1 week.

PER SERVING: 338 calories; 14 g fat (4 g sat.); 15 g protein; 40 g carbohydrate; 4 g fiber; 539 mg sodium; 48 mg cholesterol.

ditalini with chickpeas

MAKES: 4 servings. **PREP:** 5 minutes. **COOK:** 19 minutes.

- 8 ounces ditalini
- 1 teaspoon canola oil
- 4 slices turkey bacon, cut crosswise into ½-inch pieces
- 1 small onion, chopped
- 2 cups fire-roasted diced tomatoes
  Pinch red pepper flakes
- 1 can (19 ounces) chickpeas, drained and rinsed

1. Bring a large pot of salted water to a boil. Cook ditalini according to package directions. Drain, reserving ½ cup of pasta water, and return pasta to the pot.
2. Heat oil in a medium-size saucepan over medium-high heat. Add bacon and onion and cook for 3 minutes. Lower heat to medium and add tomatoes and red pepper flakes to saucepan; cook another 15 minutes. Add chickpeas to pot and cook 1 minute or until warmed through.
3. Stir sauce into pasta, adding pasta water to the sauce if necessary. Serve immediately.

PER SERVING: 406 calories; 7 g fat (1 g sat.); 16 g protein; 70 g carbohydrate; 8 g fiber; 585 mg sodium; 12 mg cholesterol.

If you like it hot, double the amount of red pepper flakes.

We cut calories by
cooking the broccoli
rabe in broth instead
of sautéing in oil.

orecchiette with sausage and broccoli rabe

MAKES: 6 servings. **PREP:** 15 minutes.
COOK: 18 minutes.

- 8 ounces orecchiette pasta
- 1¼ pounds sweet Italian turkey sausage links, casings removed
- 2 medium-size yellow squash (about 6 ounces each), cut in half horizontally and sliced into ½-inch half-moons
- 2 cloves garlic, minced
- ¼ teaspoon red pepper flakes
- 1 bunch broccoli rabe, cleaned, trimmed and cut into 1-inch pieces
- ⅓ cup low-sodium chicken broth
  Grated Parmesan cheese for sprinkling (optional)

1. Cook the orecchiette according to package directions. Drain and return pasta to the pot; keep warm.
2. While the pasta is cooking, heat a large nonstick skillet over medium heat. Crumble sausage into skillet, breaking up large pieces. Cook for 10 minutes, stirring occasionally, or until no longer pink. Stir in squash and increase heat to medium-high. Cook squash 3 minutes. Stir in garlic and red pepper flakes; cook 1 additional minute. Add the broccoli rabe and broth and cover. Cook 2 minutes, then remove cover and stir. Cook another 2 minutes or until broccoli rabe has wilted and is tender.
3. Add sausage mixture to pasta pot and stir to combine. Sprinkle with cheese, if desired.

PER SERVING: 329 calories; 10 g fat (3 g sat.); 25 g protein; 35 g carbohydrate; 2 g fiber; 624 mg sodium; 56 mg cholesterol.

mediterranean orzo

MAKES: 6 servings. **PREP:** 10 minutes. **COOK:** 12 minutes.

- 12 ounces onion-and-garlic-flavored chicken sausage (such as Al Fresco), halved lengthwise and cut into ½-inch-thick half-moons
- 1 pint grape tomatoes, halved
- 3 tablespoons red wine vinegar
- 1 teaspoon canola oil
- ¾ teaspoon dried oregano
- 8 ounces orzo
- 8 ounces green beans, trimmed and cut in half
- ½ cup crumbled fat-free feta cheese
- 1 tablespoon fresh chopped parsley
- 2 teaspoons olive oil

1. Heat a large nonstick skillet over medium-high heat. Add sausage to skillet and cook, stirring occasionally, for 5 minutes. Add tomatoes, 1 tablespoon of the vinegar, canola oil and ½ teaspoon of the oregano to pan; cook 2 minutes. Place sausage mixture in a serving bowl.
2. Meanwhile, bring large pot of salted water to a boil. Cook orzo according to package directions. Add green beans to pasta pot for final 5 minutes of cooking time. Drain and rinse under cold water.
3. Place pasta mixture in serving bowl with sausage mixture and add remaining 2 tablespoons vinegar, ¼ teaspoon oregano, the feta, parsley and olive oil. Stir to combine; serve.

PER SERVING: 301 calories; 7 g fat (2 g sat.); 22 g protein; 36 g carbohydrate; 3 g fiber; 562 mg sodium; 48 mg cholesterol.

Supermarket prepped veggies make home cooking easy. (Recipes page 58)

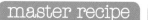 master recipe | day 2

day 3

QUICK & EASY

SUPPER

WITH ONE MASTER RECIPE AND A LITTLE KNOW-HOW, YOU CAN COOK UP MANY NIGHTS OF DELICIOUS MEALS—AND NO BORING RERUNS. **BY MICHAEL TYRRELL**

PHOTOGRAPHY BY CHARLES SCHILLER

master recipe

day 2

Store extra pork
(tightly wrapped) in
the refrigerator for
up to four days.
(Recipes page 59)

day 3

SPIN-OFFS

roast turkey breast

MAKES: 4 servings. **PREP:** 10 minutes.
ROAST: at 375° for 2¼ hours. **COOK:** 3 minutes.

- 1 whole turkey breast on the bone (about 6½ pounds)
- 2 tablespoons lemon juice
- 1 tablespoon olive oil
- 1½ teaspoons lemon pepper
- 1½ teaspoons dried Italian seasoning
- 2 tablespoons flour
- 1 can (14½ ounces) chicken broth

1. Roast **Turkey:** Heat oven to 375°. Rub turkey on all sides with lemon juice and olive oil. Rub lemon pepper and Italian seasoning over turkey.
2. Place in a roasting pan, breast-side up, and roast in oven for 2 to 2¼ hours or until internal temperature reaches 165° on an instant-read thermometer. Let rest for 15 minutes before slicing.
3. Make **Gravy:** Pour off all but 3 tablespoons of drippings. Whisk together the flour and chicken broth.

Stir into roasting pan and scrape up any browned bits. Simmer for 2 to 3 minutes. Strain and keep warm. If too thick, add a few tablespoons of water.

4. Cut one breast-half off bone and reserve for use in **Tuscan White Bean Stew** and **Smoky Turkey and Veggie Frittata** (recipes at right and below). Slice remaining turkey; serve with gravy, vegetables and stuffing, if desired.

PER SERVING: 391 calories; 5 g fat (1 g sat.); 77 g protein; 4 g carbohydrate; 0 g fiber; 668 mg sodium; 212 mg cholesterol.

tuscan white bean stew

MAKES: 4 servings.
PREP: 10 minutes. **COOK:** 5 minutes.

- 1 can (14½ ounces) chicken broth
- 2 cups shredded carrots
- 2 cans (15½ ounces each) cannellini beans, drained and rinsed
- 3 cups cubed cooked turkey (from master recipe, at left)
- ¾ teaspoon dried Italian seasoning
- ¼ cup grated Parmesan cheese
- 1 tablespoon chopped parsley Crusty bread

1. Bring chicken broth to a simmer in a large saucepan. Add carrots and one can of the beans; mash second can of beans and add to saucepan.
2. Stir in turkey and Italian seasoning. Cover and simmer 5 minutes. Stir in Parmesan and parsley. Serve with crusty bread, if desired.

PER SERVING: 409 calories; 6 g fat (2 g sat.); 50 g protein; 35 g carbohydrate; 10 g fiber; 978 mg sodium; 112 mg cholesterol.

smoky turkey and veggie frittata

MAKES: 4 servings. **PREP:** 10 minutes.
COOK: 12 minutes. **BAKE:** at 325° for 20 minutes.

- 1 tablespoon olive oil
- 2 cups assorted fresh vegetables,* cut into bite-size pieces
- 6 large eggs
- 3 tablespoons skim milk
- ¼ teaspoon salt
- ¼ teaspoon black pepper
- 2½ cups cubed cooked turkey breast (from master recipe, above)
- 1 cup diced smoked Gouda (4 ounces)
- 1 tablespoon chopped fresh parsley

1. Heat oven to 325°. Spray a 10-inch oven-safe nonstick skillet with nonstick cooking spray. Add olive oil to skillet and heat over medium heat. Add vegetables and cook 7 minutes, until tender.
2. In a large bowl, whisk together the eggs, milk, salt and pepper. Stir in turkey and ½ cup of the Gouda.

3. Pour egg mixture into skillet. Cook over medium-high heat for 5 minutes, stirring gently halfway through cooking. Sprinkle remaining ½ cup cheese over top of mixture, and transfer skillet to oven. Bake

at 325° for 20 minutes. To serve, gently slide onto plate and cut into 4 servings. Garnish with parsley.
*Note: Look for fresh, assorted, cut-up vegetables for stir-frying in your supermarket's produce department.

PER SERVING: 448 calories; 22 g fat (9 g sat.); 56 g protein; 5 g carbohydrate; 1 g fiber; 525 mg sodium; 450 mg cholesterol.

easy as 1, 2, 3

1 Spice up leftovers by keeping the pantry stocked with condiments like soy, hoisin and stir-fry sauces, as well as mustard and salsa.

2 Make sure your family gets enough fruits and veggies. Buy frozen and canned items—they're just as nutritious and always available.

3 Purchase prepared potatoes, rice and polenta for easy add-ons to any meal.

roast pork and pan-roasted potatoes

MAKES: 4 servings. **PREP:** 10 minutes. **ROAST:** at 400° for 1 hour, 20 minutes.

Pork and Potatoes:
- 1 boneless pork roast, about 4½ pounds
- 2 tablespoons olive oil
- ¼ plus ⅛ teaspoon salt
- ¼ plus ⅛ teaspoon black pepper
- 5 sprigs rosemary
- 1½ pounds red-skin potatoes, cut into 1-inch pieces

Gravy:
- 1½ cups chicken broth
- 2 tablespoons all-purpose flour
- ½ cup white wine

1. Heat oven to 400°.
2. Roast **Pork:** Rub pork roast with 1 tablespoon of the olive oil. Season with ¼ teaspoon *each* of the salt and pepper. Arrange 3 sprigs of the rosemary on top. Place in roasting pan and roast for 1 hour, 20 minutes, or until internal temperature reaches 150° on an instant-read thermometer. Remove from oven, tent with foil and allow to rest at least 10 minutes before slicing. Temperature should reach 160°. Save drippings in pan for gravy.
3. Roast **Potatoes:** On a large baking sheet, toss potatoes with remaining

1 tablespoon olive oil. Season with remaining ⅛ teaspoon *each* salt and pepper. Place remaining rosemary over potatoes.
4. After meat has been roasting for about 35 minutes, add potatoes to oven. Roast about 45 minutes or until fork-tender. Remove from oven; keep warm.
5. Make **Gravy:** Whisk together broth and flour. Stir into roasting pan and scrape up browned bits. Add wine and bring to a boil. Simmer for 3 minutes or until thickened. Strain and keep warm.

6. To serve, reserve half of roast for use in **Cuban Sandwiches** and **Pork Fried Rice** (recipes at right and below). Slice remaining half of roast and serve with gravy, potatoes and steamed spinach, if desired.

PER SERVING: 521 calories; 19 g fat (5 g sat.); 49 g protein; 31 g carbohydrate; 3 g fiber; 672 mg sodium; 118 mg cholesterol.

day 2

cuban sandwiches

MAKES: 4 sandwiches.
PREP: 10 minutes. **GRILL:** 6 minutes.

- 1 loaf (12 ounces) crusty Italian bread
- 4 dill pickles, thinly sliced lengthwise
- ½ pound roast pork, sliced (about 8 ¼-inch-thick slices; from master recipe, at left)
- 4 slices Swiss cheese (about 1 ounce each)
- 8 teaspoons yellow mustard

1. Heat grill or grill pan. Cut bread in half lengthwise, then crosswise into four equal pieces. Layer each bottom piece with a sliced pickle, 2 slices of the pork and 1 slice of cheese. Spread the cut-side of each top piece with 2 teaspoons mustard.

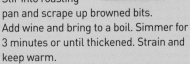

2. Stack tops onto bottom pieces, and flatten to ⅓ original thickness. Place sandwiches on heated grill and weigh down with a heavy pot. Grill for 2 to 3 minutes per side, until nicely grilled and cheese melts. Cut in half on the diagonal and serve.

PER SERVING: 422 calories; 14 g fat (6 g sat.); 28 g protein; 45 g carbohydrate; 3 g fiber; 1,033 mg sodium; 57 mg cholesterol.

day 3

pork fried rice

MAKES: 4 servings. **PREP:** 10 minutes. **COOK:** 22 minutes.

- 2 eggs, lightly beaten
- 1 box (5.2 ounces) Asian-flavored rice mix
- 1 pound pork roast, cut into ¾-inch cubes (about 2½ cups; from master recipe, above)
- 1 bag (16 ounces) frozen Asian stir-fry vegetables, thawed
- 1 can (8 ounces) sliced water chestnuts
- 2 tablespoons light soy sauce
- 1 tablespoon hoisin sauce (or ketchup)
- 2 teaspoons sesame oil
- 2 scallions, chopped

1. Add eggs to a large nonstick skillet. Cook until set and remove to a plate. Cut

into strips. Wipe out skillet; prepare rice mix in it following package directions.
2. During last 7 minutes, add pork, vegetables, water chestnuts, soy and hoisin. Stir in egg and cook, covered, for remaining 7 minutes.
3. Remove from heat and stir in sesame oil.

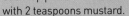

Let stand, covered, for 5 minutes before serving. Garnish with scallions.

PER SERVING: 490 calories; 15 g fat (4 g sat.); 44 g protein; 44 g carbohydrate; 6 g fiber; 726 mg sodium; 195 mg cholesterol.

master recipe

Jarred cabbage is found in the canned vegetable aisle. (Recipes opposite page)

day 2

day 3

Buying larger cuts of meat— to use over three meals— gives you more for your money and reduces prep time in the kitchen.

master recipe

old-fashioned pot roast and gravy

MAKES: 4 servings. **PREP:** 10 minutes. **COOK:** 2 hours, 45 minutes.

- 1 tablespoon vegetable oil
- 1 piece bottom-round pot roast (about 3 pounds)
- ½ teaspoon salt
- ¼ teaspoon black pepper
- 1 large onion, peeled and cut into 8 pieces
- 2 cups beef broth
- 1 can (8 ounces) tomato sauce
- 3 tablespoons all-purpose flour
- ½ pound broad egg noodles, cooked following package directions
Prepared red cabbage (optional)

1. Heat oil in a large heavy-bottomed pot over medium-high heat. Season roast with salt and pepper. Add roast and onion to pot and brown meat on all sides, about 15 minutes total.
2. Add 1½ cups of the beef broth and the tomato sauce. Bring to a boil. Lower heat to medium-low and simmer, covered, for 2 hours, 30 minutes, turning every ½ hour.
3. Remove roast from pot and allow to rest 10 minutes in a warm place.

Reserve cooking liquid. Whisk together the remaining ½ cup of the broth and the flour. Add to the liquid in the pot and bring to a simmer. Simmer for a few minutes until thickened. Strain and reserve.
4. Reserve half of the pot roast and half of the gravy for use in **Shredded Beef Shepherd's Pie** and **Beef and Cheese Melts**.
5. Slice the remaining half of the pot roast and serve with gravy, cooked egg noodles and prepared red cabbage.

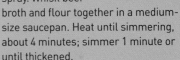

PER SERVING: 595 calories; 27 g fat (9 g sat.); 44 g protein; 42 g carbohydrate; 3 g fiber; 687 mg sodium; 153 mg cholesterol.

day 2

shredded beef shepherd's pie

MAKES: 4 servings. **PREP:** 10 minutes. **COOK:** 5 minutes. **BAKE:** at 350° for 30 minutes.

- 2 cups beef broth
- 2 tablespoons flour
- 2½ cups shredded pot roast (about 9 ounces; from master recipe, at left)
- 1 box (10 ounces) frozen peas and carrots, thawed
- ½ teaspoon dried oregano
- 1 package (21 ounces) prepared mashed potatoes (such as Country Crock)
Paprika, for sprinkling

1. Heat oven to 350°. Coat a 1½-quart casserole with nonstick cooking spray. Whisk beef broth and flour together in a medium-size saucepan. Heat until simmering, about 4 minutes; simmer 1 minute or until thickened.
2. Stir in pot roast, thawed peas and carrots, and oregano. Spoon mixture into prepared casserole.
3. Heat potatoes as per package directions. Spoon over top of meat mixture; sprinkle potatoes with a little paprika. Bake at 350° for 30 minutes. Let stand 15 minutes before serving.

PER SERVING: 389 calories; 18 g fat (8 g sat.); 21 g protein; 35 g carbohydrate; 6 g fiber; 1,105 mg sodium; 61 mg cholesterol.

day 3

beef and cheese melts

MAKES: 4 servings. **PREP:** 10 minutes. **COOK:** 3 minutes. **BROIL:** 1 minute.

- 9 ounces sliced pot roast (about 8 ¼-inch-thick slices; from master recipe, above)
- 1 cup gravy (from master recipe, above)
- 4 slices hearty white bread, lightly toasted
- 4 slices (1 ounce each) deli cheddar cheese
- 12 pickled jalapeño pepper slices
Shoestring fries and cole slaw (optional)

1. Heat broiler.
2. In a large skillet, heat pot roast and gravy over medium heat until heated through, about 3 minutes; thin gravy with a few tablespoons of water, if necessary.

3. Spread toast out on a broiler pan. Divide pot roast slices evenly among toast. Spoon most of the gravy over the meat, and top each sandwich with a slice of cheddar cheese. Spoon any remaining gravy over cheese, then top with a few jalapeño slices.
4. Broil 1 minute, until cheese is melted. Serve with fries and cole slaw, if desired.

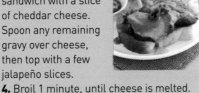

PER SERVING: 357 calories; 18 g fat (9 g sat.); 25 g protein; 24 g carbohydrate; 3 g fiber; 837 mg sodium; 70 mg cholesterol.

Food styling: Sara Neumeier. Prop styling: Loren Simons.

the family **kitchen**

ENLIST THE HELP OF EAGER YOUNGSTERS TO PREPARE A VEGGIE DISH
THEY'LL LOVE. OUR STEP-BY-STEP INSTRUCTIONS MAKE IT EASY TO COOK
UP SOME FUN WITH YOUR KIDS. **BY DEBRA PONZAK**

Raisins
balance the
spiciness of
the ginger.

other kid-friendly veggie ideas

- **MAKE WHIPPED POTATOES** and stir in roasted garlic, Parmesan cheese or caramelized onions.
- **BROIL ASPARAGUS** and top with shaved or crumbled Parmesan or another cheese of your choice.
- **STEAM BROCCOLI OR CAULIFLOWER,** or a mix of the two, and serve with a simple cheese sauce (as easy as melting cheddar in a bit of milk). Or roast cauliflower to bring out its natural sweetness.
- **BAKE SWEET POTATOES** and top with toasted pecans, brown sugar and dried cranberries. Make sweet potato fries by tossing sliced sweet potatoes in olive oil and baking in a 400° oven.

This dish has the perfect amount of sweetness for kids and adults.

glazed carrots with ginger

MAKES: 4 servings. **PREP:** 10 minutes. **COOK:** 22 minutes.

1 tablespoon unsalted butter
1 pound small carrots, well scrubbed
1 tablespoon sugar
1 cup chicken broth
2 teaspoons grated fresh ginger (photos 1 and 2)
2 tablespoons golden raisins
¼ teaspoon salt
¼ teaspoon black pepper

1. Melt butter in a large skillet over medium heat, tilting pan to coat completely.

2. Add carrots and cook for 1 minute. Add sugar and stir to combine; cook for 1 minute.

3. Add chicken broth, grated ginger, raisins, salt and pepper and cook for 20 minutes or until carrots are tender when pierced with a fork **(photo 3).** Serve warm.

PER SERVING: 107 calories; 5 g fat (2 g sat.); 1 g protein; 17 g carbohydrate; 2 g fiber; 436 mg sodium; 9 mg cholesterol.

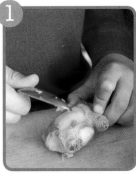

Peel ginger using the side of a spoon. The peel should flake off.

Using a sharp, fine grater, carefully grate onto a cutting board.

Stir carrots until they are tender when pierced with a fork.

cooking school

THESE ELEGANT FRENCH CUSTARDS ARE EASIER TO MAKE THAN YOU MIGHT THINK.
FOLLOW OUR STEP-BY-STEP INSTRUCTIONS FOR PERFECT POTS DE CRÈME.
BY JULIE MILTENBERGER

Be sure to chill before
serving; sweet-tart
raspberries pair well
with creamy custard.

PHOTOGRAPHY BY DAVID PRINCE

vanilla pots de crème

MAKES: 6 servings. **PREP:** 5 minutes. **COOK:** 5 minutes. **BAKE:** at 350° for 45 minutes. **REFRIGERATE:** at least 3 hours.

- ½ of a vanilla bean
- 2 cups whole milk
- 6 egg yolks
- ½ cup sugar
- 5 cups very hot tap water
- Raspberries, for garnish

1. Heat oven to 350°. Line the bottom of a 13 x 9 x 2-inch baking pan with paper towels.
2. Split vanilla bean in half. Scrape out seeds **(photo 1)**, then add seeds and bean to a small, heavy saucepan. Whisk in milk. In a medium-size bowl, whisk together egg yolks and sugar until well blended. Heat the milk gently in a small saucepan just until it reaches simmering. Remove the saucepan from the heat.
3. Whisk about 1 cup of the hot milk into yolk mixture **(photo 2)**; then whisk the yolk mixture into the hot milk in the saucepan. Pour mixture

through a fine-mesh sieve into a 4-cup glass measuring cup to remove any cooked pieces of egg **(photo 3)**.
4. Put six 6-ounce ramekins or custard cups in paper-towel-lined pan. Divide mixture equally among the ramekins **(photo 4)**.
5. Place baking pan with ramekins on middle rack in oven. Carefully pour hot water into baking pan until it reaches halfway up the sides of ramekins.
6. Bake pots de crème in water bath in a 350° oven for 45 minutes or until centers are just set. Remove baking pan from oven; carefully remove ramekins from water bath to cooling racks. Refrigerate until thoroughly chilled, 3 hours or overnight. Garnish with raspberries.

PER SERVING: 176 calories; 8 g fat (3 g sat.); 5 g protein; 21 g carbohydrate; 0 g fiber; 47 mg sodium; 224 mg cholesterol.

Split vanilla bean in half lengthwise; scrape out seeds from both halves with paring knife.

Whisking constantly, pour about 1 cup of the hot milk into egg yolk mixture.

Slowly pour egg yolk mixture through a sieve into a 4-cup measuring cup.

Pour strained mixture into six 6-ounce oven-safe custard cups or ramekins.

april

Shrimp Salad with Scallion Dressing
(Recipe page 75)

WITH SPRINGTIME IN FULL FORCE,
HEALTHFUL DINNERS PACKED WITH
GARDEN-FRESH INGREDIENTS
BRING FLAVOR—PLUS VITAMINS—
TO YOUR FAMILY'S TABLE.

Choco-Cherry Crispy Treats
page 77

**Brown-Sugar-Glazed
Salmon** page 86

3-Way Chicken Salad
page 99

Go green

ADD A LITTLE SPRING TO YOUR NEXT MEAL WITH GARDEN-FRESH RECIPES THAT ARE AS DELICIOUS AS THEY ARE NUTRITIOUS.

BY JACKIE MILLS, R.D.

Shrimp Salad with Scallion Dressing makes a satisfying one-dish meal, perfect for when you're trying to slim down. (Recipe page 75)

Food styling: Susan Spungen. Prop styling: Deborah Williams.

To ensure even roasting, choose baby potatoes— such as fingerlings— that are uniform in size.

roast chicken and veggies

MAKES: 4 servings. **PREP:** 15 minutes. **ROAST:** at 400° for 1 hour, 10 minutes.

- 1 lemon
- 1 whole chicken (about 3¼ pounds)
- 2 cloves garlic, minced
- 6 sprigs fresh tarragon
- 1 teaspoon salt
- ½ teaspoon black pepper
- 2 teaspoons olive oil
- 12 ounces baby potatoes, quartered
- 1 pound asparagus, ends trimmed and cut into 2-inch lengths
- 3 leeks, cleaned and sliced (see photo, opposite page)

1. Heat oven to 400°.

2. Grate lemon peel and set zest aside; cut lemon into quarters. Separate skin from breasts of chicken. Under skin, spread lemon zest, garlic and two of the tarragon sprigs. Season outside and cavity of chicken with ½ teaspoon of the salt and ¼ teaspoon of the pepper. Place lemon quarters and remaining 4 tarragon sprigs in cavity. Place chicken in center of a large roasting pan. Roast on lower shelf at 400° for 30 minutes.

3. Toss potatoes, 1 teaspoon of the olive oil, ¼ teaspoon of the salt and ⅛ teaspoon of the pepper in a medium-size bowl. Coat second large roasting pan with nonstick spray; add potatoes. After chicken has roasted for 30 minutes, add potatoes to top shelf; roast both 15 minutes longer.

4. Combine asparagus, leeks, remaining 1 teaspoon oil, remaining ¼ teaspoon salt, and remaining ⅛ teaspoon pepper in a medium-size bowl; toss to coat.

5. After potatoes have roasted for 15 minutes, add asparagus mixture to pan; roast chicken and vegetables 25 minutes longer, stirring once. Chicken is done when internal temperature measures 165° on an instant-read thermometer inserted in the thigh meat.

6. Let rest 10 minutes before carving. Remove and discard skin before serving.

PER SERVING: 404 calories; 13 g fat (3 g sat.); 45 g protein; 28 g carbohydrate; 5 g fiber; 708 mg sodium; 117 mg cholesterol.

meatball soup with escarole and orzo

MAKES: 6 servings. **PREP:** 15 minutes.
COOK: 23 minutes.

Meatballs:
- 1 pound 95% lean ground beef
- 1 egg
- ⅓ cup plain bread crumbs
- ¼ cup chopped fresh mint
- ¼ cup chopped fresh parsley
- 2 cloves garlic, minced
- 1 tablespoon lemon zest
- ½ teaspoon salt
- ¼ teaspoon black pepper

Soup:
- 2 teaspoons olive oil
- 2 leeks, cleaned and sliced (see photo, below right)
- 1 rib celery, sliced
- 3 cans (14.5 ounces each) low-sodium chicken broth
- 1 can (14.5 ounces) diced tomatoes
- 1 small head escarole, chopped (about 6 cups)
- ½ cup uncooked orzo
- 2 teaspoons lemon juice
- ¼ teaspoon hot pepper sauce

1. Prepare **Meatballs:** In a large bowl, combine beef, egg, bread crumbs, mint, parsley, garlic, lemon zest, salt and black pepper. Stir to mix well. Using your hands or a small scoop, shape the mixture into about 36 meatballs using about 1 heaping tablespoon for each.

2. Prepare **Soup:** Heat the oil in a large pot over medium heat. Add leeks and celery and cook 5 minutes, stirring often, until softened.

3. Stir in the broth, tomatoes and escarole and bring to a boil. Stir in the orzo and return to a boil. Carefully drop in the meatballs and return to a boil.

4. Reduce the heat to medium-low, cover, and cook about 18 minutes, stirring occasionally, until the orzo is tender and the meatballs are cooked through. Stir in lemon juice and hot pepper sauce.

PER SERVING: 282 calories; 9 g fat (3 g sat.); 22 g protein; 28 g carbohydrate; 5 g fiber; 839 mg sodium; 28 mg cholesterol.

washing leeks

Rinse leeks under cool running water, separating and lifting leaves with your fingers to be sure all the sandy grit is washed out.

grilled pork and asparagus with lemon dressing

MAKES: 4 servings. **PREP:** 10 minutes.
GRILL: 8 minutes.

- 1 **large lemon**
- 1 **tablespoon sugar**
- ½ **teaspoon Dijon mustard**
- ⅛ **teaspoon plus ½ teaspoon salt**
- ⅛ **teaspoon plus ¼ teaspoon black pepper**
- 2 **tablespoons plus 3 teaspoons olive oil**
- 1 **tablespoon minced fresh chives**
- 4 **boneless center-cut pork chops (6 ounces each), trimmed of fat**
- 2 **bunches asparagus, trimmed**

1. Cut a thin slice from the top and bottom of the lemon, exposing the flesh. Stand lemon upright, and, using a sharp knife, cut off the thick peel, following the contour of the fruit and removing all the white pith and membrane.

2. Holding lemon over a medium-size bowl, remove lemon sections from membrane (see photo, below right). Discard seeds and let sections fall into the bowl. Squeeze remaining membrane to extract juice into bowl. Break sections into pieces using two forks. Whisk **1 tablespoon water,** the sugar, the mustard, ⅛ teaspoon of the salt and ⅛ teaspoon of the pepper into the lemon. Slowly whisk in 2 tablespoons of the oil. Stir in chives; set aside.

3. Heat gas grill to medium-high or prepare charcoal grill with medium-hot coals. Brush pork with 2 teaspoons of the remaining olive oil. Sprinkle with ¼ teaspoon of the remaining salt and remaining ¼ teaspoon pepper. Grill pork about 4 minutes on each side or until internal temperature registers 155° on an instant-read thermometer.

4. Meanwhile, brush asparagus with remaining 1 teaspoon oil. Place on grill and grill 6 minutes, turning often, or until crisp-tender. Sprinkle with remaining ¼ teaspoon salt. Serve pork and asparagus topped with lemon dressing.

PER SERVING: 387 calories; 17 g fat (4 g sat.); 41 g protein; 16 g carbohydrate; 6 g fiber; 467 mg sodium; 107 mg cholesterol.

Asparagus is a good source of vitamins C and B6, and folate.

citrus sections

Cut into center between one section and membrane. Cut along other side of section next to membrane, freeing each section.

Photo (lemon): David Prince.

risotto with sugar snap peas and ham

MAKES: 4 servings. **PREP:** 10 minutes. **COOK:** 34 minutes.

½ **pound sugar snap peas, trimmed and cut in half on the diagonal**

3½ **cups low-sodium chicken broth**

2 **teaspoons olive oil**

4 **leeks, cleaned and thinly sliced (see photo, page 71)**

2 **cloves garlic, minced**

1 **cup arborio rice**

4 **ounces cubed ham (half of an 8-ounce package)**

½ **cup grated Parmesan cheese**

¼ **teaspoon black pepper**

1. Cook peas in boiling water about 4 minutes or until crisp-tender. Drain and rinse with cold water and set aside.

2. Pour broth into a medium-size saucepan and bring to a simmer over medium heat; reduce heat to low and keep broth warm.

3. Heat the oil in a large saucepan over medium heat. Add leeks and cook 6 minutes, stirring frequently, or until softened. Add garlic and cook 1 minute. Stir in rice and cook 1 more minute. Stir in broth, ½ cup at a time. Stir frequently until liquid is absorbed before adding the next ½ cup (about 20 minutes total); rice should be tender yet firm to the bite.

4. Add peas and ham and cook, stirring constantly, 2 minutes or until peas are heated through. Stir in Parmesan cheese and pepper.

PER SERVING: 421 calories; 9 g fat (4 g sat.); 20 g protein; 65 g carbohydrate; 4 g fiber; 771 mg sodium; 13 mg cholesterol.

To prep sugar snap peas before cooking, break off stem end and peel away tough string.

asparagus and spinach frittata

MAKES: 4 servings. **PREP:** 15 minutes. **COOK:** 25 minutes. **BROIL:** 4 minutes.

- 5 **large eggs**
- 4 **large egg whites**
- ½ **cup grated Parmesan cheese**
- 1 **tablespoon Dijon mustard**
- 1 **tablespoon chopped fresh dill**
- ¼ **teaspoon salt**
- ¼ **teaspoon black pepper**
- 1 **bag (6 ounces) baby spinach**
- 2 **teaspoons olive oil**
- ½ **pound new potatoes, cut into ½-inch pieces**
- 1 **bunch scallions, trimmed and sliced**
- 1 **bunch asparagus (about 1 pound), trimmed and cut into 1-inch pieces**
- ¾ **cup shredded fontina cheese**

1. Heat broiler. In a medium-size bowl, whisk eggs, egg whites, Parmesan, mustard, dill, salt and pepper.

2. Heat a 10-inch nonstick skillet with an ovenproof handle over medium heat. Add spinach and cook 4 to 5 minutes, until wilted. Remove to a strainer set over a bowl; wipe out skillet. Heat olive oil in the same skillet over medium heat. Add potatoes. Cover and cook 5 minutes, stirring occasionally. Uncover and add scallions; cook 3 minutes, stirring until softened.

3. Add asparagus to pan. Cover and cook 10 minutes, stirring occasionally.

4. Press down on spinach to remove any excess liquid. Stir spinach into pan.

5. Reduce heat to medium-low. Pour egg mixture evenly over vegetables in skillet. Cook 2 minutes or until bottom is set.

6. Place under broiler and broil 2 minutes or until top is almost set. Carefully remove from broiler (handle will be hot) and sprinkle top evenly with fontina cheese. Broil 2 minutes longer or until top is set and cheese is melted.

PER SERVING: 355 calories; 19 g fat (9 g sat.); 27 g protein; 20 g carbohydrate; 5 g fiber; 804 mg sodium; 299 mg cholesterol.

Choose firm asparagus spears with crisp tips.

Spinach is a powerhouse of nutrition—full of calcium, iron and magnesium.

almond-crusted cod with dijon spinach

MAKES: 4 servings. **PREP:** 10 minutes. **REFRIGERATE:** 30 minutes. **COOK:** 18 minutes. **BAKE:** at 400° for 13 minutes.

- **4 cod fillets (6 ounces each), about 1-inch thick**
- **1 cup dry vermouth**
- **⅔ cup slivered almonds**
- **½ teaspoon salt**
- **3 tablespoons whole-grain Dijon mustard**
- **2 teaspoons olive oil**
- **1 small onion, finely diced**
- **2 cloves garlic, minced**
- **3 bags (6 ounces each) baby spinach**
- **½ cup golden raisins**

1. Line a baking sheet with nonstick aluminum foil and set aside.
2. Place cod fillets in a large resealable plastic food storage bag; add vermouth and seal. Refrigerate for 30 minutes.
3. Toast ⅓ cup of the almonds in a small skillet over medium-high heat for about 8 minutes or until lightly browned and fragrant; set aside.
4. Heat oven to 400°. Finely chop remaining ⅓ cup almonds; place in a pie plate and set aside. Remove cod from vermouth and pat dry with paper towels. Sprinkle with the salt, then spread tops of cod with 2 tablespoons of the mustard. Sprinkle with chopped almonds and press into mustard.
5. Place cod on baking sheet, almond-side up, and bake at 400° for 13 minutes or until fish flakes easily with a fork.
6. While fish cooks, heat olive oil in a large skillet over medium heat. Add the onion and cook 5 minutes, stirring often, or until onion is softened. Add garlic and cook 1 minute. Add spinach in batches and cook 4 minutes, turning with tongs, or until spinach is just wilted.
7. Remove from heat and stir in remaining tablespoon mustard, toasted almonds and raisins. Remove cod from oven; serve with spinach.

PER SERVING: 410 calories; 15 g fat (1 g sat.); 39 g protein; 26 g carbohydrate; 6 g fiber; 756 mg sodium; 73 mg cholesterol.

shrimp salad with scallion dressing

MAKES: 6 servings. **PREP:** 10 minutes. **REFRIGERATE:** 1 hour. **COOK:** 6 minutes.

Scallion Dressing:

- **4 scallions, trimmed and sliced**
- **3 tablespoons fat-free low sodium chicken broth**
- **2 tablespoons olive oil**
- **2 tablespoons white wine vinegar**
- **1 tablespoon honey**
- **¼ teaspoon salt**
- **¼ teaspoon ground cumin**
- **⅛ teaspoon black pepper**

Salad:

- **1 tablespoon lemon zest**
- **2 cloves garlic, minced**
- **2 teaspoons olive oil**
- **½ teaspoon black pepper**
- **1½ pounds large shrimp, peeled and deveined**
- **½ teaspoon salt**
- **4 cups mixed baby salad greens**
- **1 cup grape tomatoes, halved**
- **1 large cucumber, peeled and sliced**

1. Prepare **Scallion Dressing:** Combine scallions, broth, olive oil, vinegar, honey, salt, cumin and pepper in a blender and process until smooth.
2. Prepare **Salad:** Combine lemon zest, garlic, olive oil and pepper in a resealable plastic food-storage bag. Add shrimp; toss to coat evenly. Seal and refrigerate 1 hour.

3. Remove shrimp from marinade. Coat a large nonstick skillet with nonstick cooking spray. Add shrimp and cook over medium-high heat for 6 minutes or until cooked through, turning occasionally. Sprinkle with the salt.
4. Arrange greens, tomatoes and cucumber on a large platter and toss with 3 tablespoons of the Scallion Dressing. Top with shrimp. Drizzle with more dressing and serve.

PER SERVING: 207 calories; 8 g fat (1 g sat.); 24 g protein; 9 g carbohydrate; 2 g fiber; 482 mg sodium; 172 mg cholesterol.

sweet
SUCCESS

FAMILY CIRCLE TEAMED UP WITH *SHARE OUR STRENGTH* FOR THE GREAT AMERICAN BAKE SALE. LET THEIR EFFORTS TO END CHILDHOOD HUNGER INSPIRE YOU TO HOST YOUR OWN SALE WITH THESE POPULAR TREATS.

BY CINDY HELLER

Packing goodies, such as these Oatmeal Raisin Cookies, in fun containers will boost sales. (recipe page 81)

3 00 per box

PHOTOGRAPHY BY JAMES BAIGRIE

Plastic cellophane and colorful ribbons make a simple but pretty presentation.

choco-cherry crispy treats

MAKES: 28 squares. **PREP:** 10 minutes.
COOK: 3 minutes.

- 6 cups chocolate-flavored crisped rice cereal (such as Cocoa Krispies)
- ¾ cup dried cherries
- 3 tablespoons unsalted butter
- 1 tablespoon cocoa powder
- 1 bag (10 ounces) marshmallows

1. Coat a 13 x 9-inch baking dish with nonstick cooking spray; set aside.
2. Combine cereal and cherries in a large bowl; set aside.
3. Melt butter in a large saucepan over medium-high heat. Add cocoa powder and the marshmallows and stir until completely melted, about 3 minutes. Pour over cereal mixture and stir to coat completely. Spoon cereal mixture into

prepared baking dish and, using a spatula or your hands coated with nonstick cooking spray, press mixture evenly into dish. Let cool, then cut into 2-inch squares. Place each square in a cellophane bag and tie with ribbon.

PER SQUARE: 103 calories; 2 g fat (1 g sat.); 1 g protein; 22 g carbohydrate; 1 g fiber; 75 mg sodium; 4 mg cholesterol.

Heather McAdams
Atlanta, GA

READER RECIPE

"Try doubling this recipe—buckeyes disappear faster than you can make them!"

caramel corn

MAKES: 13 cups. **PREP:** 10 minutes.
COOK: 5 minutes. **BAKE:** at 250° for 1 hour.

- 2 tablespoons vegetable oil
- ½ cup popcorn kernels
- ½ cup (1 stick) unsalted butter
- 1 cup firmly packed dark-brown sugar
- ½ cup light corn syrup
- 1 cup roasted peanuts
- ½ teaspoon vanilla extract
- ¼ teaspoon baking soda

1. Heat oven to 250°. Coat a large, deep roasting pan generously with nonstick cooking spray; set aside.
2. Combine oil and popcorn in a large saucepan. Cover and cook over medium-high heat, shaking occasionally until kernels start to pop. Shake saucepan continuously until popping stops, then pour popcorn into prepared roasting pan.
3. Melt butter in a medium-size saucepan over low heat. Add brown sugar and corn syrup and bring to a boil over medium-high heat. Boil gently without stirring for 5 minutes or until mixture reaches 260° on a candy thermometer. Remove from heat and quickly stir in peanuts, vanilla and baking soda until smooth.
4. Pour corn syrup mixture over popcorn and toss to coat evenly. Bake popcorn at 250° for 1 hour, stirring every 15 minutes. Remove from oven and cool completely. Break up into small clusters and store in small canisters.

PER CUP: 273 calories; 15 g fat (5 g sat.);
4 g protein; 34 g carbohydrate; 2 g fiber;
40 mg sodium; 19 mg cholesterol.

buckeyes

MAKES: about 48. **PREP:** 5 minutes.
FREEZE: 30 minutes.
MICROWAVE: 2 minutes. **CHILL:** 45 minutes.

- 1 cup creamy peanut butter
- ½ cup (1 stick) unsalted butter, softened
- 2 cups confectioners' sugar
- 2 cups semisweet chocolate chips

1. Line two baking sheets with waxed paper; set aside.
2. In a large bowl, beat peanut butter, butter and sugar with an electric mixer on medium speed until well combined. Roll into 1-inch balls and place on baking sheets. If mixture is sticky, wet hands with cold water and continue rolling.

Place baking sheets in freezer for 30 minutes or until balls are firm.
3. Microwave chips in a glass bowl on HIGH for 2 minutes, stirring midway.
4. Pierce each ball with a toothpick and dip into chocolate ¾ of the way deep, wiping excess chocolate on rim of bowl. Place on waxed paper; repeat with remaining balls. Return undipped buckeyes to freezer for 10 minutes if they get too soft.
5. Chill in fridge for 45 minutes, until set. Put buckeyes on a pretty paper plate, wrap in cellophane and tie with ribbon.

PER SERVING: 88 calories; 6 g fat (3 g sat.);
1 g protein; 9 g carbohydrate; 1 g fiber;
22 mg sodium; 4 mg cholesterol.

CARAMEL CORN

2 TBLS VEGETABLE OIL
1/2 C. POPCORN KERNELS
1/2 C. UNSALTED BUTTER
1 C. FIRMLY PACKED BR. SUGAR
1/2 C. LIGHT CORN SYRUP
1 C. ROASTED PEANUTS
1/2 tSP VANILLA EXTRACT
1/4 TSP BAKING SODA

Feel free to substitute any type of nut for the peanuts.

For a citrusy kick, increase the amount of lemon zest.

lemon poppy seed pound cake loaves

MAKES: 16 slices. **PREP:** 10 minutes. **BAKE:** at 350° for 48 minutes.

- 1 **box (18.25 ounces) lemon-flavored cake mix**
- 1 **package (3.4 ounces) lemon-flavored pudding mix**
- 1 **cup sour cream**
- ½ **cup vegetable oil**
- 3 **eggs**
- ¼ **cup poppy seeds**
- 1 **tablespoon lemon zest**
- 1 **tablespoon confectioners' sugar**

1. Heat oven to 350°. Coat two 8 x 4 x 3-inch loaf pans with nonstick cooking spray. Dust with flour; shake out excess.

2. In a large bowl, using an electric mixer, blend cake mix, pudding mix, sour cream, oil and eggs on low speed until moistened. Scrape down sides of bowl. Increase speed to medium and beat 2 minutes. Add poppy seeds and zest and beat until evenly distributed. Divide batter between loaf pans; smooth tops with a small spatula.

3. Bake at 350° for 48 minutes or until toothpick inserted in center comes out clean. Let loaves cool in pans on wire racks 15 minutes. Turn loaves out onto racks; let cool completely. Sift confectioners' sugar onto top. Cut each loaf into 8 slices. Wrap each slice in brightly colored plastic wrap.

PER SLICE: 274 calories; 14 g fat (4 mg sat.); 4 g protein; 33 g carbohydrate; 0 g fiber; 256 mg sodium; 50 mg cholesterol.

oatmeal raisin cookies

MAKES: about 30 cookies.
PREP: 10 minutes. **REFRIGERATE:** 15 minutes.
BAKE: at 375° for 12 minutes.

- ¾ **cup flour**
- ½ **teaspoon baking soda**
- ¼ **teaspoon cinnamon**
- ¼ **teaspoon nutmeg**
- **Pinch salt**
- ½ **cup (1 stick) unsalted butter, softened**
- 1 **cup packed light-brown sugar**
- 3 **large egg whites**
- 1 **teaspoon vanilla extract**
- 3 **cups old-fashioned rolled oats**
- ½ **cup raisins, coarsely chopped**

1. Heat oven to 375°. Lightly coat baking sheets with nonstick cooking spray or line with nonstick foil. Set aside.

2. In a large bowl, stir together flour, baking soda, cinnamon, nutmeg and salt; set aside.

3. In another large bowl, beat butter until smooth. Add sugar and beat until light and fluffy. Beat in egg whites until well combined. Beat in vanilla.

4. With mixer on lowest speed, beat in flour mixture; then stir in oats and raisins. Cover bowl with plastic wrap and refrigerate dough for 15 minutes.

5. Form dough into 1-inch balls and place on prepared cookie sheets; flatten slightly. If dough is sticky, wet hands with cold water and continue flattening. Bake at 375° for 12 minutes or until lightly golden around edges. Cool for 2 minutes on baking sheets, then transfer cookies to a wire rack and cool completely. Line Chinese take-out boxes with tissue paper and place 3 to 4 cookies inside each.

PER COOKIE: 107 calories; 4 g fat (2 g sat.); 2 g protein; 17 g carbohydrate; 1 g fiber; 40 mg sodium; 8 mg cholesterol.

baking basics

For attractive, delicious baked goods that will sell like hot-cakes, follow these simple tips; a successful sale is guaranteed!

▶ For quick cookie dough portioning, try using a spring-loaded ice cream scoop to ensure even amounts.

▶ For easier mixing, use room temperature butter and eggs.

▶ If you're baking more than one sheet of cookies at a time, use the upper-middle and lower-middle racks. Be sure to rotate pans halfway through.

▶ For clean cuts, slice room-temperature cakes or loaves using a sharp, serrated knife. When you reach the bottom of the cake, draw the knife out toward you.

▶ A great way to store pre-baked cookies and cupcakes is to freeze them in a resealable plastic bag. Press the excess air from the bag before sealing.

springtime SIMPLE

Buying a pre-baked crust, shredded cheese and washed salad greens streamlines prep. (Recipe page 87)

WITH OUR SHOPPING LIST, YOU CAN SPEED THROUGH THE SUPERMARKET, THEN COOK DELICIOUS, NUTRITIOUS MEALS—EVEN WHEN TIME IS TIGHT.
BY JULIE MILTENBERGER

PHOTOGRAPHY BY CHARLES SCHILLER

tilapia veracruz

MAKES: 4 servings. **PREP:** 5 minutes. **COOK:** 7 minutes. **BAKE:** at 350° for 25 minutes.

- 2 tablespoons olive oil
- 2 sweet bell peppers, cored and cut into strips
- 1 medium-size onion, sliced
- 1 can (14½ ounces) petite-cut diced tomatoes with jalapeños
- ½ teaspoon dried oregano
- ½ teaspoon hot pepper sauce
- 4 tilapia fillets, about 1½ pounds total
- ½ teaspoon *each* salt and black pepper
- 2 cups hot heat-and-serve white rice

1. Heat oven to 350°. Coat a 13 x 9 x 2-inch baking dish with nonstick cooking spray. Heat oil in a large skillet over medium heat. Add peppers and onion; cook 4 minutes. Add tomatoes and oregano; cook 3 minutes. Stir in hot sauce.
2. Place fish in prepared dish. Top with pepper mixture. Season with salt and pepper.

3. Bake at 350° for 25 minutes, until fish flakes easily with a fork. Spoon fish and pepper mixture onto plates; serve with rice.

PER SERVING: 443 calories; 10 g fat (2 g sat.); 56 g protein; 32 g carbohydrate; 3 g fiber; 818 mg sodium; 113 mg cholesterol.

asparagus potatoes

MAKES: 4 servings. **PREP:** 5 minutes. **MICROWAVE:** 16 minutes. **COOK:** 5 minutes. **BROIL:** at 500° for 3 minutes.

4 **large baking potatoes, scrubbed**
2 **teaspoons olive oil**
8 **ounces asparagus (about 1/2 bunch), trimmed, peeled and cut into 1-inch pieces**
1/4 **teaspoon** *each* **salt and black pepper**
4 **tablespoons margarine or unsalted butter**
2 **ounces herbed cheese bits (such as Boursin Toppers)**

1. Heat broiler. Pierce potatoes with a fork. Place on paper towels in the microwave. Microwave on HIGH for 16 minutes, turning over halfway through.

2. Meanwhile, heat oil in a medium-size skillet over medium-high heat. Add asparagus and cook 5 minutes. Season with 1/8 teaspoon *each* of the salt and pepper; remove from heat. Line a baking sheet with foil; place potatoes on foil.

3. Carefully cut open potatoes; season with remaining 1/8 teaspoon *each* salt and pepper. Dot with margarine; top with asparagus. Divide cheese evenly among potatoes. Broil for 2 to 3 minutes or until cheese is lightly browned on top.

PER SERVING: 439 calories; 20 g fat (6 g sat.); 9 g protein; 57 g carbohydrate; 7 g fiber; 414 mg sodium; 20 mg cholesterol.

See cooking tip on page 89 for instructions on peeling asparagus.

stuffed chicken breasts

MAKES: 6 servings. **PREP:** 15 minutes. **COOK:** 6 minutes. **BAKE:** at 350° for 30 minutes.

- 6 boneless, skinless chicken breast halves (2¼ pounds)
- 4 ounces (½ package) ⅓-less-fat cream cheese
- 1 package frozen chopped broccoli, thawed
- ½ cup shredded cheddar
- 2 tablespoons seasoned bread crumbs
- ½ teaspoon *each* salt and black pepper
  Hot cooked egg noodles (optional)

1. Heat oven to 350°. Remove tenders from chicken; reserve for another use. Cut a pocket into breasts, cutting into but not through. Soften cream cheese slightly.

2. In a large bowl, combine broccoli, both cheeses, bread crumbs and ¼ teaspoon *each* of the salt and pepper. Stuff a scant ⅓ cup into each chicken breast. Secure with toothpicks.

3. Season chicken with remaining ¼ teaspoon *each* salt and pepper. Brown chicken over medium-high heat in two batches in a nonstick skillet for 3 minutes. Transfer to a baking dish. Bake at 350° for 30 minutes, until cooked through. Serve with egg noodles, if desired.

PER SERVING: 351 calories; 13 g fat (6 g sat.); 52 g protein; 4 g carbohydrate; 2 g fiber; 498 mg sodium; 149 mg cholesterol.

brown-sugar-glazed salmon

MAKES: 4 servings. **PREP:** 5 minutes. **BAKE:** at 325° for 25 minutes.

4 **2-inch wide salmon fillets (about 1½ pounds total)**
¼ **cup packed dark-brown sugar**
2 **teaspoons butter**
2 **teaspoons Dijon mustard**
¼ **teaspoon** *each* **salt and black pepper**
8 **ounces steamed snow peas**
2 **cups heat-and-serve brown rice**

1. Heat oven to 325°. Line a small baking sheet with nonstick aluminum foil. Place salmon on prepared sheet.
2. In a small bowl, stir together brown sugar, butter, mustard, salt and pepper. Carefully spread over salmon pieces, dividing equally.

3. Transfer salmon to 325° oven and bake for 25 minutes, or until fish flakes easily with a fork. Serve with snow peas and rice on the side.

PER SERVING: 478 calories; 15 g fat (3 g sat.); 43 g protein; 41 g carbohydrate; 3 g fiber; 303 mg sodium; 112 mg cholesterol.

salad pizza

MAKES: 4 servings. **PREP:** 5 minutes. **BAKE:** at 450° for 13 minutes.

- 2 **plum tomatoes, cored and thinly sliced**
- 1 **whole-wheat or regular pre-baked pizza shell (10 ounces)**
- ¼ **teaspoon** *each* **salt and black pepper**
- ¾ **cup shredded part-skim mozzarella cheese**
- 3 **tablespoons grated Parmesan cheese**
- 4 **cups baby salad greens**
- 3 **tablespoons light balsamic vinaigrette**

1. Heat oven to 450°. Spread tomato slices onto paper towels. Let sit 5 minutes.
2. Place pizza shell on a large baking sheet. Top with tomatoes; sprinkle with salt and pepper. Bake at 450° for 8 minutes. Top with mozzarella and Parmesan cheese and continue to bake an additional 5 minutes.

3. Meanwhile, in a large bowl, toss salad greens with dressing. Remove pizza from oven; top with salad. Cut into wedges.

PER SERVING: 296 calories; 10 g fat (3 g sat.); 16 g protein; 40 g carbohydrate; 7 g fiber; 890 mg sodium; 17 mg cholesterol.

penne rapini

MAKES: 6 servings. **PREP:** 10 minutes. **COOK:** 12 minutes.

- 5 slices bacon
- 1 pound rapini (broccoli rabe)
- 1 pound whole-wheat penne pasta
- 4 garlic cloves, peeled and sliced
- ¼ cup sliced pitted black olives
- ¼ teaspoon crushed red pepper
- ¼ pound sliced mushrooms
- 2 tablespoons extra virgin olive oil
- 2 tablespoons grated Parmesan cheese

1. Cook bacon in a large nonstick skillet over medium heat for 6 minutes, until crisp. Cool and crumble bacon; save drippings.

2. Rinse rapini; cut into 2-inch pieces. Blanch in a large pot of lightly salted boiling water for 1 minute. Remove with a slotted spoon; scoop out ¼ cup water. Return remaining water to boiling; add pasta. Cook per package instructions.

3. While pasta cooks, reheat bacon drippings and add garlic, olives, red pepper and mushrooms to pan. Cook 3 minutes, until garlic is softened. Add reserved water and rapini. Cook 2 minutes. Toss with pasta, bacon, olive oil and Parmesan.

PER SERVING: 452 calories; 16 g fat (4 g sat.); 15 g protein; 62 g carbohydrate; 7 g fiber; 250 mg sodium; 14 mg cholesterol.

READER RECIPE

"This easy dish has the added bonus of freezing well."

Dorothy Aiken
Bradenton, FL

pantry items

- salt and pepper
- butter and margarine
- olive oil
- Dijon mustard
- seasoned bread crumbs
- dark-brown sugar
- grated Parmesan cheese
- hot pepper sauce
- crushed red pepper
- dried oregano
- garlic

shopping list

This grocery list and the pantry items are all you need to cook up a week of hearty suppers.

PRODUCE

- 2   sweet bell peppers
- 1   medium-size onion
- 1   bunch asparagus
- 1   bunch broccoli rabe
- 4   large baking potatoes
- 2   plum tomatoes
-     Assorted salad greens
- ½   pound snow peas
- ¼   pound mushrooms
- 1   package frozen chopped broccoli

DAIRY

- 1   container herbed cheese bits (Boursin Toppers)
- 1   package ⅓-less-fat cream cheese
- 1   package shredded cheddar cheese
- 1   bag shredded part-skim mozzarella cheese

MEAT, FISH AND POULTRY

- 4   tilapia fillets (1½ pounds)
- 4   salmon fillets (1½ pounds)
- 6   boneless, skinless chicken breast halves (2¼ pounds)
- 1   small package bacon

DRY GOODS

- 1   whole-wheat or regular pre-baked pizza shell
- 1   bottle light balsamic vinaigrette
- 1   package egg noodles
- 1   package whole wheat penne pasta
- 2   packages heat-and-serve cooked white rice
- 2   packages heat-and-serve cooked brown rice
- 1   can petite-cut diced tomatoes with jalapeños
- 1   can sliced black olives

cooking tip

peeling asparagus

1. Rinse asparagus well and pat dry. If using less than a bunch, store remaining spears standing upright in 1 inch of water in refrigerator.

2. Gently bend asparagus at the stem end, allowing for a natural break. Or you may simply trim about 1 inch from the stem end of each spear.

3. With vegetable peeler, peel about 1½ inches off stem end of each asparagus spear (especially if it is thicker than a pencil). Cut into pieces as recipe directs.

BEEF IT UP!

SURPRISE YOUR FAMILY WITH THESE LEAN, GREAT-TASTING WEEKNIGHT FAVORITES. BY MICHAEL TYRRELL

Vegetables add a shot of fiber to our Quick Meat Sauce and Shells. (Recipe page 91)

PHOTOGRAPHY BY DAVID PRINCE

When purchasing meat, look for ground beef that's labeled at least 90% lean.

greek meatloaf

MAKES: 6 servings. **PREP:** 10 minutes. **BAKE:** at 375° for 1 hour.

- 1½ pounds lean ground beef
- ½ cup unseasoned bread crumbs mixed with ½ cup milk
- 4 ounces basil-tomato or plain feta cheese, crumbled
- 2 eggs, lightly beaten
- 1 large onion, peeled and chopped
- 1 cup shredded carrot
- 1 teaspoon dried Greek seasoning (such as McCormick) or dried oregano
- ½ teaspoon salt
- ½ teaspoon black pepper

1. Heat oven to 375°. Spray a 13 x 9-inch baking pan with nonstick cooking spray.
2. In a large bowl, mix together beef, soaked bread crumbs, crumbled feta, eggs, onion, carrot, Greek seasoning, salt and pepper. Form into a loaf, approximately 9 x 5 inches, and place in the prepared baking pan.

3. Bake at 375° for about 1 hour or until internal temperature registers 150° on an instant-read thermometer.
4. Allow to rest, covered, for 10 minutes before slicing. Serve with oven fries, if desired. Recipe follows.

PER SERVING: 293 calories; 13 g fat (6 g sat.); 33 g protein; 11 g carbohydrate; 1 g fiber; 585 mg sodium; 156 mg cholesterol.

Oven Fries: Cut 2 pounds of baking potatoes lengthwise into eight wedges each. Toss with 1 tablespoon olive oil, ½ teaspoon dried Greek seasoning or oregano, ¼ teaspoon salt and ⅛ teaspoon black pepper. Bake at 375° for about 30 minutes or until fork tender.

PER SERVING: 126 calories; 2 g fat (0 g sat.); 3 g protein; 24 g carbohydrate; 3 g fiber; 106 mg sodium; 0 mg cholesterol.

quick meat sauce and shells

MAKES: 6 servings.
PREP: 15 minutes. **COOK:** 23 minutes.

- 1 pound lean ground beef
- 1 large sweet red pepper, cored, seeded and diced
- 1 large green bell pepper, cored, seeded and diced
- 1 medium onion, peeled and chopped
- 2 cloves garlic, peeled and chopped
- 2 cans (14½ ounces each) diced tomatoes with Italian seasoning
- 1 teaspoon sugar
- ½ teaspoon salt
- ¼ teaspoon black pepper
- 1 pound large pasta shells
- 1 cup part-skim shredded mozzarella

1. Coat a large nonstick skillet with nonstick cooking spray; heat over medium-high heat and add crumbled ground beef, peppers, onion and garlic. Cook for 8 minutes, stirring occasionally.
2. Stir in tomatoes, sugar, salt and black pepper. Cover and simmer on medium-low for 15 minutes, stirring occasionally.
3. While sauce is simmering, cook pasta following package directions. Drain.
4. Spoon sauce over pasta. Top with shredded cheese and serve.

PER SERVING: 486 calories; 9 g fat (4 g sat.); 33 g protein; 68 g carbohydrate; 5 g fiber; 697 mg sodium; 57 mg cholesterol.

"I added wheat germ to these burgers to up the fiber. They're also a great source of iron and potassium."

Suzan Wiener
Springhill, FL

cheeseburger-zucchini pie

MAKES: 6 servings. **PREP:** 10 minutes.
COOK: 6 minutes. **BAKE:** at 400° for 25 minutes.

- ¾ pound lean ground beef
- 1 medium onion, peeled and chopped
- 1 medium zucchini (about 6 ounces), shredded
- ½ teaspoon salt
- ¼ teaspoon black pepper
- 1 cup shredded Italian cheese blend
- ½ cup heart-healthy reduced-fat biscuit mix (such as Bisquick)
- 1 cup milk
- 2 eggs

1. Heat oven to 400°. Spray a 9-inch pie plate with nonstick cooking spray.
2. Spray a large nonstick skillet with nonstick cooking spray; heat over medium-high heat. Crumble in ground beef. Stir in onion and zucchini and cook for 6 minutes, stirring occasionally. Season with salt and pepper.
3. Spread beef mixture into the prepared 9-inch pie plate. Sprinkle the cheese over the top.
4. In a medium-size bowl, whisk together the biscuit mix, milk and eggs until smooth. Pour mixture over beef mixture.
5. Bake at 400° for 25 minutes or until a knife inserted in the center comes out clean. Allow to cool for 5 to 10 minutes. Cut into six wedges and serve with a green salad, if desired.

PER SERVING: 239 calories; 11 g fat (5 g sat.); 21 g protein; 13 g carbohydrate; 1 g fiber; 441 mg sodium; 123 mg cholesterol.

better burgers

MAKES: 8 servings. **PREP:** 10 minutes. **COOK:** 10 minutes.

- 2 pounds lean ground beef
- ¾ cup wheat germ
- 2 eggs
- ½ cup half-and-half
- 2 tablespoons minced onion
- 2 teaspoons Worcestershire sauce
- 1 teaspoon salt
- ¼ teaspoon dried marjoram or oregano
- ¼ teaspoon dried thyme

- 8 hamburger buns
  American cheese, lettuce and sliced tomato (optional)

1. In a large bowl, combine ground beef, wheat germ, eggs, half-and-half, onion, Worcestershire sauce, salt, marjoram and thyme. Shape into 8 patties.
2. Broil or grill for 4 to 5 minutes per side or until internal temperature registers 150° on an instant-read thermometer.

Place a slice of cheese on top during the last 2 minutes of cooking, if desired. Let stand, covered, for 5 minutes (temperature should reach 160°).
3. Place burgers on buns and top with lettuce and tomato, if desired.

PER SERVING: 351 calories; 12 g fat (5 g sat.); 34 g protein; 27 g carbohydrate; 2 g fiber; 625 mg sodium; 131 mg cholesterol.

beef and bean tortilla casserole

MAKES: 8 servings. **PREP:** 15 minutes. **COOK:** 9 minutes. **BAKE:** at 375° for 45 minutes.

1½ pounds lean ground beef
  1 large onion, peeled and chopped
  2 to 3 teaspoons hot chili powder
  ½ teaspoon ground cumin
  ¼ teaspoon salt
2½ cups prepared reduced-sodium salsa
     (such as Muir Glen Organic or Green
     Mountain Gringo)
  8 fajita-size flour tortillas
  1 can (15 ounces) red kidney beans,
     drained and rinsed
  2 cups shredded reduced-fat taco
     cheese blend (such as Sargento)

1. Heat oven to 375°. Coat a 13 x 9 x 2-inch baking dish with nonstick cooking spray. Set aside.

2. Spray a large nonstick skillet with nonstick cooking spray; heat over medium-high heat. Crumble in ground beef and onion. Cook for 8 minutes, stirring occasionally. Add chili powder, cumin and salt and cook 1 minute. Stir in 1 cup of the salsa and heat through.

3. Line the prepared baking dish with two of the tortillas. Cut a third tortilla into pieces, and use some of the pieces to completely cover bottom of dish. In a medium-size bowl, coarsely mash the beans and stir in 1 cup of the salsa. Spoon mixture evenly over the tortillas in the baking dish. Sprinkle ⅔ cup of the cheese over the top.

4. Place another layer of tortillas (and tortilla pieces) over beans and cheese. Evenly spoon beef mixture over tortillas. Sprinkle with ⅔ cup of the cheese. Place the remaining tortillas over the beef and cheese layer. Top with the remaining ½ cup salsa and the remaining cheese.

5. Cover with foil and bake at 375° for 45 minutes. Remove from oven and allow to set for at least 10 minutes before serving.

PER SERVING: 396 calories; 13 g fat (6 g sat.); 33 g protein; 36 g carbohydrate; 6 g fiber; 942 mg sodium; 73 mg cholesterol.

sloppy joes (+ 3 variations)

MAKES: 6 servings.
PREP: 5 minutes. **COOK:** 18 minutes.

- 1½ pounds lean ground beef
- 1 can (8 ounces) tomato sauce
- ⅓ cup ketchup
- 2 tablespoons white wine vinegar
- 1 tablespoon Worcestershire sauce
- 2 teaspoons sugar
- 6 hamburger buns

1. Coat a large nonstick skillet with nonstick cooking spray; heat over medium-high heat. Crumble in the ground beef and cook, stirring occasionally, for 8 minutes.
2. Stir in the tomato sauce, ketchup, vinegar, Worcestershire sauce and sugar. Simmer on medium-low for 10 minutes, stirring occasionally.
3. To serve, spoon about ½ cup of the mixture on each hamburger bun. Serve with pickles and cole slaw, if desired.

PER SERVING: 304 calories; 7 g fat (3 g sat.); 28 g protein; 29 g carbohydrate; 1 g fiber; 717 mg sodium; 70 mg cholesterol.

Variations

Asian: Add 2 cloves chopped garlic, ½ teaspoon ground ginger and substitute 2 tablespoons light soy sauce for Worcestershire. Serve over white rice or on hamburger buns.

Italian: Add 1 teaspoon dried oregano and ½ teaspoon dried Italian seasoning. Stir in marinara sauce instead of ketchup. Substitute prebaked pizza crust for hamburger buns and garnish with shredded mozzarella.

Mexican: Add 1 tablespoon chili powder and substitute prepared salsa for the ketchup. Serve in taco shells.

STORAGE CHART

	REFRIGERATOR (35° TO 40°)	FREEZER (0° OR COLDER)
ground beef	1 to 2 days	3 to 4 months
cooked ground beef	3 to 4 days	2 to 3 months

safety first

- When shopping, pick up ground beef last and make sure it's cold.
- Once home, refrigerate beef immediately. Place in plastic bag to avoid leakage and keep on plate in coldest part of refrigerator; use within two days.
- Thaw frozen ground beef in refrigerator—never on the counter.
- Cook meat to 160°, checking temp with a meat thermometer.
- Wash hands, utensils and work surfaces with soap and hot water to avoid cross-contamination.
- After meat is cooked, don't return it to raw meat platter.
- Refrigerate cooked leftovers within 2 hours of preparation.

slow-cooker solutions

GREAT-TASTING RECIPES FOR EFFORTLESS MEALS. **BY CINDY HELLER**

Food styling: Liza Jernow. Prop styling: Megan Hedgpeth.

corn chowder

MAKES: 6 servings. **PREP:** 15 minutes. **SLOW-COOK:** 2 hours, 40 minutes on HIGH; 4 hours, 10 minutes on LOW.

- 1 tablespoon vegetable oil
- 2 medium-size carrots, finely chopped
- 1 stalk celery, finely chopped
- 1 small onion, finely chopped
- 1 large Idaho potato (about 1 pound), peeled and cut into ½-inch cubes
- 3 cups low-sodium chicken broth
- 1 bay leaf
- ¾ teaspoon dried thyme
- ⅛ teaspoon paprika
- 4 cups frozen corn kernels
- 2 cups milk
- 3 tablespoons cornstarch
- 2 tablespoons white wine
- 1 tablespoon fresh thyme, chopped

- ¾ teaspoon salt
- 5 slices ready-to-serve bacon (such as Oscar Mayer), prepared according to package directions and crumbled

1. Place oil in a 4- to 6-quart stovetop-safe slow-cooker bowl over medium-high heat on stovetop. Cook carrot, celery and onion for 7 minutes or until softened.
2. Transfer to slow-cooker base and add potatoes to bowl. Pour broth over top and add bay leaf, dried thyme and paprika. Cover and cook on HIGH for 1½ hours or LOW for 3 hours, or until potatoes are cooked through.

3. Stir in corn and milk; cover and cook for 1 hour or until heated through.
4. In a small bowl, stir together cornstarch and wine and whisk into soup; cook an additional 10 minutes. Stir in fresh thyme and salt.
5. Using a potato masher, gently mash the soup until slightly thickened. Sprinkle each serving with a generous ½ tablespoon crumbled bacon and serve immediately.

PER SERVING: 304 calories; 8 g fat (3 g sat.); 12 g protein; 52 g carbohydrate; 5 g fiber; 486 mg sodium; 15 mg cholesterol.

PHOTOGRAPHY BY JAMES BAIGRIE

jambalaya

MAKES: 8 servings.
PREP: 10 minutes. **SLOW-COOK:** 4¼ hours on HIGH; 6¼ hours on LOW.

- 1 medium-size onion, chopped
- 2 stalks celery, cut into ¼-inch slices
- 1 can (14.5 ounces) no-salt-added diced tomatoes
- 2 cups low-sodium chicken broth
- 1 pound boneless, skinless chicken thighs, cut into 1-inch pieces
- ½ pound light kielbasa, cut into ½-inch slices
- ¼ teaspoon cayenne pepper
- 1 small green pepper, seeded and chopped
- ½ pound large shrimp, peeled and deveined
- 2 cups frozen cut okra
- ½ teaspoon Cajun seasoning
- 3 tablespoons cornstarch
- ¼ teaspoon salt
  Dash hot pepper sauce
  Hot cooked white rice (optional)

1. In a 4- to 6-quart slow cooker, stir onion, celery, tomatoes, broth, chicken, kielbasa and cayenne together. Cover and cook on HIGH for 3 hours or LOW for 5 hours.
2. Stir in the green pepper, shrimp, okra and Cajun seasoning and cook for 1 hour or until shrimp is cooked through.
3. Remove ¼ cup of liquid from the slow cooker and place in a small bowl; stir cornstarch into liquid. Stir back into bowl and cook an additional 15 minutes or until thickened. Stir in salt and hot sauce; serve with rice, if desired.

PER SERVING: 167 calories; 6 g fat (2 g sat.); 19 g protein; 8 g carbohydrate; 2 g fiber; 425 mg sodium; 94 mg cholesterol.

apple crisp

MAKES: 8 servings. **PREP:** 10 minutes. **SLOW-COOK:** 2 hours on HIGH; 4 hours on LOW.

Topping:
- ½ cup flour
- ¼ cup light-brown sugar
- ¼ cup granulated sugar
- ¼ teaspoon cinnamon
- ⅛ teaspoon nutmeg
  Pinch salt
- 4 tablespoons cold unsalted butter, cut into pieces
- ½ cup chopped pecans

Filling:
- 3 tablespoons granulated sugar
- 2 teaspoons lemon juice
- 1½ teaspoons cornstarch
- ¼ teaspoon ground ginger
- ¼ teaspoon ground cinnamon
- 6 large Granny Smith apples, peeled, cored and cut into ½-inch wedges (10 cups)
  Vanilla ice cream (optional)

1. Coat 2- to 4-quart slow-cooker bowl with nonstick cooking spray; set aside.
2. Prepare **Topping:** In a small bowl, mix together flour, sugars, cinnamon, nutmeg and salt. Add butter; work into flour mixture using a pastry blender or fingers until coarse crumbs form. Stir in pecans and set aside.
3. Prepare **Filling:** In a large bowl, whisk together sugar, lemon juice, cornstarch, ginger and cinnamon. Stir in apples; toss to coat.
4. Spoon apple mixture into slow cooker and sprinkle topping over it. Cover and cook on HIGH for 2 hours or LOW for 4 hours, or until apples are tender. Serve with vanilla ice cream, if desired.

PER SERVING: 240 calories; 11 g fat (4 g sat.); 2 g protein; 37 g carbohydrate; 4 g fiber; 41 mg sodium; 15 mg cholesterol.

When converting a recipe for your slow cooker, remember that liquids don't boil away like they do in conventional cooking; cut liquid amounts in the original recipe by about half.

cooking school

BRING CHICKEN SALAD TO YOUR TABLE THAT IS SURE TO SATISFY EVERYONE'S TASTES. FOLLOW OUR STEP-BY-STEP INSTRUCTIONS FOR 3-WAY CHICKEN SALAD.

BY JULIE MILTENBERGER

Combine our chicken and mayo mixture with one of three flavor options.

PHOTOGRAPHY BY JAMES BIAGRIE

3-way chicken salad

MAKES: 6 servings. **PREP:** 20 minutes. **COOK:** 12 minutes.

1½ **pounds boneless, skinless chicken
     breast halves**
2   **small bay leaves**
6   **whole peppercorns**
⅔   **cup light mayonnaise**
½   **teaspoon** *each* **salt and black pepper**

1. Place chicken breasts smooth-side down on a cutting board. Pull or cut tenders from breast halves and save for another use **(photo 1).**
2. Place a sheet of waxed paper over chicken pieces and pound lightly to an even thickness **(photo 2).**
3. Bring **8 cups water,** bay leaves and peppercorns to barely a simmer over medium heat in a large sauté pan. Add chicken and cook for 10 to 12 minutes, keeping temperature moderate so only a few bubbles appear around chicken **(photo 3).** Remove chicken when instant-read thermometer inserted in breasts registers 160°. Refrigerate until cold.
4. Cut chicken into ¾-inch cubes, stir together with mayonnaise, salt and pepper, and then with one of the flavor combinations at right.

CURRIED CHICKEN SALAD

Stir in **½ cup chopped golden raisins,
¼ cup slivered almonds, 1½ teaspoons curry
powder** and **½ teaspoon sugar.**

WALDORF SALAD

Stir in **1 Gala apple** (cored and cubed),
**½ cup chopped walnuts, 2 teaspoons cider
vinegar** and **1 teaspoon sugar.**

PER SERVING OF CURRIED OR WALDORF:
290 calories; 15 g fat (3 g sat.);
27 g protein; 8 g carbohydrate; 1 g fiber;
468 mg sodium; 73 mg cholesterol.

CLASSIC CHICKEN SALAD

Add **2 ribs celery,** trimmed and chopped,
3 tablespoons chopped fresh dill and
2 tablespoons mustard.

PER SERVING: 220 calories; 10 g fat (2 g sat.);
26 g protein; 3 g carbohydrate; 0 g fiber;
609 mg sodium; 73 mg cholesterol.

Pull tender from bottom side of breast; keep for another use.

Pound chicken to an even thickness with rolling pin or mallet.

Gently simmer chicken in water; do not boil or chicken will become tough.

may

Cookies 'n' Cream Minis
(Recipe page 104)

WITH WARM BREEZES AND COLORFUL
FLOWERS ABLOOM, IT'S A GREAT TIME TO
CELEBRATE SPRING WITH CREATIVE
CUPCAKES AND SIMPLE BUT
SPECIAL FAMILY DINNERS.

Cobb Salad
page 108

Smoky White Pizza
page115

Beef Tostadas
page 120

Billowy white icing tops lemon-poppyseed cakes, while minis are studded with cookie bits. (Recipes page 104)

the coolest
CUPCAKES

WE MAKE THE ORDINARY EXTRAORDINARY WITH FUN FLAVORS LIKE
COOKIES 'N' CREAM AND CINNAMON CARAMEL. **BY JULIE MILTENBERGER**

PHOTOGRAPHY BY CHARLES SCHILLER

Food styling: Sara Neumeier. Prop styling: Stephanie Basralian.

Pipe chocolate frosting atop caramel cakes or swirl pastel hues on chocolate ones. (Recipes page 105)

Beating the egg white–sugar mixture with an electric mixer over medium-low heat results in an easy, light and fluffy icing.

lemon-poppyseed jumbos

MAKES: 6 cupcakes. **PREP:** 20 minutes. **BAKE:** at 350° for 25 minutes. **COOK:** 7 minutes.

1⅔ cups all-purpose flour
¾ cup sugar
2 teaspoons baking powder
¼ teaspoon salt
½ cup milk
1 lemon (you will need 2 teaspoons of the zest and ¼ cup juice)
1 egg
1 egg yolk (reserve white for frosting)
¼ cup oil
2 tablespoons poppyseeds

Icing:
⅔ cup sugar
1 egg white (from above)
2 tablespoons lemon juice
1 tablespoon light corn syrup
Pinch cream of tartar
Pinch salt

1. Heat oven to 350°. Coat a popover pan* with nonstick cooking spray. Line each indentation with a paper liner, or line 6 indentations of a jumbo muffin tin with paper liners.
2. In large bowl, whisk flour, sugar, baking powder and salt.
3. In small bowl, whisk milk, lemon zest, juice, egg, egg yolk and oil. Make a well in the flour mixture; add milk mixture.

Stir until all flour mixture is moistened. Stir in poppyseeds.
4. Transfer batter to prepared pan, a heaping ⅓ cup per indentation. Bake cakes at 350° for 25 minutes.
5. Remove cakes immediately from pan; cool completely on a wire rack.
6. Prepare **Icing:** In small saucepan (not nonstick), mix sugar, egg white, lemon juice, **2 tablespoons water,** corn syrup, cream of tartar and salt. Heat over medium-low to medium heat, beating continuously with an electric mixer until medium-stiff white peaks are formed and an instant-read thermometer registers 150°, about 7 minutes. Remove from heat. Beat an additional 1 minute.
7. Spread cooled cupcakes generously with icing, about 3 tablespoons per cupcake (there will be icing left over). Slip cakes into clean cupcake liners, if desired, and tie with ribbon or string.
***Note:** Standard popover pan available from Williams-Sonoma, 877-812-6235 or visit williams-sonoma.com.

PER CUPCAKE: 456 calories; 13 g fat (2 g sat.); 7 g protein; 80 g carbohydrate; 1 g fiber; 296 mg sodium; 74 mg cholesterol.

cookies 'n' cream minis

MAKES: 36 mini cupcakes. **PREP:** 15 minutes. **BAKE:** at 350° for 15 minutes.

1½ cups all-purpose flour
2 teaspoons baking powder
¼ teaspoon salt
½ cup (1 stick) unsalted butter, softened
¾ cup sugar
2 large eggs
½ cup reduced-fat sour cream
2 tablespoons milk
½ teaspoon vanilla extract
5 chocolate and creme sandwich cookies (such as Oreos), broken up

Frosting:
2 cups confectioners' sugar
¼ cup (½ stick) unsalted butter, softened
¼ cup reduced-fat sour cream
¼ teaspoon vanilla extract
Crushed sandwich cookies (optional)

1. Heat oven to 350°. Line 36 indents of mini muffin pans (using three pans total) with paper or foil liners. If you have only one or two pans, bake batter in batches.
2. In small bowl, whisk flour, baking powder and salt. In large bowl, beat butter until smooth. Beat in sugar until fluffy. Beat in eggs, one at a time.
3. On low speed, alternately beat flour mixture and sour cream into butter mixture, beginning and ending with flour. Add milk and vanilla; fold in cookie pieces. Divide batter among prepared cups; for ease, place batter in a resealable plastic bag, snip off a corner and pipe into cups.
4. Bake at 350° for 15 minutes, until tops spring back when lightly pressed. Remove cupcakes to a rack; let cool.
5. Prepare **Frosting:** In bowl, beat sugar, butter, sour cream and vanilla until good spreading consistency.

6. Once cupcakes have cooled, spread with frosting, about 2 teaspoons for each. Top with cookie crumbs, if desired.

PER MINI CUPCAKE: 114 calories; 5 g fat (3 g sat.); 1 g protein; 16 g carbohydrate; 0 g fiber; 68 mg sodium; 24 mg cholesterol.

Have young helpers break up cookies to sprinkle over cupcakes.

cinnamon-caramel cupcakes

MAKES: 18 cupcakes.
PREP: 20 minutes. **COOK:** 20 minutes.
BAKE: at 350° for 23 minutes.

Caramel:
- ½ cup plus ¼ cup water
- 1½ cups sugar

Batter:
- 2 cups all-purpose flour
- 1½ teaspoons baking powder
- ½ teaspoon baking soda
- ½ teaspoon ground cinnamon
- ½ teaspoon salt
- ¾ cup (1½ sticks) unsalted butter, softened
- ⅔ cup granulated sugar
- 2 eggs
- ⅔ cup sour cream

Frosting:
- 6 ounces unsweetened chocolate, broken up
- 6 tablespoons unsalted butter
- ⅔ cup reserved Caramel
- 4 cups confectioners' sugar, sifted
- ½ cup milk

caramel tips

1 Remove pan from heat once caramel begins to color; watch closely—this may happen quickly. **2** Add water gradually; hold at arm's length to avoid spattering.

1. Line 18 indents of two cupcake pans with paper or foil liners. Set aside.
2. Prepare **Caramel:** Place ½ cup water near the stove. Heat sugar and ¼ cup water in a small (not nonstick) saucepan over medium-high heat until sugar starts to dissolve, 5 to 6 minutes. Swirl pan constantly as mixture continues to cook. When mixture begins to turn amber-colored, 10 to 12 minutes **(photo, bottom left),** remove from heat.
3. Very carefully add ½ cup water in 3 additions to saucepan. Stir with a metal spoon until caramel is dissolved, about a minute, returning to heat if needed. Pour into 2-cup glass measuring cup. Add water, if needed, to equal 1⅓ cups. Let stand until cooled to room temperature. Use half for batter and half for frosting.
4. Heat oven to 350°. Prepare **Batter:** Blend flour, baking powder, baking soda, cinnamon and salt in small bowl. Beat butter and sugar in large bowl for 1 minute, until light and fluffy. Beat in eggs and sour cream until blended. Alternately fold in flour mixture and ⅔ cup of the cooled caramel mixture in three additions, beginning and ending with flour. Spoon into muffin cups, a heaping ¼ cup each.
5. Bake at 350° for 21 to 23 minutes or until cupcakes spring back when lightly pressed. Cool in pans on rack 5 minutes. Remove cupcakes directly to rack and cool completely.
6. Prepare **Frosting:** In a medium-size saucepan (not nonstick), combine the chocolate and the butter. Heat over medium heat until melted and smooth, about a minute. Remove from heat and beat in caramel with mixer until smooth. Beat in half of the confectioners' sugar (mixture will be coarse), then the milk. Beat in the remaining confectioners' sugar until smooth. Let stand at room temperature until good spreading consistency, about 15 to 30 minutes. If desired, transfer frosting to a pastry bag fitted with a star tip and swirl on top of cupcake.

PER CUPCAKE: 434 calories; 19 g fat (12 g sat.); 4 g protein; 63 g carbohydrate; 2 g fiber; 94 mg sodium; 59 mg cholesterol.

chocolate cupcakes

MAKES: 18 cupcakes. **PREP:** 15 minutes.
BAKE: at 350° for 19 minutes.

- 1¾ cups all-purpose flour
- ¾ cup unsweetened cocoa powder
- 2¼ teaspoons baking powder
- ½ teaspoon salt
- 1 cup plus 2 tablespoons (2¼ sticks) unsalted butter, softened
- 1¼ cups granulated sugar
- 3 eggs
- ¾ cup milk

Frosting:
- 1 box (1 pound) confectioners' sugar
- 1 cup (2 sticks) unsalted butter, softened
- ¼ cup milk
- 1 teaspoon vanilla extract
  Assorted food colors

1. Heat oven to 350°. Line 18 indents in two cupcake pans with paper or foil liners. In a bowl, whisk flour, cocoa powder, baking powder and salt.
2. Beat butter and sugar in large bowl for 2 minutes, until light colored and smooth. Add eggs, one at a time, beating well after each. On low speed, add flour mixture, alternately with milk. Divide batter among liners, a scant ⅓ cup in each.
3. Bake at 350° for about 19 minutes or until toothpick inserted into centers comes out clean. Remove cupcakes to a rack; cool completely.
4. Prepare **Frosting:** Beat sugar, butter and milk in medium-size bowl until smooth. Beat in vanilla. Tint with desired food colors. Spread about 2 tablespoons frosting over each cupcake.

PER CUPCAKE: 406 calories; 24 g fat (14 g sat.); 4 g protein; 48 g carbohydrate; 1 g fiber; 147 mg sodium; 96 mg cholesterol.

mealtime
MAGIC

SHORT ON TIME AND EVERYONE IS STARVING? USE
OUR SHOPPING LISTS AND QUICK-TO-MAKE RECIPES
TO COOK UP SEVEN DELICIOUS, NUTRITIOUS
SPRING SUPPERS! **BY CINDY HELLER**

Buying a prepared crust,
shredded cheese and frozen
broccoli streamlines prep.
(Recipe page 113)

PHOTOGRAPHY BY TINA RUPP

fish tacos

MAKES: 4 servings. **PREP:** 10 minutes. **COOK:** 18 minutes.

- ½ cup low-fat sour cream
- 3 tablespoons minced cilantro
- ¼ cup lime juice
- 1 green pepper, finely chopped
- 1 pound cod
- ½ teaspoon salt
- ½ teaspoon chili powder
- 4 corn tortillas

1. In small bowl, stir together sour cream, 2 tablespoons of the cilantro and 1 tablespoon of the lime juice; set aside.
2. Coat an 8-inch nonstick skillet with nonstick spray; heat over medium heat. Add green pepper; cook 3 minutes. Add cod to pan and sprinkle with 2 tablespoons of the lime juice, the salt and ¼ teaspoon of the chili powder. Cover; cook 15 minutes or until fish is cooked through.

3. Flake fish in a medium-size bowl; add skillet contents. Add remaining cilantro, lime juice and chili powder to bowl; stir gently. Heat tortillas. Divide fish among tortillas and serve with sauce.

PER SERVING: 202 calories; 5 g fat (3 g sat.); 23 g protein; 15 g carbohydrate; 2 g fiber; 388 mg sodium; 64 mg cholesterol.

cobb salad

MAKES: 4 servings. **PREP:** 10 minutes. **COOK:** 18 minutes.

- 1 pound boneless, skinless chicken breasts
- 8 cups mixed salad greens
- 1 tomato (8 ounces), cut into ½-inch pieces
- ¼ cup light red wine vinaigrette
- 3 slices cooked bacon, crumbled
- ¼ cup crumbled blue cheese
- 3 hard-cooked eggs, peeled and chopped

1. Heat a large pot of water to simmering. Add chicken, cover, and cook 18 minutes or until cooked through. Cool and cut into ½-inch cubes.

2. To serve, place chicken, greens and tomatoes in a large serving bowl and pour vinaigrette over top; toss to combine. Sprinkle each serving with equal amounts bacon, blue cheese and eggs.

PER SERVING: 199 calories; 8 g fat (3 g sat.); 24 g protein; 7 g carbohydrate; 3 g fiber; 374 mg sodium; 160 mg cholesterol.

beef and chimichurri sauce

MAKES: 4 servings. **PREP:** 10 minutes. **GRILL:** 16 minutes.

1 **cup parsley leaves**
1 **shallot, coarsely chopped**
3 **cloves garlic, chopped**
3 **tablespoons red wine vinegar**
¼ **cup olive oil**
½ **teaspoon** *each* **salt and black pepper**
1 **pound boneless beef top sirloin**
3 **cups prepared white rice (optional)**

1. In a food processor, combine parsley, shallot, garlic, vinegar, olive oil, ¼ teaspoon *each* of the salt and pepper. Pulse until combined; set aside.

2. Heat a gas grill to medium-high heat or prepare a charcoal grill with medium-hot coals. Sprinkle remaining ¼ teaspoon *each* salt and pepper over steak. Grill about 8 minutes per side.

3. Remove steak from grill and place in a glass baking dish; spread the sauce over top and cover dish with foil; allow to sit for 5 minutes. Remove steak from dish and slice. Serve with sauce remaining in baking dish and rice, if desired.

PER SERVING: 287 calories; 18 g fat (4 g sat.); 26 g protein; 4 g carbohydrate; 1 g fiber; 365 mg sodium; 48 mg cholesterol.

salmon burgers

MAKES: 4 burgers. **PREP:** 10 minutes. **GRILL:** 10 minutes.

- **4   tablespoons light mayonnaise**
- **2   tablespoons chopped fresh dill**
- **1   pound salmon fillet, skin removed**
- **⅓ cup bread crumbs**
- **2   scallions, thinly sliced**
- **¼ teaspoon** *each* **salt and black pepper**
- **4   lettuce leaves**
- **4   whole-wheat hamburger buns, toasted**

1. Heat gas grill to medium-high or prepare charcoal grill with medium-hot coals. Stir together mayonnaise and 1 tablespoon of the dill; set aside.

2. In the bowl of a food processor, pulse remaining tablespoon dill, the salmon, bread crumbs, scallions, salt and pepper until combined. Form into four 3-inch round burgers and coat both sides with nonstick cooking spray.

3. Grill burgers for 5 minutes per side or until cooked through. Place lettuce leaves and burgers on buns and spread each burger with 1 tablespoon dill mayonnaise.

PER SERVING: 365 calories; 15 g fat (2 g sat.); 28 g protein; 30 g carbohydrate; 4 g fiber; 591 mg sodium; 68 mg cholesterol.

chicken nuggets

MAKES: 4 servings. **PREP:** 15 minutes. **BROIL:** for 10 minutes.

1 cup bread crumbs
½ teaspoon garlic powder
½ teaspoon dried thyme
¼ cup Dijon mustard
⅓ cup light mayonnaise
1½ pounds chicken tenders, cut into
   1-inch pieces
¾ pound green beans, washed, trimmed
   and steamed

1. Heat oven to broil. Coat baking rack with nonstick cooking spray. Place rack over baking sheet; set aside.
2. Stir together bread crumbs, garlic powder and thyme in a pie plate; set aside. Stir together mustard and mayonnaise.
3. Reserve about ½ cup of mustard mixture for dipping sauce. Brush chicken pieces with remaining mustard mix; place chicken in pie plate with bread crumb mixture, spooning crumbs on top of pieces and pressing to adhere. Transfer to prepared baking rack. Broil for 10 minutes or until cooked through. Serve with reserved dipping sauce and green beans on the side.

PER SERVING: 397 calories; 10 g fat (2 g sat.); 44 g protein; 28 g carbohydrate; 3 g fiber; 842 mg sodium; 106 mg cholesterol.

asian peanut noodles

MAKES: 4 servings. **PREP:** 10 minutes. **COOK:** 7 minutes.

- 1 **package (8.8 ounces) thin rice noodles**
- ½ **cup prepared peanut sauce**
- 1 **tablespoon rice vinegar**
- 1 **teaspoon low-sodium soy sauce**
- 1 **tablespoon olive oil**
- 1 **bag (16 ounces) frozen Asian vegetable blend**
- ⅓ **cup dry-roasted peanuts, chopped**

1. Soak noodles in hot water for 20 minutes. In a small bowl, stir together peanut sauce, vinegar and soy sauce; set aside.

2. Heat oil in a large skillet over medium-high heat. Add vegetables to pan and cook 5 minutes; stirring occasionally.

3. Drain noodles; reduce heat to medium and add noodles to skillet; pour sauce over top and toss to combine. Cook 2 minutes or until heated through. Top with chopped peanuts.

PER SERVING: 425 calories; 15 g fat (3 g sat.); 12 g protein; 63 g carbohydrate; 5 g fiber; 353 mg sodium; 0 mg cholesterol.

broccoli and ham quiche

MAKES: 6 servings. **PREP:** 10 minutes. **BAKE:** at 350° for 35 minutes.

1 refrigerated piecrust
5 eggs
5 egg whites
1 cup frozen chopped broccoli, thawed
¾ cup low-fat shredded cheddar cheese
4 slices deli ham (about 4 ounces), cut into 1-inch-long thin strips
2 scallions, sliced
½ teaspoon *each* salt and black pepper

1. Heat oven to 350°. Fit piecrust into 9-inch pie plate and flute edges; set aside.

2. In a medium-size bowl, whisk together eggs, egg whites, broccoli, ½ cup of the cheese, the ham, scallions, salt and pepper. Pour egg mixture into prepared piecrust and sprinkle with remaining ¼ cup cheese.

3. Bake on lower rack at 350° for 35 minutes or until just set. Allow to sit 5 minutes before serving.

PER SERVING: 282 calories; 15 g fat (6 g sat.); 17 g protein; 20 g carbohydrate; 1 g fiber; 779 mg sodium; 194 mg cholesterol.

shopping list

This grocery list and the pantry items are all you need to cook up a week of hearty suppers.

PRODUCE
8 cups assorted salad greens
1 bunch fresh dill
1 bunch scallions
¾ pound green beans
1 bunch fresh cilantro
1 lime
1 green pepper
1 bunch fresh parsley
1 shallot
1 head garlic
1 tomato

DAIRY
1 container crumbled blue cheese
13 eggs
1 package low-fat shredded cheddar cheese
1 container low-fat sour cream
1 refrigerated piecrust

MEAT, FISH AND POULTRY
1 pound boneless, skinless chicken breasts
1½ pounds chicken tenders
1 pound boneless top sirloin
1 small package bacon
¼ pound sliced deli ham
1 pound salmon fillet
1 pound cod

DRY GOODS
1 package whole-wheat hamburger buns
1 package tortillas
1 package (8.8 ounces) thin rice noodles
1 bottle peanut sauce
1 bag (16 ounces) frozen Asian vegetable blend
1 bottle light red wine vinaigrette
1 box frozen chopped broccoli

pantry items

- salt and pepper
- light mayonnaise
- bread crumbs
- garlic powder
- dried thyme
- Dijon mustard
- dry-roasted peanuts
- olive oil
- low-sodium soy sauce
- red wine vinegar
- chili powder
- rice vinegar
- white rice

This pizza has 50% fewer calories than a regular pie. (Recipe opposite page)

QUICK & EASY™

healthy
FAST FOOD

TAKE A BREAK FROM TAKEOUT WITH THESE GOOD-FOR-YOU VERSIONS OF YOUR FAMILY'S FAVORITES. THEY COOK UP QUICKER THAN YOU CAN SAY DRIVE-THRU. **BY MICHAEL TYRRELL**

cajun turkey quarter-pounder

MAKES: 4 servings. **PREP:** 10 minutes. **BROIL:** 10 minutes.

1 **pound ground turkey**
½ **medium green bell pepper, cored, seeded and finely chopped**
3 **ounces white mushrooms, shredded (about 1 cup shredded)**
1 **egg**
2 **tablespoons dry unseasoned bread crumbs**
2 **tablespoons ketchup**
1 **tablespoon dried minced onion**
2 **teaspoons Cajun seasoning (such as McCormick)**
1 **teaspoon garlic powder**
2 **whole-wheat pitas, cut in half crossways**
4 **slices tomato**
4 **slices red onion**
 Pickles (optional)

1. Heat broiler. Spray a broiler pan with nonstick cooking spray.
2. In a large bowl, mix together turkey, green pepper, mushrooms, egg, bread crumbs, ketchup, minced onion, Cajun seasoning and garlic powder. Form into 4 burgers, about 3 inches in diameter.
3. Place burgers on the prepared broiler pan and broil for about 5 minutes per side or until internal temperature reads 160° on an instant-read thermometer.
4. In each pita half, place a burger, a slice of tomato and a slice of onion. Serve with additional ketchup and pickles, if desired.

PER SERVING: 325 calories; 12 g fat (3 g sat.); 27 g protein; 29 g carbohydrate; 4 g fiber; 719 mg sodium; 142 mg cholesterol.

Most fast food burgers have 500 calories; our delicious version has just 325.

smoky white pizza

MAKES: 12 slices. **PREP:** 10 minutes. **BAKE:** at 450° for 16 minutes.

1 **tube (13.8 ounces) refrigerated pizza dough**
1 **package (4 ounces) light garlic and herb spreadable cheese (such as Alouette)**
2 **cups part-skim shredded mozzarella cheese**
1 **cup part-skim ricotta cheese**
2 **ounces deli smoked turkey, sliced into thin ribbons Basil for garnish (optional)**

1. Heat oven to 450°. Grease a cookie sheet with nonstick cooking spray.
2. Spread pizza dough on baking sheet. Bake at 450° for 8 minutes.
3. Remove from oven and evenly spread herb and garlic cheese over the pizza dough. Sprinkle the mozzarella over the top; dollop the ricotta evenly over the mozzarella. Scatter the sliced turkey over the cheeses. Bake for 8 minutes or until crust is nicely golden.
4. Garnish with fresh basil leaves, if desired. Cut into 12 squares to serve.

PER SLICE: 195 calories; 9 g fat (5 g sat.); 11 g protein; 18 g carbohydrate; 0 g fiber; 505 mg sodium; 31 mg cholesterol.

Food styling: Michael Pederson. Prop styling: Denise Canter.

vegetable curry

MAKES: 4 servings.
PREP: 15 minutes.
COOK: 23 minutes.

- 1 tablespoon canola oil
- 1 medium onion, peeled and sliced
- 2 teaspoons hot curry powder
- 1 cup vegetable broth
- 1 tablespoon cornstarch
- 1 can (8 ounces) no-salt-added tomato sauce
- 1 head cauliflower (about 2 pounds), trimmed and cut into florets
- 1 medium green bell pepper, cored, seeded and cut into ½-inch pieces
- 2 large carrots, peeled and cut into ¼-inch coins
- 1 can (15 ounces) chickpeas, drained and rinsed
- ¼ teaspoon salt
- 2 tandoori nan from a 14-ounce package (such as Kontos), cut in half crossways, or 4 small whole-wheat pitas

1. In a large nonstick pot, heat oil over medium-high heat. Add onion and cook, stirring occasionally, for 5 minutes or until golden brown. Stir in curry powder and cook 1 minute.
2. In a small glass measuring cup, mix together ¼ cup of the vegetable broth and the cornstarch. Set aside.
3. Into the onion-curry mixture, add the remaining ¾ cup broth, **1 cup water,** the tomato sauce, cauliflower, green pepper, carrots, chickpeas and salt. Stir to combine.
4. Bring to a boil. Reduce heat to medium-low and simmer, partially covered, for 15 minutes, stirring occasionally. Stir in cornstarch mixture and cook for an additional 1 to 2 minutes or until thickened.
5. Spoon vegetable curry into bowls and serve with nan or pita; use the bread to soak up any juices.

PER SERVING: 358 calories; 8 g fat (2 g sat.); 14 g protein; 59 g carbohydrate; 12 g fiber; 931 mg sodium; 0 mg cholesterol.

Our curry contains at least a third less saturated fat than takeout.

italian panko "fried" chicken

MAKES: 4 servings.
PREP: 10 minutes.
BAKE: at 450° for 25 minutes.

- 3 **egg whites**
- 1 **tablespoon Dijon mustard**
- 1 **cup Italian-style panko bread crumbs (such as Progresso) or 1 cup plain bread crumbs mixed with 1 teaspoon Italian seasoning**
- ¼ **cup reduced-fat grated Parmesan cheese**
- ½ **cup all-purpose flour**
- 4 **boneless, skinless chicken breasts, about 6 ounces each**
- ¾ **cup prepared marinara sauce, heated French fries and cole slaw (optional)**

1. Heat oven to 450°. Place a rack on a baking sheet and spray with nonstick cooking spray.
2. Whisk together egg whites and mustard in a shallow dish. In a second dish, blend the panko and cheese. Place the flour in a third dish.
3. Coat the chicken with the flour, shaking off the excess. Dip in the egg mixture and then coat well with the panko. Place on prepared rack.
4. Bake at 450° for 15 minutes and turn over. Bake an additional 10 minutes or until internal temperature registers 160° on an instant-read thermometer. Broil for 1 minute if you wish to lightly brown.
5. Serve with heated marinara sauce. Accompany with cooked french fries and prepared cole slaw, if desired.

PER SERVING: 392 calories; 7 g fat (1 g sat.); 49 g protein; 31 g carbohydrate; 2 g fiber; 937 mg sodium; 106 mg cholesterol.

Made from crustless bread, panko crumbs have a crispy texture.

easy microwave shrimp nachos

MAKES: 6 servings.
PREP: 10 minutes.
MICROWAVE: 4 minutes.

- 6 ounces reduced-fat tortilla chips, from an 8½-ounce bag (such as Tostitos)
- 1 cup lower-sodium salsa (such as Muir Glen Organic)
- ½ pound cooked shrimp, coarsely chopped
- 1 can (15 ounces) white beans, drained and rinsed
- 1 cup reduced-fat shredded pepper-Jack cheese
- 2 scallions, trimmed and thinly sliced
- 1 small sweet red pepper, cored, seeded and thinly sliced

1. Line the bottom of a large microwave-safe serving dish with half of the tortilla chips. Evenly spoon on half of the salsa. Layer half each of the shrimp, beans, cheese, scallions and red pepper.
2. Microwave on HIGH for 2 minutes, until hot and bubbly.
3. Repeat with the remaining ingredients on a second serving dish.

PER SERVING: 276 calories; 9 g fat (3 g sat.); 17 g protein; 37 g carbohydrate; 6 g fiber; 902 mg sodium; 70 mg cholesterol.

Swapping shrimp for meat adds a hit of omega-3s to our easy nachos.

chili dogs

MAKES: 8 chili dogs. **PREP:** 15 minutes. **COOK:** 5 minutes. **GRILL:** 5 minutes.

- 1 can (15 ounces) red kidney beans, drained, rinsed and coarsely mashed
- 1 can (8 ounces) no-salt-added tomato sauce
- 2 teaspoons sugar
- 1 teaspoon chipotle chili powder (such as McCormick) or regular chili powder
- ½ teaspoon ground cumin
- ½ teaspoon dried oregano
- 8 fat-free hot dogs (such as Ball Park)
- 8 hot dogs rolls
- ½ cup reduced-fat 4-cheese Mexican-blend shredded cheese
- 1 small onion, peeled and finely chopped

1. In medium-size saucepan, combine beans, tomato sauce, sugar, chili powder, cumin and oregano. Simmer on medium heat for 5 minutes, stirring.
2. Spray a stovetop grill pan or skillet with nonstick cooking spray and heat over medium-high heat. Grill hot dogs for about 5 minutes, turning halfway.
3. To serve, place hot dogs in rolls. Spoon chili over the top of each. Sprinkle each with 1 tablespoon of the cheese and some of the chopped onion.

PER CHILI DOG: 276 calories; 4 g fat (2 g sat.); 17 g protein; 43 g carbohydrate; 4 g fiber; 966 mg sodium; 15 mg cholesterol.

No one will guess these dogs, topped with our healthy homemade chili, are low fat.

general tso's chicken

MAKES: 4 servings. **PREP:** 15 minutes.
COOK: 8 minutes.

- 1 cup chicken broth
- 2 tablespoons low-sodium soy sauce
- 1 tablespoon chopped fresh ginger
- 2 teaspoons rice vinegar
- 2 teaspoons sugar
- 2 teaspoons cornstarch
- 1 teaspoon Asian chili paste
- 2 tablespoons canola oil
- 1½ pounds boneless, skinless chicken breast, cut into 1½-inch pieces
- 2 scallions, trimmed and sliced
- 2 cups cooked brown rice
- 1 head fresh broccoli, steamed

1. In a medium-size bowl, whisk together chicken broth, soy sauce, ginger, vinegar, sugar, cornstarch and chili paste; set aside.

2. Heat the oil in a large nonstick skillet over medium-high heat. Add the chicken and cook for about 6 minutes, turning halfway through cooking, or until internal temperature reaches 160° on an instant-read thermometer. Remove to a plate and keep warm.

3. In the same skillet, add the chicken broth mixture. Bring to a simmer and add chicken and scallions. Stir to coat chicken with sauce and heat through, about 1 to 2 minutes.

4. Serve over brown rice with steamed broccoli on the side.

PER SERVING: 414 calories; 11 g fat (1 g sat.); 45 g protein; 33 g carbohydrate; 3 g fiber; 706 mg sodium; 99 mg cholesterol.

We slashed the calories of this restaurant favorite from 1,300 to 414.

slow-cooker solutions
GREAT-TASTING RECIPES FOR EFFORTLESS MEALS. BY CINDY HELLER

Food styling: Liza Jernow. Prop styling: Megan Hedgpeth.

beef tostadas
MAKES: 12 tostadas. **PREP:** 15 minutes. **SLOW-COOK:** 6 hours on HIGH or 8 hours on LOW. **MICROWAVE:** 1½ minutes.

1½ **pounds boneless beef round steak**
 ½ **teaspoon salt**
 ½ **teaspoon black pepper**
 ¼ **cup lime juice**
  3 **garlic cloves, finely chopped**
  1 **jalapeño, seeded and finely chopped**
  1 **large onion, chopped**
  1 **tablespoon chili powder**
 ¼ **teaspoon cumin**
 ⅛ **teaspoon cayenne pepper**
 12 **packaged tostada or hard taco shells**
 ¾ **cup fat-free refried beans**
1½ **cups shredded iceberg lettuce**
  1 **cup reduced-fat shredded**
     Mexican-blend cheese
 ¾ **cup salsa**

1. Sprinkle steak with salt and pepper. Place 3 tablespoons of the lime juice, the garlic, jalapeño, onion, chili powder, cumin and cayenne in a slow cooker. Place beef on top and cook on HIGH for 6 hours or LOW for 8 hours.
2. Remove beef to a cutting board and when cool enough to handle, shred with fingers or using two forks. Place shredded beef in a large bowl.
3. Strain remaining liquid in slow cooker over a bowl or measuring cup, discarding solids. Add strained liquid and remaining 1 tablespoon lime juice to beef in bowl and stir to combine. Cover; keep warm.

4. Warm tostada shells in oven according to package directions. While tostadas are baking, heat refried beans in microwave for 1½ minutes on HIGH, stirring halfway through until warm and spreadable.
5. Spread each tostada with 1 tablespoon refried beans. Place ⅓ cup beef over beans and divide lettuce equally among tostadas. Top each with 1 heaping tablespoon cheese and 1 tablespoon salsa.

PER TOSTADA: 187 calories; 8 g fat (3 g sat.); 18 g protein; 13 g carbohydrate; 2 g fiber; 152 mg sodium; 41 mg cholesterol.

PHOTOGRAPHY BY JAMES BAIGRIE

thai coconut chicken

MAKES: 6 servings. **PREP:** 10 minutes. **SLOW-COOK:** 3 hours on HIGH or 5 hours on LOW.

- ⅓ cup low-sodium chicken broth
- 2½ tablespoons green curry paste (such as Thai Kitchen)
- 1 tablespoon fish sauce
- 1 tablespoon brown sugar
- 1¾ pounds boneless, skinless chicken thighs
- ½ teaspoon salt
- ½ teaspoon black pepper
- 3 cups cauliflower florets
- 2 large carrots, sliced
- 1 large sweet red pepper, chopped
- ½ pound green beans, halved
- 1 can (14 ounces) coconut milk
- 12 basil leaves, chopped
- 3 cups cooked jasmine rice (optional)

1. In a small bowl, stir together broth, 2 tablespoons of the curry paste, the fish sauce and brown sugar; set aside.
2. Sprinkle chicken with salt and pepper. Place chicken in slow cooker with cauliflower and carrots. Pour curry mixture on top and cover. Cook on HIGH for 3 hours or on LOW for 5 hours or until internal temperature of chicken registers 160° on an instant-read thermometer.
3. Add red pepper and green beans to slow cooker for last hour of cook time.
4. Heat coconut milk in a small saucepan over medium-high heat and whisk in remaining curry paste. Add coconut milk mixture and basil leaves to slow cooker for last 15 minutes of cook time. Serve with rice, if desired.

PER SERVING: 383 calories; 25 g fat (14 g sat.); 30 g protein; 15 g carbohydrate; 5 g fiber; 785 mg sodium; 129 mg cholesterol.

lemony lamb ragu

MAKES: 4 servings. **PREP:** 15 minutes.
SLOW-COOK: 4½ hours on HIGH or 6 hours on LOW. **COOK:** 12 minutes.

- 1 tablespoon olive oil
- 1 tablespoon lemon zest
- 2 teaspoons Greek seasoning (such as McCormick)
- 3 garlic cloves, finely chopped
- ½ teaspoon salt
- ½ teaspoon black pepper
- 3 lamb shanks (about 3 pounds), excess fat removed
- 4 small leeks, rinsed, trimmed, white and light-green parts thinly sliced (about 2 cups)
- ½ cup low-sodium chicken broth
- ¼ cup lemon juice
- 1 tablespoon cornstarch
- 8 ounces cholesterol-free egg noodles (such as No Yolks)
- 2 tablespoons chopped parsley

1. In a small bowl, stir together olive oil, lemon zest, Greek seasoning, garlic, salt and pepper. Rub over lamb shanks.
2. Place lamb shanks in slow cooker and sprinkle leeks around them. Pour ¼ cup of the broth and 2 tablespoons of the lemon juice over shanks. Cover and cook on HIGH for 4½ hours or LOW for 6 hours.
3. Remove shanks to a cutting board and let cool. Shred meat with fingers or two forks and set aside.
4. Strain liquid in slow cooker into a fat separator and pour de-fatted liquid into a medium-size saucepan; bring to a boil over medium-high heat. Meanwhile, stir together remaining ¼ cup broth, remaining 2 tablespoons lemon juice and cornstarch. Whisk cornstarch mixture into liquid and boil for 1 minute or until thickened. Cover and keep warm.
5. Bring a large pot of salted water to a boil over high heat. Cook noodles according to package directions, about 11 minutes. Drain and return to pot. Add lamb meat and sauce, and stir to combine. Sprinkle with parsley and serve.

PER SERVING: 626 calories; 18 g fat (6 g sat.); 60 g protein; 53 g carbohydrate; 3 g fiber; 650 mg sodium; 217 mg cholesterol.

cooking school

BECAUSE THEY ADD HEARTINESS—PLUS EXTRA FIBER AND NUTRIENTS—TO ANY MEAL, WHOLE-WHEAT ROLLS MAKE DINNER SPECIAL. FOLLOW OUR STEP-BY-STEP INSTRUCTIONS FOR THESE ALWAYS-DELICIOUS SIDES. **BY JULIE MILTENBERGER**

Whole wheat is a good source of fiber, as well as selenium, potassium and magnesium.

PHOTOGRAPHY BY TINA RUPP

whole-wheat rolls

MAKES: 16 rolls. **PREP:** 10 minutes. **KNEAD:** 10 minutes. **RISE:** 1½ hours total. **BAKE:** at 375° for 20 minutes.

⅓ cup warm water (105° to 115°)
1 tablespoon honey
1 envelope (¼ ounce) active dry yeast
4 tablespoons flax seeds (regular or golden)
2¼ cups all-purpose flour
1¾ cups whole-wheat flour
1 cup warm skim milk
2 tablespoons olive oil
1½ teaspoons salt
1 egg white, lightly beaten

1. In a small bowl, whisk together the warm water and honey. Stir yeast into the water mixture and let stand until foamy, about 7 minutes.

2. Meanwhile, place 3 tablespoons of the flax seeds in a mini chopper or spice grinder. Grind until medium-fine. Transfer to a large bowl and add all-purpose flour and whole-wheat flour. Whisk to blend, then make a well in the center of the mixture.

3. In a small bowl, stir together milk, olive oil and salt. Pour into well of flour mixture, along with yeast mixture. Stir until dough comes together **(photo 1).** Knead until smooth, 5 to 10 minutes **(photo 2).**

4. Place dough in a lightly greased bowl, turning to coat. Cover with a damp, clean towel and allow to rise 45 minutes. Punch down dough **(photo 3),** then knead lightly. Divide into 16 pieces, then roll each into ball, tucking any seams under **(photo 4).** Place on a large nonstick baking sheet and cover with damp towel. Let rise in a warm place for 45 minutes.

5. Heat oven to 375°. Uncover dough, brush rolls with egg white, then sprinkle with remaining 1 tablespoon flax seeds. Bake at 375° for 20 minutes, until lightly browned and hollow-sounding when tapped lightly. Serve warm.

PER ROLL: 162 calories; 3 g fat (0 g sat.); 6 g protein; 28 g carbohydrate; 3 g fiber; 229 mg sodium; 0 mg cholesterol.

Once liquid is added, stir mixture until dough begins to hold together.

Knead dough by folding and pushing it down until it is smooth and elastic.

Once dough has risen, gently punch down and knead once or twice.

Roll and pinch dough into balls, tucking any seams under bottom.

june

Chipotle
Mini Burgers
(Recipe page 145)

AS THE WARM DAYS OF SUMMER SET IN, CHILL
OUT WITH SIMPLE, EASY-TO-MAKE DINNERS
AND LUSCIOUS, BERRY-FILLED DESSERTS.

Shrimp with Bean-Tomato Ragu
page 137

Strawberry-Rhubarb Pie
page 130

Stuffed Flank Steak
page 151

The cream cheese–
white chocolate
filling is the perfect
base for berries.

KEEP IT SIMPLE WITH THIS QUICK AND CREAMY NO-BAKE CROWD-PLEASER.
BY KAREN TACK

white chocolate mousse pie

MAKES: 12 servings. **PREP:** 15 minutes. **COOK:** 5 minutes. **REFRIGERATE:** 3 hours or overnight.

Crust:
- 13 chocolate cream-filled sandwich cookies, ground (such as Oreo)
- 3 tablespoons unsalted butter, melted
- 17 oval vanilla-and-chocolate sandwich cookies (such as Pepperidge Farm Milano)

Filling:
- 1¼ teaspoons unflavored gelatin
- 1¼ cups heavy cream
- 4 ounces cream cheese, softened
- 12 ounces white chocolate, chopped
- 1 teaspoon vanilla extract

Garnish:
- 1 pint strawberries, hulled and halved
- 2 cups frozen whipped topping (such as Cool Whip), thawed

1. Prepare **Crust:** Set aside 1 tablespoon of ground chocolate cookies for garnish. Stir together remaining ground cookies and butter in a bowl until combined. Press the mixture evenly over the bottom of a 9-inch pie plate. Arrange oval cookies around the edge of pie plate, alternating with vanilla and chocolate facing out.

2. Prepare **Filling:** In a small glass measuring cup, sprinkle gelatin over ¼ cup of the cream and let stand 5 minutes to soften.

3. Combine cream cheese, white chocolate and gelatin mixture in small saucepan. Heat over medium-low heat for 6 minutes, stirring constantly, until smooth. Remove from heat and stir in vanilla. Pour into large bowl; place over ice bath. Stir until thickened and cooled.

4. Whip remaining 1 cup heavy cream in a large bowl until soft peaks form. Fold a third of the whipped cream into the white chocolate mixture until well-combined. Gently fold in the remaining whipped cream until just blended.

5. Spoon mixture into prepared crust and refrigerate at least 3 hours or overnight.

6. To **Garnish:** Before serving mound whipped topping in center of pie. Sprinkle with berries and reserved cookie crumbs.

PER SERVING: 489 calories; 34 g fat (20 g sat.);
5 g protein; 40 g carbohydrate; 2 g fiber;
166 mg sodium; 63 mg cholesterol.

PHOTOGRAPHY BY RITA MAAS

FRESH-PICKED
desserts

PHOTOGRAPHY BY TINA RUPP

WE'VE WHIPPED UP FIVE
BERRY DELICIOUS WAYS
TO ENJOY THIS SEASON'S
SWEETEST TREATS.
BY JULIE MILTENBERGER

**Pile berries—
tossed with jam for
shine—atop fruit-
filled cheesecake.**

Food styling: Susan Spungen. Prop styling: Deborah Williams.

blueberry cheesecake

MAKES: 12 servings. **PREP:** 30 minutes.
BAKE: at 350° for 1 hour.
REFRIGERATE: 3 hours or overnight.

Crust and Filling:
- 12 graham cracker boards
- 6 tablespoons unsalted butter, melted
- 2 tablespoons plus 1½ cups sugar
- 3 packages (8 ounces each) Neufchâtel cream cheese, softened
- 1 container (7 ounces) 2% plain low-fat Greek yogurt (such as Fage)
- 3 tablespoons lemon juice
- 2 teaspoons lemon zest
- 3 eggs
- ¾ cup blueberries
- ¼ cup all-purpose flour

Topping:
- 1 cup strawberries, trimmed
- ½ cup blueberries
- ½ cup raspberries
- 1 tablespoon seedless raspberry jam

1. Heat oven to 350°. Prepare **Crust:** Crush graham crackers. Add butter and 2 tablespoons of the sugar; mix until all crumbs are moist. Press into bottom and up side of a 9-inch round springform pan.
2. Prepare **Filling:** In a large bowl, beat together cream cheese and yogurt. Beat in remaining 1½ cups sugar, lemon juice and zest. Add eggs and beat until smooth. Rinse ¾ cup blueberries; place in a small bowl. Sprinkle with 1 tablespoon of the flour; toss to coat. Fold berries and any flour in the bowl, along with remaining 3 tablespoons flour, into the cream cheese mixture. Pour into prepared crust, smoothing top.
3. Bake at 350° for 1 hour or until lightly browned around edges. Remove to a wire rack and run a thin knife between pan and cheesecake. Cool 1 hour at room temperature, then refrigerate 3 hours.
4. Prepare **Topping:** Just before serving, quarter strawberries, and combine with ½ cup blueberries and the raspberries in a bowl. Microwave jelly on HIGH for 15 seconds, until melted. Toss jelly with berries and pile atop cheesecake. Remove side of pan, slice and serve.

PER SERVING: 407 calories; 21 g fat (13 g sat.); 11 g protein; 44 g carbohydrate; 1 g fiber; 352 mg sodium; 109 mg cholesterol.

strawberry-rhubarb pie

MAKES: 12 servings. **PREP:** 20 minutes.
BAKE: at 400° for 50 minutes.

- 1 package (15 ounces) refrigerated rolled pie crusts (2 per package)
- 3 cups fresh or frozen rhubarb pieces (about 1 pound)
- 3 cups trimmed and quartered strawberries (about 1 pound)
- 1 cup sugar mixed with ¼ cup cornstarch
- 1 tablespoon lemon juice
- 1 tablespoon milk
- 1 teaspoon sugar
- Vanilla ice cream (optional)

1. Heat oven to 400°. Fit one of the pie crusts into a 9-inch pie plate. Set aside.

2. In a large bowl, toss rhubarb, strawberries, sugar-cornstarch mixture and lemon juice. Let stand 5 minutes.

3. Pour strawberry mixture into crust-lined pie dish, leveling slightly.

4. Using a knife or pizza cutter, cut remaining crust into 1-inch strips. Interweave into a lattice pattern (see photos). Crimp strip edges with bottom crust to seal. Brush crust with milk, then sprinkle with 1 teaspoon sugar.

5. Bake at 400° for 50 minutes, covering edge of pie with foil if browning too quickly. Cool to room temperature. Serve slightly warm with ice cream, if desired.

PER SERVING: 256 calories; 10 g fat (4 g sat.); 2 g protein; 41 g carbohydrate; 1 g fiber; 136 mg sodium; 7 mg cholesterol.

When cooking with fresh rhubarb, be sure to use only the stem of the plant.

For a sweet surprise, spoon berry yogurt into meringues before filling with fruit.

meringue berry bowls

MAKES: 8 servings.
PREP: 20 minutes.
BAKE: at 250° for 50 minutes.

    4   egg whites, at room temperature
    ¼   teaspoon cream of tartar
    ¾   cup sugar
    1   cup raspberries
    ½   cup blueberries
    ½   cup blackberries
    ¼   cup sugar
    2   tablespoons orange juice

1. Heat oven to 250°. Cover two baking sheets with nonstick foil.
2. Combine egg whites and cream of tartar in large bowl. With electric mixer on medium speed, beat whites to soft peaks. Gradually add sugar a few tablespoons at a time, beating constantly, until fully incorporated, 5 to 7 minutes; meringue should form glossy, stiff peaks, without sugar granules.

3. Transfer meringue to large resealable plastic bag. Snip off a corner and pipe eight 3½-inch round outlines onto prepared baking sheets. Fill in outlines with a small amount of meringue, spreading with spatula. Build walls on top of base at edges using a continuous stream of meringue. Do not pipe higher than 1¼ inches, as walls may fall over. There should be a total of 8 bowls.
4. Bake at 250° for 50 minutes; the meringues should be firm but not yet brown. Remove baking sheets to wire racks to cool. Once meringues have cooled, gently peel them from the foil. If meringues are sticking, cut around them and remove from the baking sheet, with the foil attached to the meringue, then slowly and carefully peel the foil from the bottom of the meringue. To prepare ahead, bake, cool and store meringues in airtight container at room temperature for a day or two. If meringues are soft or moist, return to a 250° oven for 10 minutes.

5. Meanwhile, toss together berries, sugar and orange juice in large bowl.
6. Place a meringue bowl on a dessert plate. Fill with ¼ cup of the berry mixture. Repeat with all bowls and berries.

PER SERVING: 125 calories; 0 g fat (0 g sat.); 2 g protein; 30 g carbohydrate; 2 g fiber; 28 mg sodium; 0 mg cholesterol.

HOW TO PICK 'EM

Farmers' markets and grocery stores Look for dry, plump fruit with no visible signs of mold. Use locally grown berries within two days of purchase.
A bushel basket Beginning in June, many farms will offer a variety of berries for you to pick yourself. Visit pickyourown.org for listings arranged by state.

mixed-berry jelly roll

MAKES: 10 servings. **PREP:** 20 minutes. **COOK:** 10 minutes. **BAKE:** at 350° for 14 minutes.

Filling and Frosting:
- ½ cup sugar
- 1 tablespoon cornstarch
- ¾ cup blackberries, halved
- ¾ cup blueberries
- ¾ cup raspberries
- 1½ cups frozen whipped topping, thawed

Cake:
- 1 cup all-purpose flour
- 1 teaspoon baking powder
- Pinch salt
- 4 large eggs
- ¾ cup granulated sugar
- 2 teaspoons vanilla extract
- 2 tablespoons confectioners' sugar

1. Heat oven to 350°. Prepare **Filling:** In a small saucepan, stir together the sugar and cornstarch. Stir in berries and **1 tablespoon water** and heat over medium heat. Cook 9 to 10 minutes, until thickened, bubbly and most of the berries have popped. Break up remaining berries with a spoon. Remove from heat; cool.

2. Prepare **Cake:** Coat a 15 x 10 x 1-inch jelly roll pan with nonstick cooking spray. Line bottom of pan with waxed paper. Spray paper. In a medium-size bowl, stir together the flour, baking powder and salt. In a large bowl, beat eggs with an electric mixer for 5 minutes, until very light yellow. Add granulated sugar in batches, beating until smooth. Beat in vanilla extract.

3. Fold flour mixture into egg mixture until no lumps remain. Pour into prepared pan, spreading level. Bake at 350° for 12 to 14 minutes or until lightly browned.

4. Meanwhile, dust a clean kitchen towel with confectioners' sugar. When cake is done, turn out onto towel. Roll up towel and cake; cool completely.

5. Unroll cake; spread with filling. Roll up again, without the towel. Prepare **Frosting:** Transfer cake to a platter; spread with thawed whipped topping. Slice and serve.

PER SERVING: 228 calories; 4 g fat (2 g sat.); 4 g protein; 43 g carbohydrate; 2 g fiber; 69 mg sodium; 85 mg cholesterol.

The mixed-berry filling in this jelly roll can double as an ice cream topper.

This dessert reminds us of strawberry shortcake blended with banana pudding.

strawberry-banana trifle

MAKES: 16 servings.
PREP: 30 minutes. **COOK:** 20 minutes.
BAKE: at 350° for 35 minutes.
REFRIGERATE: 3 hours or overnight.

Cake:
- 2 bananas, peeled
- 3 egg whites
- 2 tablespoons oil
- 1 box (18.25 ounces) white cake mix

Filling and fruit:
- 2 boxes (3 ounces each) cook-and-serve vanilla or banana pudding mix
- 3½ cups 2% low-fat milk
- 2 bananas, peeled and sliced
- 2 cups sliced strawberries, plus more for garnish
- 1 cup heavy cream, whipped with 1 tablespoon sugar

1. Heat oven to 350°. Line a 13 x 9 x 2-inch baking pan with nonstick foil. Set aside.
2. Prepare **Cake:** In a blender, combine **1⅓ cups water**, the bananas, egg whites and oil. Blend until smooth, about 1 minute. Place cake mix in a large bowl and add mixture from blender. With an electric mixer, beat on low speed for 30 seconds, then increase speed to high and beat 2 minutes. Pour into prepared pan and bake at 350° for 33 to 35 minutes.
3. Cool cake in pan on a wire rack for 15 minutes, then, using foil, lift cake from pan and cool completely.
4. Prepare **Filling and Fruit:** Meanwhile, cook pudding mix with milk for 15 to 20 minutes over medium heat, until thickened and bubbly. Transfer to a bowl and refrigerate 30 minutes.
5. Trim edges from cooled cake. Cut in half, then cut one half into cubes (about 20). Place in a trifle dish or bowl and press slightly to compress. Spoon 2 cups pudding over cake. Top with 1 sliced banana and 1 cup of the sliced strawberries. Cut second cake half into cubes and continue layering cake, pudding, bananas and strawberries. Top with heavy cream. Refrigerate at least 3 hours or overnight.

PER SERVING: 314 calories; 12 g fat (5 g sat.); 5 g protein; 48 g carbohydrate; 2 g fiber; 339 mg sodium; 25 mg cholesterol.

SUMMERTIME *easy*

IT'S SUMMER AND WE
MAKE THE LIVING—
AND EATING—EASY.
OUR QUICK-TO-MAKE
RECIPES SOLVE YOUR
DINNER DILEMMAS AND
THE SHOPPING LIST
SPEEDS YOU THROUGH
THE AISLES.

BY MICHAEL TYRRELL

Find out the secret
ingredient in this light
and luscious pasta
dish on page 139.

PHOTOGRAPHY BY JAMES BAIGRIE

cheesy flounder fillets

MAKES: 4 servings. **PREP:** 5 minutes. **BAKE:** at 400° for 20 minutes.

⅓ cup light mayonnaise
⅓ cup shredded cheddar cheese
4 flounder fillets, about
   6 ounces each
1 package (6.1 ounces) tomato lentil
   couscous mix (such as Near East)
1 box (10 ounces) frozen spinach

1. Heat oven to 400°. Spray a baking dish with nonstick cooking spray.
2. Mix together the mayonnaise and cheddar cheese. Place the fillets in the baking dish and fold in half. Evenly divide the mayonnaise mixture over each and spread evenly.
3. Bake fillets at 400° for 20 minutes or until fish flakes easily.

4. While fish is baking, prepare couscous and spinach following package directions.
5. Serve fish fillets alongside couscous and spinach.

PER SERVING: 436 calories; 14 g fat (4 g sat.); 42 g protein; 37 g carbohydrate; 4 g fiber; 901 mg sodium; 98 mg cholesterol.

Food styling: Heidi Johannsen. Prop styling: Megan Hedgpeth.

apricot-dijon chicken

MAKES: 4 servings. **PREP:** 10 minutes. **COOK:** 30 minutes. **BAKE:** at 400° for 25 minutes.

⅓ cup apricot preserves
2 tablespoons ketchup
1 tablespoon Dijon mustard
½ teaspoon ground ginger
4 boneless, skinless chicken breasts
   (6 ounces each)
¼ cup toasted hazelnuts, chopped
1 box (6 ounces) long grain and
   wild rice mix
1 tablespoon olive oil

1. Heat oven to 400°. Spray a baking dish with nonstick cooking spray.

2. Whisk together the apricot preserves, ketchup, mustard and ginger. Reserve ¼ cup of the mixture.

3. Place chicken in the prepared baking dish; spread remaining apricot mixture over top. Bake at 400° for 20 to 25 minutes or until internal temperature reaches 160° on an instant-read thermometer.

4. Make rice following package directions, using the olive oil.

5. To serve, sprinkle the hazelnuts over the chicken breasts and stir the reserved apricot mixture into the cooked rice.

PER SERVING: 483 calories; 10 g fat (1 g sat.); 45 g protein; 52 g carbohydrate; 2 g fiber; 854 mg sodium; 99 mg cholesterol.

shrimp with bean-tomato ragu

MAKES: 4 servings. **PREP:** 15 minutes. **COOK:** 9 minutes.

- 5 ounces uncooked whole-wheat angel-hair pasta
- 2 tablespoons olive oil
- 1½ pounds large, frozen shrimp, thawed and deveined (see photos, page 141)
- ¾ teaspoon lemon pepper
- 3 cloves garlic, chopped
- 1 can (15 ounces) white beans
- 1 pound cherry tomatoes, halved
- ½ teaspoon dried Italian seasoning
- ½ teaspoon crushed red pepper
- Basil, for garnish

1. Cook pasta following package directions. Drain and toss with 1 tablespoon of the olive oil. Keep warm.
2. While pasta is cooking, season shrimp with ½ teaspoon of the lemon pepper. Heat remaining tablespoon oil in a nonstick skillet over medium-high heat. Add shrimp and garlic; cook 4 minutes or until cooked through, turning once. Remove and keep warm.
3. Drain and rinse the beans and add to the skillet along with tomatoes, Italian seasoning, red pepper and the remaining ¼ teaspoon lemon pepper. Cook 5 minutes over medium heat.
4. Serve the ragu over the pasta and shrimp. Garnish each serving with basil.

PER SERVING: 458 calories; 11 g fat (2 g sat.); 47 g protein; 50 g carbohydrate; 10 g fiber; 644 mg sodium; 259 mg cholesterol.

filet with mushroom sauce

MAKES: 4 servings. **PREP:** 5 minutes. **COOK:** 8 minutes. **BROIL:** 8 minutes.

4 filet mignon steaks, 5 to 6 ounces each
¼ teaspoon salt
¼ teaspoon black pepper
1 tablespoon olive oil
8 ounces presliced mixed mushrooms
3 cloves garlic, chopped
¼ cup steak sauce, such as A-1
1 tablespoon onion flakes
2 teaspoons brown sugar
Green salad and asparagus (optional)

1. Heat broiler. Coat a broiler pan with nonstick spray.

2. Season steaks with salt and pepper. Place on prepared pan and broil for 3 to 4 minutes per side for medium rare or until internal temperature reads 130° on an instant-read thermometer. Keep warm and allow to rest for 5 minutes.

3. Meanwhile, heat a large nonstick skillet over medium-high heat. Add the olive oil, mushrooms and garlic and cook, stirring occasionally, for 5 minutes. Stir in steak sauce, onion flakes, brown sugar and **¼ cup water.** Cook, stirring occasionally, for about 3 minutes, until thickened.

4. Serve with salad and asparagus, if desired.

PER SERVING: 364 calories; 15 g fat (5 g sat.); 43 g protein; 14 g carbohydrate; 1 g fiber; 474 mg sodium; 112 mg cholesterol.

spaghetti with tomato, green pepper and anchovy

MAKES: 6 servings. **PREP:** 10 minutes. **COOK:** 8 minutes.

- 3 tablespoons olive oil
- 1 large green pepper, seeded and thinly sliced
- 4 cloves garlic, chopped
- 2 tins (2 ounces each) anchovies in oil, drained*
- 2 pints grape tomatoes, halved (about 4 cups)
- ¼ teaspoon salt
- ¼ teaspoon black pepper
- 1 pound uncooked spaghetti
- ½ cup shredded Parmesan cheese

1. Bring a large pot of lightly salted water to a boil.

2. Heat 2 tablespoons of the olive oil in a large skillet over medium heat. Add green pepper and cook 2 minutes. Add garlic and anchovies and cook for 1 minute, mashing anchovies with spoon.

3. Add tomatoes, salt and pepper. Cook 5 minutes, stirring.

4. While sauce is cooking, prepare pasta following package directions. Drain, reserving 1 cup cooking water.

5. Toss pasta with tomato mixture and remaining tablespoon olive oil. Add ¼ cup pasta water if needed. Serve with cheese.

***Note:** If desired, use a 6-ounce can of tuna instead of anchovies.

PER SERVING: 437 calories; 13 g fat (3 g sat.); 19 g protein; 62 g carbohydrate; 3 g fiber; 660 mg sodium; 18 mg cholesterol.

pork and peppers

MAKES: 4 servings. **PREP:** 10 minutes. **COOK:** 61 minutes.

- 2 tablespoons olive oil
- 3 cloves garlic, chopped
- 1½ pounds boneless pork, cut into 1-inch pieces
- 4 sweet peppers, cut into 1-inch pieces
- 1 large onion, chopped
- 1 can (28 ounces) plum tomatoes
- 1½ teaspoons dried oregano
- ½ teaspoon parsley flakes
- ¼ teaspoon black pepper
- 6 ounces uncooked egg noodles

1. Heat olive oil in a large pot; add garlic and cook 1 minute. Add pork and cook 5 minutes, until lightly browned, being careful not to let garlic burn. Stir in peppers and onion and cook for an additional 5 minutes, stirring occasionally.

2. Add tomatoes and break up with a wooden spoon. Stir in the oregano, parsley and black pepper.

3. Bring to a boil over high heat. Lower to medium-low heat and simmer, with the lid ajar, for 50 minutes, stirring occasionally.

4. Meanwhile, cook egg noodles following package directions. Drain.

5. Serve pork and peppers over noodles.

PER SERVING: 527 calories; 13 g fat (3 g sat.); 48 g protein; 53 g carbohydrate; 8 g fiber; 581 mg sodium; 143 mg cholesterol.

Heather Janwich
Freehold, NJ

"My grandmother always made this for me and gave me the recipe. It's even better the second day."

pantry items

- apricot preserves
- ketchup
- Dijon mustard
- light mayonnaise
- ground ginger
- olive oil
- lemon pepper
- dried Italian seasoning
- crushed red pepper
- salt and pepper
- onion flakes
- brown sugar
- shredded Parmesan cheese
- dried oregano
- dried parsley flakes

cooking tip

shrimp cleaning how-to

1. Gently remove shell with fingers.

2. With a small paring knife, cut along inside of shrimp to expose vein.

3. With small paring knife, cut along rounded part of shrimp to expose vein.

4. Run under cold water to rinse away veins.

- 1½ pounds of shrimp with shells = 1 pound cleaned shrimp.
- Buy frozen shrimp with shells on to protect them from freezer burn.
- Thaw shrimp in refrigerator; use within two days and never refreeze.

shopping list

This grocery list and the pantry items are all you need to cook up a week of hearty suppers.

PRODUCE
1 pound cherry tomatoes
8 ounces presliced mixed mushrooms
5 assorted sweet bell peppers
2 pints grape tomatoes
1 large yellow onion
2 heads garlic

DAIRY
1 package shredded cheddar cheese

MEAT, FISH AND POULTRY
4 boneless, skinless chicken breasts, about 6 ounces each
4 flounder fillets, about 6 ounces each
4 beef filet mignon steaks, about 6 ounces each
1½ pounds thick-cut boneless pork chops

FROZEN
1½ pounds large, frozen shrimp
1 box (10 ounces) frozen spinach

DRY GOODS
1 small bag shelled hazelnuts
1 box (6 ounce) long grain and wild rice mix
1 box whole-wheat angel-hair pasta
1 pound spaghetti
1 can (15 ounces) white beans
1 box (6.1 ounces) tomato and lentil couscous mix
1 bottle steak sauce
2 tins (2 ounces each) anchovies packed in oil
1 can (28 ounces) plum tomatoes
1 bag (12 ounces) egg noodles

the thrill of the grill

FIRE UP THE BARBECUE! WE'VE CREATED SIX DISHES THAT NEED A MERE 15 MINUTES TO PREP. FROM SHRIMP AND BURGERS TO A PINEAPPLE SHORTCAKE, THESE BACKYARD RECIPES MAKE FOR A DELICIOUSLY GOOD TIME. **BY PEGGY KATALINICH**

Delight your guests with our smoky Chipotle Mini Burgers. (Recipe page 145)

PHOTOGRAPHY BY TINA RUPP

blue cheese potato salad

MAKES: 8 servings. **PREP:** 10 minutes.
COOK: 20 minutes.

- 5 pounds Yukon gold potatoes
- 1 pound green beans, trimmed and cut into 1-inch pieces
- 4 ounces reduced-fat cream cheese, softened
- 1 bottle (8 ounces) light blue cheese dressing
- 1¼ cups light mayonnaise
- ½ teaspoon salt
- ½ teaspoon black pepper
- 1 medium-size red onion, diced
- 3 cloves garlic, minced
  Chives or dill, for garnish (optional)

1. Bring a large pot of salted water to a boil. Scrub potatoes and add to pot; if potatoes are not uniform in size, add largest first then smaller ones, waiting a few minutes between additions. Cook about 20 minutes or until tip of knife can be inserted easily into center of potatoes. Drain and rinse under cool water.

2. While potatoes are cooking, bring a pot of salted water to a boil; add green beans. Cook 5 minutes or until crisp-tender. Drain; rinse under cool water.

3. In a large bowl, stir cream cheese, dressing, mayonnaise, salt and pepper; mix well. When potatoes are cool enough to handle, peel, if desired, and cut into cubes. Stir into mayonnaise mixture along with drained green beans, onion and garlic. Refrigerate until ready to serve. Garnish with chives or dill, if desired.

PER SERVING: 274 calories; 12 g fat (3 g sat.); 6 g protein; 37 g carbohydrate; 5 g fiber; 660 mg sodium; 14 mg cholesterol.

Yukon gold potatoes are yellower, sweeter and heartier than regular potatoes.

Emily Prieto
Columbus, OH

READER RECIPE

"It's great for summer picnics but also a nice side in cooler months."

shrimp bruschetta

MAKES: 8 servings.
PREP: 15 minutes. **MARINATE:** 30 minutes.
COOK: 3 minutes. **GRILL:** 12 minutes.

- 1¼ pounds small shrimp, cleaned
- ½ cup white wine
- 6 teaspoons minced garlic
- 2 containers (1 pint each) mixed red and yellow grape tomatoes
- 4 tablespoons olive oil
- 6 leaves fresh basil, finely chopped
- 1 small loaf Italian bread
  Sea salt, for sprinkling (optional)

1. Place shrimp in a large resealable plastic bag. Add wine and 2 teaspoons of the minced garlic. Marinate at room temperature 30 minutes or in refrigerator for a few hours.
2. Cut grape tomatoes in quarters. Heat oil in medium-size skillet over medium-low heat. Add the remaining garlic and cook 1 minute; add tomatoes and cook 1 to 2 minutes or until slightly softened. Stir in basil then remove from heat.
3. Heat gas grill to medium or prepare charcoal grill with medium coals. Remove shrimp from marinade; discard marinade. Place shrimp in a grill basket and grill 6 minutes, stirring occasionally. Remove and cut in half crosswise, if desired; stir into tomato mixture.
4. Cut 8 slices bread, about ½ inch thick. Brush both sides with a little of the oil from the tomato-garlic skillet. Grill bread 3 minutes per side, until golden-brown. Serve topped with shrimp-tomato mixture; sprinkle with a little sea salt, if desired.

PER SERVING: 178 calories; 8 g fat (1 g sat.); 13 g protein; 10 g carbohydrate; 1 g fiber; 154 mg sodium; 86 mg cholesterol.

chicken appetizer kebabs

MAKES: 8 servings (3 kebabs each).
PREP: 15 minutes. **REFRIGERATE:** 2 hours. **GRILL:** 12 minutes.

Kebabs:
- 1 pound boneless, skinless chicken thighs
- 3 tablespoons lime juice
- 1 tablespoon sugar
- 1 clove garlic, minced
- 1 large red pepper
- 24 large fresh sage leaves

Pepper dip:
- 3 cloves garlic, peeled
- 3 leaves fresh sage
- ¼ cup jarred roasted pepper
- ½ cup light mayonnaise
- 1 tablespoon sugar
- 1 tablespoon lime juice
- ½ teaspoon salt
- ¼ teaspoon black pepper

1. Kebabs: Cut chicken thighs into 1-inch pieces. Place in resealable plastic bag; add lime juice, sugar and garlic. Press to combine. Refrigerate at least 2 hours.
2. Pepper dip: Smash garlic cloves and place in a food processor; blend until minced. Add sage leaves and roasted pepper; process until smooth. Add mayonnaise, sugar, lime juice, salt and pepper and process until smooth. Remove to a bowl; cover with plastic and refrigerate until ready to serve.
3. Soak 24, 6-inch bamboo skewers in water for 30 minutes. Heat gas grill to medium-high or prepare charcoal grill with medium-hot coals. Cut pepper into 1-inch pieces. Thread a pepper piece onto skewer. Wrap chicken in a sage leaf and thread onto skewer. Repeat using all ingredients, for a total of 24 kebabs.
4. Grill about 12 minutes, turning often, until chicken is nicely crisped. Remove and serve with pepper dip; kebabs can be served at room temperature.

PER SERVING: 153 calories; 8 g fat (1 g sat.); 14 g protein; 6 g carbohydrate; 1 g fiber; 751 mg sodium; 64 mg cholesterol.

These bite-size kebabs are easy to handle and are bursting with fresh flavor.

chipotle mini burgers

MAKES: 16 burgers.
PREP: 10 minutes. **COOK:** 16 minutes.
GRILL: 12 minutes.

- 1½ pounds sweet onion (such as Vidalia or Maui, about 1 very large bulb)
- 4 teaspoons cinnamon-chipotle rub (such as McCormick Grill Mates*)
- 2 pounds ground beef, chuck (17% fat)
- 1 tablespoon oil
- ½ cup bourbon
- ⅔ cup ketchup
- 2 tablespoons brown mustard
- 16 mini hamburger buns or dinner rolls

1. Cut onion in half, then into thin slices. Finely chop some of the slices to equal ¼ cup chopped onion; set the slices aside. Heavily coat a small nonstick pan with nonstick spray; heat over medium heat, then add chopped onion and 1 teaspoon of the cinnamon chipotle rub. Cook 1 minute or until fragrant. Combine seasoned onion with ground beef in a large bowl. Shape into 16 small burgers, each about 1-inch thick. Can be made ahead and covered with plastic wrap; refrigerate for up to 6 hours.

2. Heat oil in a large nonstick skillet over medium heat. Add reserved onion slices and cook, stirring often, 10 minutes or until lightly golden. Sprinkle remaining 3 teaspoons cinnamon-chipotle rub and cook 1 minute. Add bourbon and cook 2 minutes, until liquid is reduced. Stir in ketchup and mustard; simmer 2 minutes. Can be made ahead; cover and refrigerate for several hours.

3. Heat gas grill to medium-high or prepare charcoal grill with medium-hot coals. Grill burgers about 6 minutes per side or until instant-read thermometer registers 160°. Reheat onions if necessary. Place patties on buns, topping each burger with a tablespoon of onions; serve remaining onions on the side.

*Note: If you cannot find the rub, stir together 1 teaspoon ground cinnamon and 4 teaspoons chipotle or chili powder (you'll have a little extra).

PER BURGER: 232 calories; 11 g fat (4 g sat.); 13 g protein; 16 g carbohydrate; 2 g fiber; 332 mg sodium; 39 mg cholesterol.

The bourbon-laced onions also make a tangy topping for steak.

grilled pineapple shortcake

MAKES: 8 servings. **PREP:** 10 minutes. **COOK:** 12 minutes. **GRILL:** 7 minutes.

¾ cup orange-pineapple juice
1 tablespoon cornstarch
¾ cup coconut-flavored rum*
3 tablespoons dark-brown sugar
1 teaspoon rum extract
½ teaspoon coconut extract
1 peeled and cored pineapple (about 9 ounces)
1 small prepared pound cake (about 11 ounces)
1 pint light pineapple-coconut ice cream (such as Häagen-Dazs)

1. Stir together 1 tablespoon of the juice and the cornstarch. Set aside. In a small saucepan, combine the remaining juice, rum and brown sugar. Bring to a boil over medium-high heat and simmer for 10 minutes. Stir in cornstarch mixture and extracts. Cook another 2 minutes. Set sauce aside.
2. Cut pineapple into 8 slices, each about ¾ inch thick. Cut pound cake into 8 slices, each about 1 inch thick. Heat gas grill to medium or prepare charcoal grill with medium-hot coals.

3. Brush pineapple with some of the rum sauce. Grill 5 minutes, turning once, until grill marks form. Set aside. Grill pound cake slices 2 minutes or until grill marks appear, turning once.
4. Serve pound cake slices, topped with grilled pineapple and a scoop of ice cream. Drizzle with remaining sauce.
***Note:** Substitute additional juice for the rum, if desired.

PER SERVING: 289 calories; 9 g fat (5 g sat.); 5 g protein; 46 g carbohydrate; 1 g fiber; 164 mg sodium; 78 mg cholesterol.

Smoky grill flavors balance well with sweet pineapple.

Grilled fresh corn gives this creamy summertime pudding amazing flavor.

grilled corn pudding

MAKES: 8 servings. **PREP:** 15 minutes.
GRILL: 12 minutes.
BAKE: at 350° for 30 minutes.

- 4 large ears corn, shucked
- 5 eggs
- ¼ cup all-purpose flour
- 1 cup heavy cream
- ½ cup milk
- ¼ to ½ teaspoon hot pepper sauce
- 1 tablespoon sugar
- 1 teaspoon salt
- ¼ teaspoon black pepper

1. Heat gas grill to medium heat or prepare charcoal grill with medium-hot coals. Coat corn with nonstick spray for grilling. Grill about 12 minutes, turning frequently, or until ears are lightly charred. Remove and let cool. Cut kernels from ears; you need 2½ cups total; save any extra for another use. This step can be done several hours ahead.
2. Heat oven to 350°. In large bowl, lightly beat eggs, then beat in flour, cream, milk, hot pepper sauce, sugar, salt and pepper. Stir in corn. Coat a 2-quart baking dish with nonstick spray. Add corn mixture.
3. Bake at 350° for about 30 minutes or until pudding is set in middle. Let sit at least 15 minutes before serving.

PER SERVING: 234 calories; 15 g fat (8 g sat.); 7 g protein; 19 g carbohydrate; 2 g fiber; 358 mg sodium; 176 mg cholesterol.

slow-cooker solutions

GREAT-TASTING RECIPES FOR EFFORTLESS MEALS. **BY CINDY HELLER**

Food styling: Toni Brogan. Prop styling: Chiara Milott.

pulled pork sandwiches

MAKES: 6 servings. **PREP:** 10 minutes. **REFRIGERATE:** at least 1 hour. **SLOW-COOK:** 6 hours on HIGH or 8 hours on LOW. **COOK:** 2 minutes.

2½ **tablespoons dark-brown sugar**
1 **tablespoon paprika**
1 **teaspoon chili powder**
1 **teaspoon ground cumin**
1 **teaspoon black pepper**
1 **boneless pork butt or shoulder (about 2½ pounds), trimmed**
1 **cup low-sodium chicken broth**
2 **tablespoons cider vinegar**
2 **tablespoons ketchup**
6 **hamburger buns**

1. In a small bowl, stir together 1 tablespoon of the sugar, the paprika, chili powder, cumin and pepper; set aside.
2. Lay pork on work surface and sprinkle on all sides with spice rub; rub well into meat. Wrap in plastic wrap and refrigerate for 1 hour or overnight.
3. Unwrap pork and place in slow cooker with chicken broth. Cover and cook on HIGH for 6 hours or LOW for 8 hours. Remove pork from slow cooker and cut into large chunks; let stand 20 minutes or until cool enough to handle.

4. While pork is cooling, pour cooking liquid into a fat separator. Pour de-fatted liquid into small saucepan. Heat over medium-high heat. Whisk in vinegar, ketchup and remaining 1½ tablespoons brown sugar. Cook until sugar has dissolved, about 2 minutes; set aside.
5. Using forks or your hands, pull meat into shreds, discarding excess fat, and place in bowl. Stir in sauce and put ½ cup meat on each bun. Serve immediately.

PER SERVING: 366 calories; 12 g fat (4 g sat.); 39 g protein; 22 g carbohydrate; 1 g fiber; 424 mg sodium; 114 mg cholesterol.

PHOTOGRAPHY BY KATE MATHIS

chilled red pepper soup

MAKES: 4 servings. **PREP:** 10 minutes. **COOK:** 8 minutes. **SLOW-COOK:** 3 hours on HIGH or 4½ hours on LOW.

- 1 tablespoon olive oil
- 1 small onion, chopped
- 2 garlic cloves, finely chopped
- 1 teaspoon smoked paprika
- 4 medium-size red peppers, seeded and cut into 1-inch pieces (about 4 cups)
- 3 cups low-sodium chicken broth
- 1 teaspoon sugar
- ½ teaspoon salt
- ¼ teaspoon white pepper
  Basil, for garnish

1. Heat oil in a large nonstick skillet over medium-high heat. Cook onion and garlic for 3 minutes or until softened. Stir in paprika and cook for 1 minute. Add red pepper to skillet and cook, stirring occasionally, for 4 minutes.

2. Scrape contents of skillet into slow-cooker bowl and pour in chicken broth. Cover and cook on HIGH for 3 hours or LOW for 4½ hours or until red peppers are completely soft.

3. Working in batches, puree soup in a blender until completely smooth. Stir in sugar, salt and white pepper. Cover and chill overnight. Garnish each serving with basil and serve.

PER SERVING: 88 calories; 4 g fat (1 g sat.); 3 g protein; 12 g carbohydrate; 3 g fiber; 747 mg sodium; 3 mg cholesterol.

cooking school

FOLLOW OUR STEP-BY-STEP INSTRUCTIONS TO PREPARE THIS EYE-CATCHING STUFFED FLANK STEAK FOR A SPECIAL DINNER. ROUND OUT YOUR MEAL BY SERVING IT ALONGSIDE ROASTED VEGGIES. **BY JULIE MILTENBERGER**

This showy main dish is easy to keep rolled; tie at 2-inch intervals with twine.

stuffed flank steak

MAKES: 6 servings. **PREP:** 20 minutes. **ROAST:** at 425° for 35 minutes. **BROIL:** 10 minutes.

1 flank steak (1½ to 2 pounds)
1 package frozen chopped spinach, thawed
½ cup crumbled blue cheese
1 jar (7 ounces) roasted red peppers, drained and chopped
2 tablespoons seasoned dry bread crumbs
1 egg yolk
¾ teaspoon garlic salt
¾ teaspoon ground black pepper
1 tablespoon olive oil

1. Heat oven to 425°.

2. Lay steak on work surface. Holding sharp knife parallel to work surface and starting at a long side, slice flank steak in half to opposite long side, without cutting all the way through **(photo 1)**; open up the steak like a book. Flatten slightly to an even thickness.

3. Squeeze liquid from spinach; discard liquid. In medium-size bowl, combine spinach, cheese, peppers, bread crumbs, egg yolk, ¼ teaspoon *each* of the garlic salt and the pepper.

4. Season steak with an additional ¼ teaspoon *each* of the garlic salt and pepper. Press filling onto steak, leaving a 1-inch border on all sides **(photo 2)**. Roll up steak to enclose filling **(photo 3)**, beginning on a short side; the grain of the meat will be running from left to right. Tuck any loose filling back into ends.

5. Tie steak with cotton twine at 2-inch intervals to secure. Rub outside with oil, then sprinkle with remaining ¼ teaspoon *each* garlic salt and pepper.

6. Roast at 425° for 35 minutes, then increase heat to broil and broil for 10 minutes, turning once. Let meat rest 15 minutes. Remove twine, slice and serve.

PER SERVING: 305 calories; 15 g fat (6 g sat.); 36 g protein; 7 g carbohydrate; 2 g fiber; 588 mg sodium; 92 mg cholesterol.

Starting on a long side, split steak in half (not all the way through), and open like a book.

Spread spinach filling over flattened meat, leaving a 1-inch border around all edges.

Roll up meat, starting at a short end, until you enclose all of the spinach filling.

july

Caesar Salad with Steak
(Recipe page 166)

AS SUMMER TEMPERATURES SOAR,
HELP YOUR FAMILY BEAT THE HEAT WITH
LIGHT, REFRESHING SALADS AND
DECADENT BAKED ALASKA.

Moo-Shu Chicken
page 160

Pasta Salad with Chicken
page 168

Baked Alaska
page 171

A FAVORITE TREAT JUST GOT BIGGER—NOW THERE'S ENOUGH FOR EVERYONE!
BY KAREN TACK

giant cupcake

MAKES: 16 servings. **PREP:** 15 minutes. **BAKE:** at 325° for 1 hour.

Cake:
- 3 cups all-purpose flour
- ¼ cup poppy seeds
- ¾ teaspoon baking soda
- ½ teaspoon salt
- 1 cup (2 sticks) unsalted butter, softened
- ½ of an 8-ounce package cream cheese, softened (save other half for frosting)
- 2 cups granulated sugar
- 3 large eggs
- ¾ cup buttermilk
- ¼ cup fresh lemon juice
- 2 tablespoons fresh grated lemon zest

Glaze:
- 3 cups confectioners' sugar
- 4 tablespoons lemon juice
- 2 drops blue food coloring

Frosting:
- ½ cup (1 stick) unsalted butter, softened
- 4 ounces cream cheese, softened
- 2 cups confectioners' sugar
- 1 tablespoon fresh lemon juice
- Raspberries, blueberries and assorted sprinkles (optional)

1. Heat oven to 325°. Grease and flour giant cupcake pan and set aside.

2. Cake: Whisk together flour, poppy seeds, baking soda and salt in a medium bowl. Set aside.

3. Beat butter and cream cheese with an electric mixer in a large bowl until smooth. Add granulated sugar and beat on medium until light and fluffy, about 3 minutes. Add eggs, one at a time, beating well after each until well combined.

4. Combine the buttermilk, lemon juice and zest in a liquid measuring cup. Add the flour mixture, alternating with the buttermilk mixture, to the butter mixture, starting and ending with the dry ingredients. Beat until just blended.

5. Divide batter evenly between prepared pan halves. Bake at 325° until a toothpick inserted in centers comes out clean, about 1 hour. Transfer to a wire rack and cool 10 minutes. Invert; cool.

6. Trim cakes if necessary. Place bottom part of the cupcake on a wire rack over a jelly roll pan, top-side down.

7. Prepare **Glaze:** In a medium-size bowl, whisk together the confectioners' sugar, lemon juice and food coloring until smooth. Pour glaze over the bottom half of cake to cover completely; use a spatula to help spread it onto side of cake. Let dry 5 minutes, then repeat, scraping up glaze from the pan and reusing excess. Let stand until glaze is set, about 15 minutes.

8. Meanwhile, prepare **Frosting:** In a large bowl, beat together butter and cream cheese. Add the confectioners' sugar and lemon juice and beat on low speed until smooth and good spreading consistency.

9. Turn over cupcake bottom and spread with a little frosting. Attach top of cupcake (trimmed level if needed) and spread with remaining frosting. Decorate with berries and sprinkles and add candles or sparklers, if desired.

PER SERVING: 539 calories; 22 g fat (13 g sat.); 5 g protein; 82 g carbohydrate; 1 g fiber; 183 mg sodium; 93 mg cholesterol.

To make our cover cupcake at home, purchase the Wilton Large Cupcake pan. Visit wilton.com to order.

Food styling: Karen Tack. Prop styling: Leslie Siegel.

PHOTOGRAPHY BY RITA MAAS

worldly DINNERS

SPICE UP MEALTIME WITH DELICIOUS AND NUTRITIOUS RECIPES FROM AROUND THE WORLD—OUR SHOPPING LIST MAKES YOUR TRIP TO THE SUPERMARKET EASY AND FAST.
BY MICHAEL TYRRELL

Moo-Shu Chicken filling also goes great with rice. (Recipe page 160)

PHOTOGRAPHY BY ALEXANDRA GRABLEWSKI

greek-style roasted vegetables

MAKES: 4 servings. **PREP:** 20 minutes. **ROAST:** at 425° for 45 minutes.

- 1 **pound small red potatoes, quartered**
- 2 **small eggplants, cut into ½-inch half-moons**
- 1 **medium-size sweet onion, sliced**
- 1 **medium-size green bell pepper, sliced**
- 3 **tablespoons olive oil**
- 1 **teaspoon garlic salt**
- ½ **teaspoon black pepper**
- 1 **lemon**
- 1 **can (15 ounces) chickpeas, drained and rinsed**
- 1 **tablespoon fresh chopped oregano**
- 1 **tablespoon chopped mint**
- 2 **ounces reduced-fat feta crumbles**

1. Heat oven to 425°. In a large roasting pan, toss together the potatoes, eggplants, onion, green pepper, 2 tablespoons of the olive oil, the garlic salt and pepper. Peel off the lemon zest with a peeler and add to mixture. Reserve lemon. Roast vegetables at 425° for 30 minutes, stirring twice.

2. Add chickpeas and roast an additional 15 minutes.

3. Stir in juice from lemon, oregano and mint. Top with feta crumbles and drizzle with remaining tablespoon olive oil.

PER SERVING: 356 calories; 14 g fat (3 g sat.); 12 g protein; 48 g carbohydrate; 12 g fiber; 775 mg sodium; 4 mg cholesterol.

Food styling: Michael Pederson. Prop styling: Lynda White.

pesto scallops with toasted walnuts

MAKES: 4 servings. **PREP:** 15 minutes. **COOK:** 10 minutes. **SAUTÉ:** 8 minutes.

½ pound whole-wheat bowtie pasta
1 pound sea scallops
¼ teaspoon salt
¼ teaspoon black pepper
1 tablespoon olive oil
¼ cup jarred basil pesto
¼ cup shredded Parmesan cheese
¼ cup chopped, toasted walnuts
Fresh basil (optional)

1. Cook pasta following package directions, about 10 minutes. Drain, reserving 1 cup of the cooking liquid.

2. While pasta is cooking, season scallops with salt and pepper. Heat olive oil in a large nonstick skillet over medium-high heat. Sauté 3 to 4 minutes per side, until cooked through and no longer translucent.

3. Add the pesto to drained pasta. Stir in some of the reserved cooking liquid until pasta is evenly coated with pesto.

4. Stir in the cheese and the toasted walnuts. Serve with the scallops, and garnish with fresh basil, if desired.

PER SERVING: 487 calories; 19 g fat (3 g sat.); 31 g protein; 48 g carbohydrate; 6 g fiber; 550 mg sodium; 47 mg cholesterol.

jerk chicken and rice

MAKES: 4 servings. **PREP:** 15 minutes. **COOK:** 25 minutes. **BAKE:** at 450° for 15 minutes.

1 **cup long-grain, parboiled rice**
2 **cups reduced-sodium chicken broth**
4 **teaspoons jerk seasoning**
1 **can (15 ounces) red kidney beans, drained and rinsed**
1½ **pounds boneless, skinless chicken breasts**

1. Heat oven to 450°. Coat a baking dish with nonstick cooking spray.

2. Cook rice following package directions, about 25 minutes, replacing water with the broth and adding 1 teaspoon of the jerk seasoning. Gently stir in kidney beans during the last 5 minutes of cooking.

3. Meanwhile, cut the chicken into 1-inch pieces and toss with remaining 3 teaspoons of jerk seasoning. Place in prepared pan and bake at 450° for 15 minutes or until internal temperature reaches 160° on an instant-read thermometer, turning once halfway through cooking.

4. Serve the chicken with the rice and beans on the side.

PER SERVING: 487 calories; 4 g fat (1 g sat.); 52 g protein; 59 g carbohydrate; 12 g fiber; 623 mg sodium; 99 mg cholesterol.

moo-shu chicken

MAKES: 10 rolls. **PREP:** 10 minutes. **COOK:** 10 minutes.

- 1 tablespoon sesame oil
- 2 cloves garlic, chopped
- 1 bag (10 ounces) shredded coleslaw mix
- 1 bag (8 ounces) shredded carrots
- 4 scallions, sliced
- ¼ cup hoisin sauce
- 2 tablespoons reduced-sodium soy sauce
- 10 flour tortillas (6 inches)
- 3 cups shredded cooked chicken (from a rotisserie chicken)

1. In a large nonstick skillet, heat the oil over medium heat. Add the garlic, coleslaw mix, carrot and scallions. Cook, stirring occasionally, for 8 minutes, until vegetables are softened.

2. Stir in the hoisin and soy sauce and cook 2 minutes. Add chicken; stir to combine with vegetables and heat through.

3. To serve, heat tortillas following package directions. Spoon ½ cup of chicken mixture down center of tortilla and roll up.

PER ROLL: 190 calories; 5 g fat (1 g sat.); 12 g protein; 25 g carbohydrate; 3 g fiber; 897 mg sodium; 19 mg cholesterol.

chili flank steak

MAKES: 4 servings. **PREP:** 5 minutes. **MARINATE:** 8 hours or overnight. **GRILL:** medium-high heat for 12 minutes.

⅔ cup brown sugar
⅔ cup reduced-sodium soy sauce
⅔ cup V-8 juice
½ cup olive oil
2 tablespoons chili powder
4 cloves garlic, chopped
¼ teaspoon ground cumin
1 flank steak, about 1½ pounds
 Corn tortillas and salad (optional)

1. In a large resealable plastic bag, combine the brown sugar, soy sauce, V-8, olive oil, chili powder, garlic and cumin.
2. Add the steak and marinate in the refrigerator at least 8 hours or overnight.
3. Remove steak from bag and discard the marinade.
4. Heat a grill to medium-high. Grill steak for 5 to 6 minutes per side, until internal temperature reads 150° on an instant-read thermometer. Remove steak from grill and cover with foil. Let stand 5 minutes before thinly slicing against the grain. Serve with warmed corn tortillas and salad, if desired.

Broiler Method: Heat broiler; place steak on broiler pan and broil for 5 to 6 minutes per side.

PER SERVING: 471 calories; 23 g fat (7 g sat.); 48 g protein; 14 g carbohydrate; 1 g fiber; 344 mg sodium; 94 mg cholesterol.

READER RECIPE

Debbie Krygeris Downers, IL

"Perfect for busy summer days. Marinate steak in the morning and it's ready to grill for dinner."

pork chops provençal

MAKES: 4 servings. **PREP:** 15 minutes. **COOK:** 14 minutes.

1 tablespoon olive oil
4 boneless pork chops, about 4 ounces each, ¾ inch thick
¼ teaspoon black pepper
⅛ teaspoon salt
1 cup dry white wine
2 cloves garlic, chopped
3 plum tomatoes, seeded and chopped
1 tablespoon grainy Dijon mustard
⅓ cup pitted and coarsely chopped Niçoise olives
1 tablespoon capers

2 tablespoons chopped fresh parsley
½ pound orzo, cooked according to package directions

1. Heat oil in a large nonstick skillet over medium-high heat. Season chops with pepper and salt. Add to skillet and cook 4 minutes per side. Remove to plate.
2. Reduce heat to medium and add wine and garlic, stirring up brown bits in pan. Cook 3 minutes. Stir in tomatoes, mustard, olives and capers. Cook 3 minutes, stirring occasionally. Stir in parsley.
3. To serve, spoon sauce over chops. Serve orzo on the side.

PER SERVING: 482 calories; 12 g fat (3 g sat.); 33 g protein; 49 g carbohydrate; 3 g fiber; 477 mg sodium; 70 mg cholesterol.

pantry items

- olive oil
- salt and pepper
- Parmesan cheese
- dry white wine
- garlic salt
- brown sugar
- reduced-sodium soy sauce
- chili powder
- ground cumin
- grainy Dijon mustard
- capers

family circle tips

need a quick side?

Easy Rice Pilaf → Prepare white rice following package directions. During last 3 minutes, stir in some thawed frozen peas, chopped dried apricots and chopped salted cashews. Serve warm or at room temperature.

~

pump up prepared potato salad

Antipasto Potato Salad → Stir a bit of prepared pesto into your favorite potato salad. Fold in strips of salami, provolone cheese and chopped pitted olives.

~

leftover rotisserie chicken?

Spicy Chicken Ramen Soup → Prepare ramen noodle soup. Stir in shredded rotisserie chicken, sliced scallions and hot sauce to taste.

~

extra cooked shrimp?

Quick Mexican Pizza → Spread Boboli pizza crust with prepared salsa; scatter cooked shrimp over top. Sprinkle with a little chili powder and shredded Mexican cheese blend. Bake at 450° for 10 minutes.

shopping list

This grocery list and the pantry items are all you need to cook up a week of hearty suppers.

PRODUCE
- 2 heads garlic
- 1 bag (10 ounces) shredded coleslaw mix
- 1 bag (8 ounces) shredded carrots
- 1 bunch scallions
- 3 plum tomatoes
- 1 bunch fresh parsley
- 1 pound small red potatoes
- 1 medium-size sweet onion
- 1 medium-size green pepper
- 1 lemon
- 1 bunch fresh oregano
- 1 bunch fresh mint
- 2 small eggplants

DAIRY
- 1 package large flour tortillas
- 1 package (4 ounces) reduced-fat feta crumbles

MEAT, FISH AND POULTRY
- 1½ pounds boneless, skinless chicken breasts
- 1 pound sea scallops
- 1 fully cooked rotisserie chicken
- 4 boneless pork chops, about 4 ounces each, ¾ inch thick
- 1½ pounds flank steak

DRY GOODS
- sesame oil
- hoisin sauce
- jerk seasoning
- 2 cans reduced-sodium chicken broth
- 1 can red kidney beans
- 1 box whole-wheat bowtie pasta
- 1 jar prepared basil pesto
- 1 small package shelled walnuts
- 1 jar Niçoise olives
- 1 box orzo pasta
- 1 small can V-8 juice
- 1 can chickpeas
- 1 box parboiled brown rice

SALAD
days

OUR FIVE SEASONAL SUPPERS—
INCLUDING AN EDAMAME-SHRIMP COMBO
AND CHICKEN PASTA SALAD—ARE SATISFYING
AND SLIMMING: EACH WEIGHS IN AT FEWER
THAN 375 CALORIES.

BY JULIE MILTENBERGER

shrimp and cabbage salad

MAKES: 6 servings. **PREP:** 10 minutes. **COOK:** 5 minutes.

Salad:
- 1 pound frozen edamame
- 2 oranges
- 1 pound frozen fully cooked medium-size shrimp, thawed
- 1 medium-size head napa cabbage, trimmed and shredded (about 6 cups)
- 3 scallions, trimmed and thinly sliced

Dressing:
- ¼ cup rice vinegar
- 1 tablespoon mandarin-style hoisin sauce
- 2 teaspoons sugar
- 2 teaspoons sesame oil
- 1 teaspoon reduced-sodium soy sauce
- ½ teaspoon salt
- ⅓ cup extra-virgin olive oil

1. Prepare **Salad:** Heat a medium-size pot of water to boiling. Add edamame and cook according to package directions, about 5 minutes. Drain, cool and shell beans from pods (you will have about 1¼ cups).

2. With a sharp knife, cut peel and white pith from oranges. Following membranes, cut out orange sections and place in a small bowl. Squeeze any extra juice from membranes into bowl, then discard membranes.

3. In a large bowl, combine edamame, orange sections, shrimp, cabbage and scallions. Prepare **Dressing:** In small bowl, whisk together vinegar, hoisin, sugar, sesame oil, soy sauce and ¼ teaspoon of the salt. While whisking, add oil in a thin stream. Add dressing to bowl; toss to combine. Season with remaining ¼ teaspoon salt; serve.

PER SERVING: 303 calories; 17 g fat (2 g sat.); 24 g protein; 14 g carbohydrate; 3 g fiber; 548 mg sodium; 153 mg cholesterol.

Edamame, or fresh soy beans, are high in protein, low in carbs and add texture to salads.

caesar salad with steak

MAKES: 4 servings.
PREP: 20 minutes. **GRILL:** 12 minutes.

- ½ cup light mayonnaise
- ¼ cup grated Parmesan cheese
- ¼ cup fresh squeezed lemon juice (from 1 large lemon)
- 2 anchovy fillets (from a 3-ounce can)
- ½ plus ¼ teaspoon garlic powder
- ½ teaspoon salt
- ½ teaspoon black pepper
- 1 package (18 ounces) romaine hearts, trimmed, rinsed and dried
- 2 medium-size beef filet mignon steaks (about ¾ pound total)

1. In a mini chopper or a blender, combine mayonnaise, Parmesan cheese, lemon juice, anchovies, ½ teaspoon of the garlic powder, ¼ teaspoon of the salt and ¼ teaspoon of the pepper. Puree until smooth and well combined, scraping down side of bowl if necessary.
2. Heat gas grill or grill pan to medium-high heat. Season steaks with remaining ¼ teaspoon garlic powder, ¼ teaspoon salt and ¼ teaspoon pepper.
3. Stack large leaves of romaine, and cut in half lengthwise along the rib. Then cut crosswise into 1-inch pieces. Repeat with remaining lettuce leaves and transfer lettuce to a large bowl.

4. Grill steaks for 4 to 6 minutes per side, depending on thickness or until meat registers 130° on an instant-read thermometer for medium-rare. Grill an additional minute per side for medium. Remove steaks to a cutting board and tent with foil. Let rest 5 minutes.
5. Pulse dressing again to blend, then toss with lettuce. Divide salad equally among four plates. Thinly slice steak, then fan over salad on each plate, dividing evenly.

PER SERVING: 333 calories; 22 g fat (7 g sat.); 26 g protein; 8 g carbohydrate; 3 g fiber; 588 mg sodium; 89 mg cholesterol.

If filet is too pricey, look for specials from your butcher or opt for sirloin instead.

broccoli-turkey salad

MAKES: 6 servings. **PREP:** 20 minutes.
COOK: 4 minutes. **MICROWAVE:** 7 minutes.

- ⅔ cup light mayonnaise
- 2 tablespoons red wine vinegar
- 2 teaspoons sugar
- ¼ teaspoon salt
- ¼ teaspoon black pepper
- 1 large head broccoli (1½ pounds), cut into florets or 6 cups broccoli florets
- 1 package turkey breast cutlets, about ¾ to 1 pound
- 1 package (6 ounces) turkey bacon
- ½ small red onion, chopped
- ½ cup golden raisins

1. In a small bowl, whisk together the mayonnaise, red wine vinegar, sugar, salt and pepper. Set aside.

2. Heat a medium-size pot of water to boiling and a large skillet of water to simmering. Add broccoli to boiling water and cook 3 minutes, until tender but still crisp. Drain. Meanwhile, add turkey to skillet of simmering water and poach for 3 to 4 minutes or until cooked through. Remove to a cutting board and cool.

3. While broccoli and turkey cool, stack bacon slices on a paper-towel-lined plate (about 5 slices per layer; paper towels between each layer). Microwave on HIGH for 7 minutes, checking and removing any crisp slices after 5 minutes. Cool slightly, then crumble.

4. Cut turkey into bite-size pieces, then transfer to a large bowl. Add broccoli, bacon, red onion and raisins. Toss with mayonnaise mixture until combined. Serve or refrigerate until serving.

PER SERVING: 283 calories; 15 g fat (3 g sat.); 20 g protein; 18 g carbohydrate; 3 g fiber; 693 mg sodium; 71 mg cholesterol.

Raisins add sweetness and a touch of fiber, while bacon lends crunch and flavor.

pasta salad with chicken

MAKES: 6 servings.
PREP: 15 minutes. **COOK:** 8 minutes.

Dressing:
- 3 tablespoons white vinegar
- 2 tablespoons light mayonnaise
- 1 tablespoon honey
- ¼ teaspoon salt
- ¼ teaspoon black pepper
- ¼ cup extra-virgin olive oil
- ¼ cup loosely packed fresh dill, chopped

Pasta Salad:
- 8 ounces mini wagon wheel, bowties or fusilli pasta (such as Barilla Piccolini)
- 2 cups white meat from rotisserie chicken, cut into bite-size pieces
- 1 sweet red pepper, cored and diced
- 2 celery ribs, trimmed and chopped
- ½ cup crumbled feta cheese

1. Prepare **Dressing:** In a medium-size bowl, whisk together vinegar, mayonnaise, honey, salt and pepper. Whisk in olive oil and dill and set aside.

2. Prepare **Pasta Salad:** Heat a medium-size pot of lightly salted water to boiling. Add pasta and cook according to package directions, about 8 minutes. Drain and rinse with cool water; let cool until room temperature.

3. In a large bowl, combine cooled pasta, chicken, red pepper, celery and crumbled feta. Drizzle with dressing and toss to coat. Serve immediately, or refrigerate until ready to serve; toss to blend dressing and ingredients before serving.

PER SERVING: 338 calories; 17 g fat (4 g sat.); 17 g protein; 30 g carbohydrate; 2 g fiber; 454 mg sodium; 68 mg cholesterol.

Using store-bought rotisserie chicken saves time; leftover meat makes a great filling for tacos or quesadillas.

To reduce their sodium levels, rinse canned beans thoroughly before using.

3-bean caprese salad

MAKES: 6 servings.
PREP: 20 minutes. **COOK:** 4 minutes.

Dressing:
- ⅓ cup balsamic vinegar
- 1 tablespoon honey Dijon mustard
- ¼ teaspoon salt
- ¼ teaspoon black pepper
- ¼ cup extra-virgin olive oil

Salad:
- ½ pound green beans, trimmed and cut into 1-inch pieces
- 1 cup loosely packed basil leaves
- 1¼ pounds tomatoes, cored and chopped
- ½ pound fresh mozzarella, cut into ½-inch cubes
- 1 can (15 ounces) red kidney beans, drained and rinsed
- 1 can (15 ounces) small white beans, drained and rinsed

1. Prepare **Dressing:** In a medium-size bowl or measuring cup, whisk together the vinegar, mustard, salt and pepper. While whisking, add oil in a thin stream until blended. Set aside.

2. Prepare **Salad:** Heat a medium-size pot of water to boiling. Add green beans and cook 4 minutes or until crisp-tender. Drain and rinse with cold water.

3. Tear basil into bite-size pieces. In a large bowl, toss basil, green beans, tomatoes, mozzarella, and the kidney and white beans. Whisk dressing, then drizzle over salad. Toss gently to coat and serve.

PER SERVING: 368 calories; 20 g fat (7 g sat.); 18 g protein; 35 g carbohydrate; 11 g fiber; 650 mg sodium; 27 mg cholesterol.

mix it up

Dress up an everyday salad with these greens. They'll add texture and flavor, and you'll save money buying whole heads instead of pre-prepped bags.

bibb lettuce
Part of the butter lettuce family, the leaves are sweet and succulent; handle gently as they are fragile.

watercress
This lettuce belongs to the mustard family and adds a crisp, peppery bite. Discard thickest stems before eating.

red leaf
Frilly, loosely packed leaves and a fuller flavor than head lettuce define this sister of the green leaf.

napa cabbage
Also called Chinese cabbage, this crinkly, white-and-pale-green head has a mild, crunchy texture.

cooking school

GRAND IN APPEARANCE—AND IN FLAVOR—THIS CLASSIC DESSERT IS THE PERFECT TREAT AT ANY SUMMER GET-TOGETHER. FOLLOW OUR STEP-BY-STEP INSTRUCTIONS FOR SUMPTUOUS BAKED ALASKA. **BY JULIE MILTENBERGER**

It may look difficult, but you can make this impressive dessert with a little advance planning.

PHOTOGRAPHY BY KATE MATHIS

baked alaska

MAKES: 8 servings. **PREP:** 30 minutes. **FREEZE:** overnight. **BAKE:** at 350° for 18 minutes; at 475° for 4 minutes.

- 2 **pints strawberry ice cream, softened**
- ¼ **cup all-purpose flour**
- ¼ **cup unsweetened cocoa powder**
- ⅛ **teaspoon baking powder**
  Pinch salt
- 1 **egg**
- ⅔ **cup sugar**
- ½ **teaspoon vanilla extract**
- ⅓ **cup pasteurized powdered egg whites**

1. Line a 1-quart round bowl with plastic wrap, allowing some to overhang edge of bowl. Spoon ice cream into bowl, spreading until level **(photo 1).** Freeze overnight.

2. Heat oven to 350°. Coat an 8-inch round baking pan with nonstick cooking spray. Trace outline of pan on a sheet of waxed paper, then cut out with scissors **(photo 2).** Fit into bottom of pan and coat paper with cooking spray. Whisk together flour, cocoa, baking powder and salt in a bowl.

3. Beat egg and **2 tablespoons water** in a large bowl for 1 minute. Add ⅓ cup of the sugar and the vanilla. Beat 5 minutes, until sugar is dissolved and mixture is pale in color. Sift flour mixture over egg mixture, then fold in. Spread into prepared pan.

4. Bake at 350° for 15 to 18 minutes, until cake just begins to pull away from side of pan. Invert onto wire rack to cool.

5. Combine powdered egg whites and **⅔ cup warm water** in a large bowl. Beat until soft peaks form, then gradually beat in remaining ⅓ cup sugar, until stiff peaks form **(photo 3).**

6. Increase oven temperature to 475°. Place cooled cake layer on a baking sheet. Remove ice cream from freezer and invert onto cake layer (if it sticks, press a warm kitchen towel against bottom of bowl). Remove plastic wrap. Spread whipped egg whites over ice cream and cake to cover, swirling decoratively **(photo 4).** Bake at 475° for 4 minutes, until browned. Slice into wedges and serve immediately. Cover and return any leftover slices to freezer.

PER SERVING: 240 calories; 8 g fat (4 g sat.); 7 g protein; 36 g carbohydrate; 1 g fiber; 95 mg sodium; 46 mg cholesterol.

Line a 1-quart bowl with plastic wrap, then spoon in softened ice cream; spread until level.

Trace pan onto a sheet of waxed paper, then cut out with scissors to fit into baking pan.

Beat powdered egg whites on high speed, gradually adding sugar, until stiff peaks form.

Spread whipped egg whites on ice cream and cake to cover, swirling decoratively.

august

Beijing Chicken Stir-Fry
(Recipe page 189)

THE DOG DAYS OF SUMMER ARE HERE—
AND SO IS THE GARDEN'S BOUNTY.
IT'S THE PERFECT TIME TO TREAT YOUR
FAMILY TO FARM-FRESH MEALS AND
FRUIT-FILLED DESSERTS.

Apple and Cheddar Crumble page 185

Sparkling Sangria page 195

Coconut- or
pineapple-flavored
fruit curd also
works great
in this recipe.

WE'VE UPDATED A CLASSIC WITH FRESH FLAVORS THAT ARE GUARANTEED TO WOW YOUR FAMILY AND FRIENDS. **BY KAREN TACK**

tropical ambrosia
MAKES: 16 servings. **PREP:** 25 minutes. **COOK:** 8 minutes. **REFRIGERATE:** 1 hour.

Passion Fruit Filling:
- 5 large egg yolks
- ⅔ cup sugar
- ¾ cup frozen passion fruit pulp (such as Goya), thawed
- ½ cup (1 stick) unsalted butter, cut up
- Pinch salt
- 1 container (8 ounces) frozen whipped topping (such as Cool Whip), thawed

Assembly:
- 1 mango, peeled
- 3 kiwi, peeled
- ½ fresh pineapple, peeled and cored
- 1 can (15 ounces) mandarin oranges
- 1 cup sweetened flaked coconut, plus more for garnish
- 1 frozen pound cake (10.75 ounces), thawed
- 2 cups plus 1 tablespoon mini marshmallows
- 1 cup raspberries

1. Prepare **Passion Fruit Filling:** Combine egg yolks, sugar, passion fruit pulp, butter and salt in a small saucepan. Cook over medium heat for 8 minutes, stirring constantly, or until mixture thickens and registers 160° on an instant-read thermometer. Do not let the mixture come to a boil or it will curdle.

2. Transfer mixture to a medium-size bowl set over an ice bath (a larger bowl filled with ice and cold water). Stir with a wooden spoon until chilled.

3. Fold whipped topping into chilled curd. Cover with plastic wrap and refrigerate until ready to assemble.

4. Assembly: Cut mango into ¾-inch chunks. Cut 1 kiwi in half lengthwise, then crosswise into ¼-inch-thick slices. Cut remaining kiwis into ½-inch chunks. Cut pineapple into ½-inch-thick slices, then cut slices into ¾-inch chunks.

5. Drain mandarin oranges. Set aside about 14 pieces of the nicest looking oranges and pineapple and all of the kiwi slices. Toss remaining mango, kiwi chunks, oranges and pineapple with 1 cup coconut to blend (makes about 6 cups).

6. Cut cake into ½-inch-thick slices (14 total). Using a 1½-inch round cookie cutter, cut a semicircle from the bottom edge of each cake slice. Cut remaining pound cake scraps into ¾-inch pieces.

7. Spread 1 cup of the fruit mixture in an even layer on the bottom of trifle dish. Arrange a row of the reserved kiwi slices, cut-edge down, along bottom, pressed against the side of dish. Add reserved pieces of pineapple in between each kiwi slice and mandarin oranges on top of kiwi. Set aside 1 cup of the fruit mixture; spread remaining fruit into the serving dish. Spread level.

8. Sprinkle 2 cups of the mini marshmallows in an even layer on top of fruit, making sure they reach the side of the dish. Place raspberries in a single layer along outer edge of dish. Add any leftover berries to the reserved fruit.

9. Place the semicircles of pound cake on top of raspberries, straight-side down, pressing against the side of the dish. Add the cubed pound cake scraps to help support the semicircles. Press down slightly so top is level.

10. Spread passion fruit curd evenly over cake layer. Mound remaining chopped fruit on top and sprinkle with remaining 1 tablespoon mini marshmallows. Garnish with coconut. Refrigerate at least 1 hour or until ready to serve.

PER SERVING: 302 calories; 15 g fat (10 g sat.); 3 g protein; 38 g carbohydrate; 2 g fiber; 94 mg sodium; 100 mg cholesterol.

PHOTOGRAPHY BY RITA MAAS

farm-fresh FLAVORS

CORN AND TOMATOES EARN TOP
BILLING IN OUR 7 NO-FUSS RECIPES,
INCLUDING A CLASSIC CORN CHOWDER
AND A NEW TWIST ON THE BLT.

BY CINDY HELLER

For a spicy kick, add
a seeded and finely
chopped jalapeño to
the corn salsa.
(Recipe page 177)

PHOTOGRAPHY BY DAVID PRINCE

corn fritters
with tomato-corn salsa

MAKES: 8 fritters.
PREP: 10 minutes. **COOK:** 4 minutes.

Salsa:

-   2 medium-size ears of corn
-   1 medium-size tomato (½ pound),
    cored, seeded and finely diced
-   1 scallion, thinly sliced
-   1 tablespoon chopped parsley
-   1 clove garlic, minced
-   1½ tablespoons lime juice
-   1½ tablespoons vegetable oil
-   ½ teaspoon salt
-   ¼ teaspoon black pepper

Fritters:

-   3 medium-size ears of corn
-   ¼ cup cornmeal
-   ¼ cup flour
-   1 egg, lightly beaten
-   ¼ cup buttermilk
-   ¾ teaspoon baking soda
-   ½ teaspoon salt
-   ¼ teaspoon black pepper
-   ⅛ teaspoon cayenne pepper
-   ¼ cup vegetable oil for frying

1. Prepare **Salsa:** Cut kernels off corn; you should have about 1½ cups. Toss with tomato, scallion, parsley, garlic, lime juice, oil, salt and pepper. Set aside.
2. Prepare **Fritters:** Cut kernels off two ears of corn (about 1½ cups). Grate kernels off remaining ear of corn using a box grater. Use the dull side of a knife to scrape any remaining pulp into bowl; you should have about ½ cup grated kernels and pulp. Add cornmeal, flour, egg, buttermilk, baking soda, salt, pepper and cayenne to bowl; stir until combined.
3. Heat oil in large skillet over medium-high heat. Drop batter by ¼-cupfuls into skillet and press with spatula to flatten. Fry 1 to 2 minutes per side or until golden brown. Remove to a paper-towel-lined plate and serve warm with salsa.

PER FRITTER: 196 calories; 11 g fat (1 g sat.); 4 g protein; 23 g carbohydrate; 3 g fiber; 439 mg sodium; 27 mg cholesterol.

Food styling: Sara Neumeier. Prop styling: Megan Hedgpeth.

Starting with fresh tomatoes keeps sodium levels low.

pasta with fresh tomato sauce

MAKES: 8 servings. **PREP:** 10 minutes. **COOK:** 12 minutes.

-   1 pound penne
-   3 tablespoons extra-virgin olive oil
-   2 cloves garlic, minced
-   7 medium-size ripe tomatoes
    (about 2½ pounds), peeled,
    seeded and cut into ½-inch
    pieces (about 3 cups)
-   1½ tablespoons balsamic vinegar
-   1 teaspoon Worcestershire sauce
-   ¾ teaspoon salt
-   ½ teaspoon black pepper
-   ½ teaspoon tomato paste
-   1 tablespoon chopped fresh basil
-   2 tablespoons grated Parmesan
    cheese, plus more for serving

1. Cook pasta according to package directions. Drain and set aside.

2. While pasta is cooking, heat 2 tablespoons of the olive oil in a medium-size saucepan over medium heat. Add garlic and cook for 2 minutes or until fragrant.
3. Add tomatoes, vinegar, Worcestershire sauce, salt, pepper and tomato paste to pan and turn heat to medium-high. Cook for about 10 minutes or until tomatoes begin to soften. Stir in remaining tablespoon olive oil and the basil.
4. Place pasta in large bowl; stir in sauce and Parmesan cheese.

PER SERVING: 299 calories; 7 g fat (1 g sat.); 9 g protein; 50 g carbohydrate; 3 g fiber; 272 mg sodium; 1 mg cholesterol.

Try doubling this recipe and freezing half for an easy meal this winter.

corn chowder

MAKES: 6 servings.
PREP: 15 minutes. **COOK:** 28 minutes.

- 8 medium-size ears of corn
- 4 slices thick-cut bacon, cut into ½-inch pieces
- 1 medium-size onion, finely chopped
- 2 cloves garlic, minced
- 3 tablespoons all-purpose flour
- 3 cups low-sodium chicken broth
- 2 medium-size red skin potatoes (about ¾ pound), cut into ¼-inch pieces
- 1 teaspoon minced fresh thyme
- 2 cups milk
- 1 cup heavy cream
- 1 teaspoon salt
- ¼ teaspoon black pepper
- ⅓ cup shredded white cheddar cheese

1. Cut kernels from 4 ears of corn (about 3 cups of kernels); set aside. Working over a bowl, grate remaining 4 ears of corn on the large holes of a box grater. Scrape pulp from cobs (about ¾ cup) using the dull side of a knife; set aside.
2. In a large pot over medium-high heat, cook bacon for about 6 minutes or until crisp. Remove with a slotted spoon and drain on a paper-towel-lined plate.
3. Add onion to pot and cook for about 4 minutes, stirring occasionally, or until golden brown. Add garlic and cook for 1 minute. Add flour and stir constantly for 2 minutes.

4. Whisk in chicken broth. Add potatoes, thyme, milk and grated corn and pulp. Bring to a boil. Reduce heat to medium-low and simmer for about 10 minutes or until potatoes are tender. Using a potato masher, press down on the potatoes 4 to 5 times. Stir in cooked bacon.
5. Add whole corn kernels and heavy cream and cook an additional 5 minutes or until corn is tender but still crunchy. Stir in salt and pepper. Ladle chowder into bowls. Top each serving with a little cheddar cheese, dividing equally.

PER SERVING: 453 calories; 25 g fat (14 g sat.); 15 g protein; 48 g carbohydrate; 5 g fiber; 636 mg sodium; 81 mg cholesterol.

This chutney is also great spooned over grilled pork tenderloin.

grilled chicken breast with tomato chutney

MAKES: 4 servings. **PREP:** 15 minutes.
COOK: 22 minutes. **GRILL:** 14 minutes.

  2 pounds ripe tomatoes, peeled,
     seeded and cut into ½-inch pieces
  ¾ cup cider vinegar
  ½ cup packed dark-brown sugar
  1 small onion, finely chopped
  1½ teaspoons salt
  4 teaspoons ground ginger
  1½ teaspoons ground cumin
  2 tablespoons vegetable oil
  1 teaspoon ground coriander
  ¼ teaspoon cayenne pepper
  4 small boneless, skinless chicken
     breasts (about 1½ pounds total)

1. In a medium-size saucepan, stir together tomatoes, vinegar, brown sugar, onion, 1 teaspoon of the salt, 1 teaspoon of the ground ginger and ½ teaspoon of cumin. Bring to a boil over high heat. Boil for 18 to 22 minutes, stirring occasionally, or until the liquid has cooked off; set aside and keep warm.
2. Meanwhile, place vegetable oil, remaining 3 teaspoons ground ginger, 1 teaspoon cumin, the coriander and cayenne in a shallow glass dish; stir to combine. Place chicken in the mixture and turn to coat.
3. Heat gas grill to medium-high or prepare charcoal grill with medium-hot coals. Sprinkle chicken with remaining ½ teaspoon salt and grill for about 7 minutes per side or until internal temperature registers 160° on an instant-read thermometer. Serve chicken with a heaping ¼ cup chutney.

PER SERVING: 425 calories; 10 g fat (1 g sat.); 42 g protein; 44 g carbohydrate; 4 g fiber; 1,017 mg sodium; 99 mg cholesterol.

blt salad

MAKES: 4 servings.
PREP: 15 minutes. **COOK:** 14 minutes.

- 8 slices bacon, cut into ½-inch pieces
- 1 ripe avocado, pitted and skinned
- ⅓ cup buttermilk
- ¼ cup chopped red onion
- 2 teaspoons lime juice
- ¾ teaspoon salt
- ½ teaspoon black pepper
- ½ teaspoon cayenne pepper
- ½ cup cornmeal
- ⅓ cup all-purpose flour
- 1 egg, lightly beaten
- 2 medium-size firm, unripe tomatoes (about ¾ pound), cored and cut into ½-inch slices
- 2 tablespoons canola oil
- 3 romaine lettuce hearts, chopped

1. Cook bacon in a large skillet over medium-high heat for 8 minutes or until crisp. Remove bacon and drain on a paper-towel-lined plate; pour off drippings and reserve. Wipe out skillet.
2. While cooking bacon, prepare dressing: Place avocado, buttermilk, onion, lime juice, ¼ teaspoon *each* of the salt, black pepper and cayenne in a blender and puree until smooth; set aside.
3. Stir together cornmeal, remaining ½ teaspoon salt and ¼ teaspoon *each* black pepper and cayenne in shallow dish; place flour and egg in separate shallow dishes.
4. Dip tomato slices in flour, then egg, then cornmeal mixture to coat.
5. Heat canola oil and 1 tablespoon of the reserved bacon drippings in skillet over medium-high heat. Fry tomatoes in a single layer for about 2 to 3 minutes per side or until golden brown. Repeat with remaining tomatoes.
6. Place romaine lettuce in a large bowl and toss with bacon and ⅔ cup of the avocado dressing. Place about 2 cups salad on each plate and top with 2 to 3 fried tomato slices. Dollop with a little of the remaining dressing and serve.

PER SERVING: 425 calories; 26 g fat (8 g sat.); 13 g protein; 34 g carbohydrate; 7 g fiber; 1,019 mg sodium; 77 mg cholesterol.

For a real BLT experience, cut white bread into cubes and toast for croutons.

grilled tomato and cheese

MAKES: 4 sandwiches.
PREP: 10 minutes. **COOK:** 6 minutes.

- 8 slices 12-grain bread
- 8 ounces sharp white cheddar cheese, grated (about 2½ cups)
- 4 ripe tomatoes (about 1 pound), cored and cut into ½-inch slices
- 16 basil leaves
- 2 tablespoons unsalted butter, melted

1. On 1 piece of bread, layer a heaping ¼ cup grated cheese, 4 tomato slices, 4 basil leaves and another heaping ¼ cup grated cheese.

Top with another slice of bread; brush with melted butter.
2. Heat a large nonstick skillet over medium heat. Place sandwich, butter-side down, in pan and brush top slice of bread with butter.* Press with spatula.
3. Cook for about 3 minutes or until golden brown. Flip and cook for another 3 minutes. Remove from skillet and serve immediately. Repeat with remaining sandwiches.
***Note:** You also could prepare in a panini grill, omitting butter.

PER SANDWICH: 503 calories; 28 g fat (16 g sat.); 21 g protein; 42 g carbohydrate; 5 g fiber; 723 mg sodium; 75 mg cholesterol.

spicy skillet cornbread

MAKES: 8 servings.
PREP: 10 minutes.
BAKE: at 450° for 20 minutes.

- 2 medium-size ears of corn
- ¾ cup all-purpose flour
- ½ cup cornmeal
- 1 tablespoon sugar
- 1 teaspoon baking powder
- 1 teaspoon salt
- ¼ cup milk
- ¼ cup buttermilk
- 2 tablespoons unsalted butter, melted
- 1 egg
- 1 jar (2 ounces) pimiento, drained and chopped
- 1 small jalapeño, seeded and chopped
- ¼ teaspoon cayenne pepper, or more, to taste

1. Heat oven to 450°. Place an 8-inch ovenproof nonstick skillet in oven to heat.
2. Cut kernels off corn and set aside; you should have about 1½ cups kernels.
3. In a medium-size bowl, mix flour, cornmeal, sugar, baking powder and salt.
4. In a large measuring cup, combine milk, buttermilk, butter and egg; add to flour mixture and stir until just blended. Fold in corn, pimiento, jalapeño and cayenne and stir until evenly distributed.
5. Using a hot pad, remove skillet from oven and coat generously with nonstick cooking spray. Pour batter into skillet and spread to edges of pan.
6. Bake at 450° for about 20 minutes or until top is golden and slightly cracked.
7. Cool on a wire rack for 10 minutes. Carefully slide cornbread out of skillet and cut into 8 wedges. Serve warm.

PER SERVING: 143 calories; 4 g fat (2 g sat.); 4 g protein; 22 g carbohydrate; 2 g fiber; 364 mg sodium; 36 mg cholesterol.

Make this special grilled cheese when tomatoes and basil abound at your local farmer's market.

COBBLERS, CRUMBLES & CRISPS

WHETHER IT'S LAYERS OF STRAWBERRIES AND BLUEBERRIES WITH COOKIES OR MOUNDS OF SWEET DOUGH ATOP NECTARINES AND CHERRIES, THESE SIX DELICIOUS DESSERTS SERVE UP THE CLASSIC FLAVORS OF SUMMER.

BY MICHAEL TYRRELL

Dollops of pastry give this dessert its cobblestone look. (Recipe page 183)

PHOTOGRAPHY BY RICK LEW

Using a boxed cake mix makes this fresh-fruit treat extra quick and easy.

mixed berry cobbler

MAKES: 8 servings. **PREP**: 20 minutes.
BAKE: at 350° for 40 minutes.

Filling:
3½ cups blackberries (2 packages, about 6 ounces each)
2 cups blueberries (2 packages, 4.4 ounces each)
1½ cups raspberries (6-ounce package)
½ cup sugar
½ cup coarsely chopped walnuts
¼ cup orange liqueur or orange juice
2 tablespoons quick-cooking tapioca

Topping:
1 cup all-purpose flour
¼ cup plus 1 tablespoon sugar
¼ teaspoon baking soda
¼ teaspoon salt
6 tablespoons milk
¼ cup sour cream
2 tablespoons unsalted butter, melted
Whipped cream (optional)

1. Heat oven to 350°. Coat a 6-cup oval baking dish with nonstick cooking spray.
2. Prepare **Filling:** In a large bowl, gently mix blackberries, blueberries, raspberries, sugar, walnuts, orange liqueur and tapioca. Spoon into prepared dish.
3. Prepare **Topping:** In a large bowl, whisk flour, ¼ cup of the sugar, the baking soda and salt. Mix together milk, sour cream and butter. Add to the flour mixture;stir until a batter forms.
4. Dollop batter over the fruit. Sprinkle batter with remaining 1 tablespoon sugar. Bake at 350° for 35 to 40 minutes, until nicely browned.
5. Serve warm or at room temperature with whipped cream, if desired.

PER SERVING: 329 calories; 10 g fat (3 g sat.); 5 g protein; 55 g carbohydrate; 6 g fiber; 125 mg sodium; 13 mg cholesterol.

Food styling: Sara Neumeier. Prop styling: Loren Simons.

strawberry-rhubarb cobbler

MAKES: 8 servings. **PREP:** 15 minutes. **BAKE:** at 350° for 50 minutes.

6 cups sliced rhubarb (about 1½ pounds)
½ cup granulated sugar
1 package (3 ounces) strawberry-flavored gelatin
1 package (9 ounces) yellow cake mix (such as Jiffy)
⅓ cup unsalted butter, melted
2 teaspoons confectioners' sugar, for garnish
Whipped topping (optional)

1. Heat oven to 350°. Coat an 11 x 7 x 2-inch baking dish with nonstick cooking spray.

2. Place rhubarb in the prepared baking dish and sprinkle with granulated sugar and then with gelatin. Sprinkle the cake mix over the gelatin and then drizzle with **¾ cup water** and melted butter.
3. Bake at 350° for 50 minutes. Remove from oven and cool on a wire rack for 10 to 15 minutes.
4. Serve warm or at room temperature. Dust with confectioners' sugar and serve with whipped topping, if desired.

PER SERVING: 275 calories; 8 g fat (4 g sat.); 4 g protein; 50 g carbohydrate; 2 g fiber; 235 mg sodium; 14 mg cholesterol.

Called a slump in some regions, a grunt is a version of fruit cobbler that is cooked on the stovetop.

nectarine-cherry grunt

MAKES: 8 servings. PREP: 20 minutes. COOK: 28 minutes.

Fruit:
- 4 cups peeled and sliced nectarines (about 1¾ pounds)
- 3 cups pitted sweet cherries (about 1 pound)
- 1 cup granulated sugar
- 2 tablespoons lemon juice
- 1 teaspoon lemon zest

Dumplings:
- ¾ cup all-purpose flour
- 3 tablespoons granulated sugar
- 1 teaspoon chai seasoning (such as McCormick)
- ¾ teaspoon baking powder
- ¼ teaspoon baking soda
- ¼ teaspoon salt
- ⅔ cup buttermilk
- 2 tablespoons unsalted butter, melted

Whipped cream:
- 1 cup heavy cream
- 1 tablespoon granulated sugar
- ½ teaspoon chai seasoning
  Confectioners' sugar, for dusting

1. Prepare **Fruit:** In a large nonstick skillet, stir together nectarines, cherries, sugar, lemon juice and lemon zest. Simmer over medium-high heat for 3 minutes.

2. Prepare **Dumplings:** In a large bowl, whisk flour, sugar, chai seasoning, baking powder, baking soda and salt. Stir in buttermilk and melted butter until a sticky dough forms.

3. Dollop heaping tablespoonfuls of the dough over the simmering fruit. Cover tightly and simmer on medium-low for 25 minutes. Cool for at least 15 minutes.

4. Prepare **Whipped cream:** In a large bowl, beat cream, sugar and chai seasoning until stiff peaks form.

5. To serve, dust with confectioners' sugar and spoon dumplings and fruit into individual bowls. Serve with whipped cream.

PER SERVING: 376 calories; 15 g fat (9 g sat.); 4 g protein; 60 g carbohydrate; 3 g fiber; 181 mg sodium; 50 mg cholesterol.

strawberry-blueberry cookie crisp

MAKES: 8 servings. PREP: 10 minutes.
BAKE: at 375° for 25 minutes.

- 4 cups hulled and quartered strawberries (about 1 pound)
- 2 cups blueberries (2 packages, 4.4 ounces each)
- ½ cup pecans, coarsely chopped
- ⅓ cup sugar
- 1 tablespoon cornstarch
- 3 tablespoons orange juice
- 12 pecan shortbread cookies, crumbled (such as Keebler Pecan Sandies)

1. Heat oven to 375°. Coat a shallow 2-quart casserole with nonstick cooking spray.

2. In a large bowl, toss together strawberries, blueberries, pecans, sugar and cornstarch. Spoon into the prepared baking dish and drizzle with orange juice.

3. Sprinkle cookie crumbs over fruit mixture. Bake at 375° for 20 to 25 minutes or until bubbly and topping is nicely browned. Cool; serve warm.

PER SERVING: 246 calories; 11 g fat (2 g sat.); 3 g protein; 36 g carbohydrate; 3 g fiber; 106 mg sodium; 5 mg cholesterol.

peach melba buckle

MAKES: 12 servings. **PREP:** 15 minutes.
BAKE: at 350° for 1 hour.

- 2 cups all-purpose flour
- 1 cup granulated sugar
- 1 teaspoon salt
- ¾ cup (1½ sticks) cold unsalted butter, cut into ½-inch pieces
- ⅓ cup slivered almonds
- ⅓ cup packed light-brown sugar
- 2 teaspoons baking powder
- ½ cup milk
- 1 egg
- 1 teaspoon vanilla extract
- 3 cups peeled and chopped peaches (about 1¾ pounds)
- 1½ cups raspberries (6-ounce package)
- ¼ cup raspberry preserves

1. Heat oven to 350°. Coat a 10-inch springform pan with nonstick cooking spray.
2. In a large bowl, whisk flour, granulated sugar and salt. Cut in butter until mixture becomes crumbly. Remove 1 cup of the mixture to a small bowl and stir in almonds and light-brown sugar; reserve for topping.
3. Stir baking powder into the remaining flour mixture. In a small bowl, whisk milk, egg and vanilla. Stir into the flour mixture until batter forms.
4. Spoon half the batter into the prepared pan. Scatter peaches and raspberries over the batter. Drop the remaining batter in tablespoons over the fruit and sprinkle with the reserved topping.
5. Bake at 350° for 1 hour, until golden-brown and toothpick inserted in the center comes out clean.
6. Cool slightly on wire rack. Run knife around edge and remove side of pan.
7. Gently heat preserves until just liquid enough to drizzle over buckle. Serve warm or at room temperature.

PER SERVING: 343 calories; 14 g fat (8 g sat.); 4 g protein; 50 g carbohydrate; 3 g fiber; 276 mg sodium; 50 mg cholesterol.

apple and cheddar crumble

MAKES: 8 servings.
PREP: 15 minutes.
BAKE: at 375° for 30 minutes.

- 6 cups peeled and coarsely chopped apples (about 2 pounds)
- 1 lemon, juiced
- 8 ounces shredded sharp cheddar cheese (about 2 cups)
- ½ cup golden raisins
- ½ cup packed light-brown sugar
- ⅓ cup all-purpose flour
- ⅓ cup quick-cooking oats
- ¼ cup (½ stick) unsalted butter, softened
- 1 teaspoon pumpkin pie spice

1. Heat oven to 375°. Coat a 13 x 9 x 2-inch baking dish with nonstick cooking spray.
2. In a large bowl, fold together apples, lemon juice, cheddar cheese and raisins. Spoon into prepared baking dish.
3. In another bowl, combine sugar, flour, oats, butter and pumpkin pie spice; mix until crumbly. Scatter over apple mixture.
4. Bake at 375° for 30 minutes or until nicely browned and apples are tender. Cool at least 15 minutes. Serve warm.

PER SERVING: 326 calories; 15 g fat (9 g sat.); 9 g protein; 42 g carbohydrate; 2 g fiber; 190 mg sodium; 46 mg cholesterol.

This fruit-filled dessert buckles as it bakes, hence the name.

gold-worthy DINNERS

BRING HOME THE GOLD WITH OLYMPIC-INSPIRED MEALS TO HONOR THE BEIJING SUMMER GAMES. OUR QUICK-TO-MAKE RECIPES AND SHOPPING LIST WILL HELP YOU PUT NUTRITIOUS SUPPERS ON THE TABLE IN RECORD TIME.

BY JULIE MILTENBERGER

A classic medley of white beans, escarole and sausage gets a fiber hit from whole-grain pasta. (Recipe page 192)

PHOTOGRAPHY BY TINA RUPP

athens veggie burgers

MAKES: 4 servings. **PREP:** 10 minutes. **GRILL OR COOK:** 8 minutes.

1½ **cups loosely packed baby spinach**
½ **cucumber, peeled, seeded and diced**
2 **scallions, chopped**
1 **plum tomato, cored and diced**
¼ **cup crumbled reduced-fat feta cheese**
2 **tablespoons bottled light vinaigrette**
4 **veggie burger patties**
4 **whole-wheat mini pitas**
¼ **cup light mayonnaise**

1. Stack baby spinach leaves and cut into thin strips, discarding stems. Place in a large bowl and combine with cucumber, scallions, tomato and feta cheese. Toss gently to combine, then add dressing and toss. Set aside.

2. Heat veggie burgers for 8 minutes or according to package directions (either on grill or in skillet). Warm pitas in a toaster oven or toaster. Spread each pita with 1 tablespoon of the light mayonnaise. Top each with a veggie burger, then with ¼ of the salad topping (½ cup per burger). Serve immediately.

PER SERVING: 282 calories; 11 g fat (3 g sat.); 17 g protein; 30 g carbohydrate; 6 g fiber; 814 mg sodium; 15 mg cholesterol.

ATHENS 2004

atlanta pork and potato salad

MAKES: 4 servings. **PREP:** 10 minutes. **COOK:** 14 minutes. **GRILL OR BROIL:** 20 minutes.

⅓ cup light mayonnaise
1 tablespoon creamy horseradish sauce
2 scallions, chopped
1 teaspoon sugar
½ teaspoon salt
1½ pounds red new potatoes, quartered
1 pork tenderloin (about 1¼ to 1½ pounds)
2 teaspoons Montreal chicken seasoning

1. Heat grill or broiler to medium-high heat. In a small bowl, whisk together mayonnaise, horseradish, scallions, sugar and salt. Set aside.

2. Place potatoes in a saucepan and add enough water to cover. Bring to a boil and boil 12 to 14 minutes, until potatoes are tender when pierced with a knife. Drain, rinse and cool.

3. Meanwhile, rub pork with Montreal seasoning. Grill or broil pork for 20 minutes, turning occasionally, or until meat is cooked through and registers 145° on an instant-read thermometer. Cover and let rest at least 5 minutes before slicing. Gently combine potatoes and dressing. Slice pork and serve with potato salad.

PER SERVING: 396 calories; 13 g fat (3 g sat.); 34 g protein; 35 g carbohydrate; 4 g fiber; 814 mg sodium; 102 mg cholesterol.

beijing chicken stir-fry

MAKES: 4 servings. **PREP:** 15 minutes. **COOK:** 12 minutes.

- **1 pound boneless, skinless chicken breasts**
- **6 tablespoons jarred Asian black bean sauce**
- **1 tablespoon canola oil**
- **3 cloves garlic, sliced**
- **½ pound green beans, stems trimmed**
- **1 head bok choy (¾ pound), trimmed and chopped**
- **2 small carrots, peeled and cut into coins**
- **8 ounces lo mein noodles**
- **⅛ teaspoon cayenne pepper**

1. Bring a pot of water to boiling. Slice chicken into thin strips. Toss with 2 tablespoons of the black bean sauce. Heat oil in a large nonstick skillet over medium-high heat. Add chicken and garlic. Cook 4 minutes. Transfer to a plate; keep warm.

2. Reduce heat to medium and add green beans, bok choy and carrots to skillet. Sauté 3 minutes, then add **¼ cup water** and cover skillet. Cook 5 minutes or until beans and carrots are crisp-tender.

3. Meanwhile, boil noodles 5 minutes. Drain and transfer to a platter. Uncover vegetables, add chicken and any juices, remaining 4 tablespoons black bean sauce and cayenne. Toss well to combine, then spoon over noodles and serve warm.

PER SERVING: 483 calories; 13 g fat (2 g sat.); 33 g protein; 59 g carbohydrate; 4 g fiber; 871 mg sodium; 63 mg cholesterol.

Beijing 2008

mexico city beef and bean burritos

MAKES: 6 servings. **PREP:** 10 minutes. **COOK:** 10 minutes. **MICROWAVE:** 2 minutes.

½ head iceberg lettuce
2 plum tomatoes, cored and chopped
1 pound ground sirloin
2 teaspooons chili powder
½ teaspoon dried oregano
2 green peppers, chopped
1 small onion, chopped
1 can (15 ounces) fat-free refried beans
4 whole-grain burrito-size tortillas
¾ cup reduced-fat shredded
   cheddar cheese
⅓ cup light sour cream

1. Shred the lettuce (you will need 3 cups) and core and chop the tomatoes. Set aside. Coat a large nonstick skillet with nonstick cooking spray and heat over medium-high heat. Crumble in sirloin and season with chili powder and oregano. Cook 3 minutes. Reduce heat to medium and add green peppers and onion. Cook an additional 7 minutes, until vegetables are softened (add **½ cup water** if pan is dry).

2. Place beans in a bowl; microwave on HIGH for 2 minutes, stirring halfway.
3. Spread a tortilla with ¼ cup beans. Spoon ⅔ cup of the meat mixture in center of tortilla. Top with 2 tablespoons cheese, ⅔ cup lettuce and ¼ cup tomato. Fold up tortilla, burrito-style; repeat, using all ingredients. Serve with sour cream.

PER SERVING: 462 calories; 14 g fat (6 g sat.); 29 g protein; 55 g carbohydrate; 8 g fiber; 999 mg sodium; 57 mg cholesterol.

mexico68

sydney shrimp and barley

MAKES: 4 servings. **PREP:** 15 minutes. **MARINATE:** 20 minutes. **COOK:** 10 minutes. **GRILL:** 9 minutes.

1¼ **pounds cleaned raw shrimp**
⅓ **cup plus ½ cup light lime vinaigrette**
1⅓ **cups quick-cooking barley**
1 **sweet red pepper, diced**
2 **carrots, peeled and diced**
2 **ribs celery, trimmed and diced**

1. Combine shrimp and ⅓ cup of the vinaigrette in a large resealable bag. Marinate in refrigerator for 20 minutes.

2. Meanwhile, soak 8 bamboo skewers in warm water. Bring a medium-size pot of lightly salted water to boiling. Add barley and cook 10 minutes. Drain and rinse with cool water.

3. Heat gas grill to medium-high or charcoal grill to medium-hot coals. Thread shrimp onto skewers, about 3 or 4 per skewer. Discard shrimp marinade. Grill shrimp 7 to 9 minutes, turning once. While shrimp grills, combine barley, red

pepper, carrots, celery and remaining ½ cup dressing in a large bowl. Toss to coat all ingredients with dressing.

4. To serve: Spoon about 1 cup barley salad onto a plate. Top with two shrimp skewers. Serve hot or at room temperature.

PER SERVING: 365 calories; 5 g fat (1 g sat.); 34 g protein; 50 g carbohydrate; 6 g fiber; 695 mg sodium; 215 mg cholesterol.

Sydney 2000

torino turkey sausage and penne

MAKES: 6 servings. **PREP:** 10 minutes. **COOK:** 15 minutes.

12 ounces whole-wheat penne pasta
1 large head escarole
2 tablespoons olive oil
1 small onion, chopped
1 package (20 ounces) hot Italian turkey sausage
½ teaspoon garlic salt
½ teaspoon black pepper
1 can small white beans, drained and rinsed
Parmesan cheese, for serving (optional)

1. Heat a large pot of salted water to boiling. Add pasta and cook 12 minutes. Clean, trim and chop escarole.

2. While pasta cooks, heat olive oil in a large skillet over medium heat. Add onion and cook 3 minutes, stirring occasionally. Remove sausage from its casing and crumble into pan. Cook 5 minutes, breaking apart with a spoon.

3. Drain pasta, reserving 1 cup pasta water. Keep warm. Increase heat under skillet to medium-high. Add escarole, garlic salt and pepper. Cook 3 minutes, until greens are wilted. Add beans and ½ cup of the pasta water (if necessary). Add drained pasta to the pan and toss to combine. Garnish with Parmesan cheese, if desired.

PER SERVING: 431 calories; 12 g fat (2 g sat.); 31 g protein; 58 g carbohydrate; 10 g fiber; 936 mg sodium; 66 mg cholesterol.

torino 2006

august

pantry items

- salt and pepper
- sugar
- olive and canola oils
- cayenne pepper
- garlic bulb
- garlic salt
- dried oregano
- light mayonnaise
- light vinaigrette
- horseradish sauce

shopping list

This grocery list and the pantry items are all you need to cook up a week of hearty suppers.

PRODUCE
- 1 head iceberg lettuce
- 3 plum tomatoes
- 1 sweet red pepper
- 2 green peppers
- 2 small onions
- 1 large head escarole
- 1 bag baby spinach
- 1 cucumber
- 1 bunch scallions
- ½ pound green beans
- 1 bunch carrots
- 1½ pounds new potatoes
- 1 bunch celery hearts
- 1 head bok choy

DAIRY AND FROZEN
- 1 bag shredded reduced-fat cheddar cheese
- 1 container reduced-fat feta cheese
- 1 container light sour cream
- 4 veggie burgers

MEAT, FISH AND POULTRY
- 1 pound boneless, skinless chicken breast halves
- 1¼ pounds cleaned shrimp
- 1½ pound pork tenderloin
- 1 package hot Italian turkey sausage links
- 1 pound ground sirloin

DRY GOODS
- 1 can fat-free refried beans
- 4 large whole-grain tortillas
- 1 box whole-wheat penne
- 1 can small white beans
- 1 jar Asian black bean sauce
- 1 box quick-cooking barley
- 1 bottle light lime vinaigrette (Newman's Own)
- 1 pack whole-wheat mini pitas
- 1 jar Montreal chicken seasoning (McCormick)
- 1 package lo mein noodles

fun olympic facts

10,500
Number of athletes who competed (from 205 nations) in the 2008 Olympic Games in Beijing.

6
Number of additional cities cohosting Olympic events: Hong Kong, Qinhuangdao, Qingdao, Shanghai, Shenyang and Tianjin.

30,000
Pounds of fruit consumed each year at the Olympic Training Facility in Colorado Springs, Colorado.

75,000
Pounds of protein (supplied by Tyson Foods) the athletes will consume during training, qualifying events and competition.

8
Number of times the Olympic Games have been held in the U.S., from 1904 (summer; St. Louis) to 2002 (winter; Salt Lake City).

85,000
Number of miles (approximately) the Olympic torch traveled on its worldwide journey to Beijing.

Source: U.S. Olympic Committee

cooking **school**

LOOKING FOR A CLASSY COCKTAIL TO SERVE AT YOUR NEXT GET-TOGETHER? USE OUR STEP-BY-STEP INSTRUCTIONS TO TREAT YOUR GUESTS TO DELICIOUS SPARKLING SANGRIAS. **BY JULIE MILTENBERGER**

Add lemon-lime and club sodas right before serving for maximum fizz.

sparkling sangria

MAKES: 12 servings. **PREP:** 10 minutes.
REFRIGERATE: 2 hours or overnight.

- 1 750-ml bottle dry white wine
- 1 cup pomegranate juice
- 1 cup red wine
- ½ cup peach schnapps (or apricot brandy)
- 1 Granny Smith apple, cored and diced
- 1 regular or white peach, pitted and diced
- 1 can diet lemon-lime or grapefruit soda
   (such as 7 UP or Fresca)
- 1 can club soda
   Oranges, for garnish

Combine white wine, pomegranate juice, red wine, schnapps, apple pieces and peach pieces in a large pitcher. Stir well to blend flavors. Refrigerate for at least 2 hours or overnight. Before serving, add diet soda and club soda. Serve over ice with orange curlicue garnish (see photos).

PER SERVING: 118 calories; 0 g fat; 0 g protein; 11 g carbohydrate; 0 g fiber; 13 mg sodium; 0 mg cholesterol.

sangria starters

When selecting white wine for Sangria, look for inexpensive (under $10) bottles that you would normally enjoy drinking. A good rule of thumb is to choose wine that echos some of the flavors that you are using in your sangria cocktail. For our Sparkling Sangria, look for a bottle that advertises fruity flavors, such peach or apple.

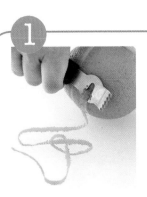

1 With a channel knife zester, separate long, thin strips of peel from an orange.

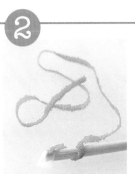

2 Tape one end of the peel to the bottom of a chopstick or drinking straw.

3 Carefully wrap peel around chopstick, evenly spacing to form a curlicue.

4 Tape other end of peel to chopstick; freeze overnight. Slip off chopstick; garnish drink.

Food styling: Sara Neumeier. Prop styling: Megan Hedgpeth.

september

Pork with Pear Compote
(Recipe page 215)

WITH AUTUMN COMES COOL BREEZES AND
THE START OF A NEW SCHOOL YEAR. IT'S A
GREAT TIME TO SAVOR THE LAST OF THE
SEASON'S FRESH PRODUCE IN SIMPLE AND
QUICK WEEKNIGHT DINNERS.

FAN FARE

plus

HEALTHY FAMILY DINNERS

QUICK AND EASY

SLOW-COOKER SOLUTIONS

COOKING SCHOOL

Rub spices onto the steak the night before you go tailgating—all the great flavor will seep into the meat.

FAN FARE

Get ready for NASCAR, football or even an afternoon at the Little League field with these tailgating recipes! Finger-licking ribs, spicy macaroni salad and checkered flag cookies are all surefire winners. **By Julie Miltenberger** »

PHOTOGRAPHY BY ALISON MIKSCH

september

steak and pepper hoagies

MAKES: 6 servings. **PREP:** 10 minutes.
MARINATE: at least 4 hours or overnight.
GRILL: peppers for 10 minutes; steak
for 10 minutes.

- 2 teaspoons chili powder
- 1 teaspoon onion powder
- 1 teaspoon dried oregano
- ½ teaspoon garlic powder
- ½ teaspoon ground black pepper
- 1 tablespoon olive oil
- 1½ pounds flank steak
- 3½ sweet red and green peppers (use remaining pepper half for Macaroni Salad)
- ½ teaspoon salt
- 1 cup mild or medium salsa
- 6 medium-size hoagie or submarine-style rolls

1. In a small bowl, combine chili powder, onion powder, oregano, garlic powder and pepper. Stir to blend. Add oil and stir until combined. Rub into both sides of flank steak and transfer to a resealable plastic bag. Refrigerate 4 hours or overnight.

2. Heat charcoal grill to medium-hot coals or gas grill to medium-high. Cut and core peppers; grill 10 minutes, turning, until slightly charred.

3. Season both sides of steak with salt and then grill steak 8 to 10 minutes (depending on thickness), turning once.

4. Meanwhile, slice peppers into thin strips and transfer to a bowl. Toss with salsa and cover to keep warm.

5. Once steak is finished, allow to rest 5 minutes (keep warm). Thinly slice steak against the grain. Toss steak and any accumulated juices with the pepper-salsa mixture. Spoon about ⅔ to 1 cup mixture onto each roll and serve warm.

PER SERVING: 428 calories; 13 g fat (4 g sat.); 25 g protein; 52 g carbohydrate; 6 g fiber; 1,075 mg sodium; 39 mg cholesterol.

macaroni salad

MAKES: 8 servings. **PREP:** 15 minutes. **COOK:** 7 minutes.

- 8 ounces elbow macaroni, or other pasta shape
- ½ cup light mayonnaise
- 2 tablespoons ketchup
- 1 tablespoon sweet pickle relish
- ½ to 1 teaspoon hot pepper sauce
- ¼ teaspoon ground black pepper
- ⅛ teaspoon salt
- 1 cup grape tomatoes, halved
- 3 stalks celery, trimmed and sliced (1 cup)
- 2 large carrots, trimmed, peeled and grated (about 1 cup)
- 4 ounces pepper-Jack cheese, cut into ¼-inch pieces
- ½ of a sweet green pepper, seeded and chopped (⅔ cup; use remaining half for Hoagies)

1. Heat a medium-size pot of lightly salted water to boiling. Add macaroni and cook for 7 minutes or until desired tenderness. Drain and rinse with cool water to halt cooking.

2. Meanwhile, in a small bowl, whisk together mayonnaise, ketchup, pickle relish, hot sauce, pepper and salt.

3. Transfer drained pasta to a serving bowl. Add tomatoes, celery, carrots, cheese, green pepper and slightly more than half of the mayonnaise mixture. Stir gently to combine and coat all ingredients with dressing. Refrigerate. Just before serving, stir in reserved dressing.

PER SERVING: 234 calories; 10 g fat (4 g sat.); 8 g protein; 28 g carbohydrate; 2 g fiber; 345 mg sodium; 20 mg cholesterol.

Food styling: Megan Schlow. Prop styling: Loren Simons.

barbecued baby back ribs

MAKES: 2 rib slabs. **PREP:** 15 minutes.
MARINATE: at least 8 hours. **BOIL:** 3 minutes.
GRILL: 1½ hours or bake at 375° 1 hour.*

- 2 racks of back ribs (about 5 pounds)
- ¼ cup honey
- 1 jar (7 to 8 ounces) hoisin sauce
- 2 tablespoons reduced-sodium soy sauce
- 1 tablespoon ketchup
- 1 tablespoon minced, peeled ginger
- 1 tablespoon minced garlic
- 1½ teaspoons black bean sauce
- ¼ teaspoon hot-pepper sauce
- ¼ teaspoon liquid smoke
- ½ teaspoon ground black pepper
- ¼ teaspoon cayenne pepper
- ¼ teaspoon onion powder
- ¼ teaspoon garlic powder

1. Trim any excess fat from racks of ribs. Cut ribs in half, to form 4 pieces total. Place two in one gallon-size zip-top plastic bag, and the other two in a second zip-top bag. In a large measuring cup or bowl, combine honey and hoisin sauce. Whisk in soy sauce. Add ketchup, ginger, garlic, black bean sauce, hot pepper sauce, liquid smoke, black pepper, cayenne, onion powder and garlic powder to measuring cup. Whisk to blend, then divide evenly between bags of ribs, about ¾ cup marinade in each.

2. Seal bags and refrigerate, turning occasionally. Marinate overnight (or for at least 8 hours).

3. Heat gas grill to medium heat, or prepare charcoal grill with briquettes piled to one side. When ready to cook, turn off half of the burners (on gas grill). Remove ribs from marinade, pouring remaining marinade into a small saucepan. Place ribs over turned-off burners or on side without coals. Bring sauce to a boil; boil 3 minutes.

4. Cook for 1 to 1½ hours, turning and basting with sauce. When done, slice ribs apart and enjoy.

***Note:** Ribs can be cooked in the oven before traveling. Place ribs on a rack over a foil-lined pan. Bake at 375° for 1 hour, turning and basting several times. Heat on grill before serving.

PER RIB: 181 calories; 12 g fat (4 g sat.); 10 g protein; 7 g carbohydrate; 0 g fiber; 238 mg sodium; 47 mg cholesterol.

chunky salsa

MAKES: 3½ cups. **PREP:** 10 minutes. **STAND:** about 30 minutes.

- 2 medium tomatoes (about 1 pound total), cored, seeded and diced
- 1 can (15.5 ounces) black beans, drained and rinsed
- ⅔ cup fresh corn kernels (from 1 ear corn)
- ½ cup finely chopped red onion (½ of 1 small onion)
- ¼ cup fresh-squeezed lime juice (about 1 large lime)
- 2 tablespoons chopped flat-leaf parsley
- 1 teaspoon garlic powder
- 3 dashes hot pepper sauce
- ¾ teaspoon salt
- ¼ teaspoon ground black pepper
  Tortilla chips, for serving

In a medium-size bowl, stir together diced tomato, beans, corn, onion, lime juice, parsley, garlic powder, hot pepper sauce, salt and pepper. Let stand at room temperature for 30 minutes to blend flavors. Serve with chips.

PER ¼ CUP: 42 calories; 0 g fat (0 g sat.); 2 g protein; 10 g carbohydrate; 3 g fiber; 241 mg sodium; 34 mg cholesterol.

READER RECIPE

"When I was 16, I went to a party at Trader Vic's in NYC and ordered the spareribs. When I had a family, I started trying to duplicate the flavor—it took years, but I finally created something that's darn close!"

Ellen Ryan
Skillman, NJ

light bites on the fast track

» Try trimmer takes on our trio of dips: Instead of crackers, serve blanched broccoli spears alongside warm Cheddar-Onion Dip; pull apart endive leaves or cut up celery spears to plunge into the Spinach-Bean Dip; reach for baked or whole-grain chips to scoop up salsa.

» Offer a mixed lettuce or cucumber salad with low-cal dressing to keep friends and family full while watching 500 miles of NASCAR racing.

» Our spicy macaroni salad is loaded with celery, grape tomatoes and green peppers, and you could trim calories by using low-fat pepper-jack cheese. Use fiber-rich or whole-wheat macaroni to make this carb-heavy picnic fave a more efficient source of energy.

» When prepping the Steak and Pepper Hoagies, consider using thin-sliced chicken cutlets instead. Rub cutlets with spices and marinate. Or for a vegetarian option, grill veggie burgers and place on rolls. Top with a spoonful of the pepper-salsa mixture.

» For a sweet finish to your meal, have bowls of cherries and strawberries ready to eat alongside Checkered Flag Cookies. You can even freeze seedless grapes for a cool late-summer treat.

cheddar-onion dip

MAKES: 3 cups. **PREP:** 10 minutes.
COOK: 5 minutes.

- 1 large Vidalia onion, trimmed and grated (about 1 cup)
- 8 ounces sharp cheddar cheese, grated
- 1 package (8 ounces) light cream cheese (Neufchâtel)
- 1 teaspoon garlic powder
- ¼ teaspoon ground cayenne pepper
  Chopped scallions (optional)
  Assorted crackers, for serving

In a medium-size cast-iron or oven-safe skillet, combine onion, cheeses, garlic powder and cayenne pepper. Cook over grill heated to medium heat, stirring until cheese is melted, about 5 minutes. Garnish with scallions, if desired, and serve with crackers.

PER ¼ CUP: 130 calories; 10 g fat (6 g sat.); 7 g protein; 2 g carbohydrate; 0 g fiber; 203 mg sodium; 34 mg cholesterol.

spinach-bean dip

MAKES: 3 cups. **PREP:** 5 minutes.
REFRIGERATE: 2 hours.

- 1 box frozen chopped spinach, thawed
- 1 can (15 ounces) white beans, drained and rinsed
- 1 cup sour cream
- 1 envelope vegetable soup mix (from a 1.8-ounce pack)
- ¼ cup milk

Drain spinach; squeeze out excess liquid. Place beans in a food processor. Puree until smooth. Add sour cream, soup mix and milk. Pulse until blended. Transfer to a portable container or bowl and stir in chopped spinach. Refrigerate 2 hours or until serving.

PER ¼ CUP: 94 calories; 5 g fat (3 g sat.); 4 g protein; 10 g carbohydrate; 3 g fiber; 285 mg sodium; 11 mg cholesterol.

checkered flag cookies

MAKES: 32 cookies. **PREP:** 10 minutes. **REFRIGERATE:** 4 hours or overnight.
BAKE: at 350° for 12 minutes. **DECORATE:** 1 hour.

- 2 cups all-purpose flour
- ½ teaspoon baking powder
- ⅛ teaspoon salt
- ½ cup (1 stick) unsalted butter, softened
- ¾ cup granulated sugar
- 1 egg
- 2 tablespoons milk
- 1 teaspoon vanilla extract

Royal Icing:

- 1 box (1 pound) confectioners' sugar
- 3 tablespoons powdered egg whites
- 7 to 8 tablespoons water
  Black and green gel food coloring

1. In a medium-size bowl, whisk together flour, baking powder and salt.
2. In a large bowl, beat butter and granulated sugar until smooth, about 2 minutes. Beat in egg, milk and vanilla. On low speed, beat in flour mixture until just combined.
3. Gather dough; divide in half. Flatten into two disks. Wrap tightly in plastic wrap. Refrigerate 4 hours or overnight.
4. Heat oven to 350°. Roll out one disk to a 10½-inch square (about ⅛ inch thick). Trim slightly; then divide into 16 cookies. Place on ungreased baking sheets; bake at 350° for 12 minutes. Repeat with second half of dough, rerolling scraps. Remove cookies from baking sheets; cool on rack.
5. Royal Icing: In large bowl, combine confectioners' sugar, powdered egg whites and water. Beat on high power with electric mixer until good spreading consistency. Transfer ⅓ to a small bowl. Tint black. Tint a second ⅓ of the frosting green. Leave remaining ⅓ white. Decorate cookies, making white, green and checkered flags (use pastry bags for icing to outline flags and make checkerboards). Dry cookies on rack.

PER COOKIE: 112 calories; 3 g fat (2 g sat.); 1 g protein; 21 g carbohydrate; 0 g fiber; 345 mg sodium; 20 mg cholesterol.

Your kids can wave these checkered flags to signal the finish of the race.

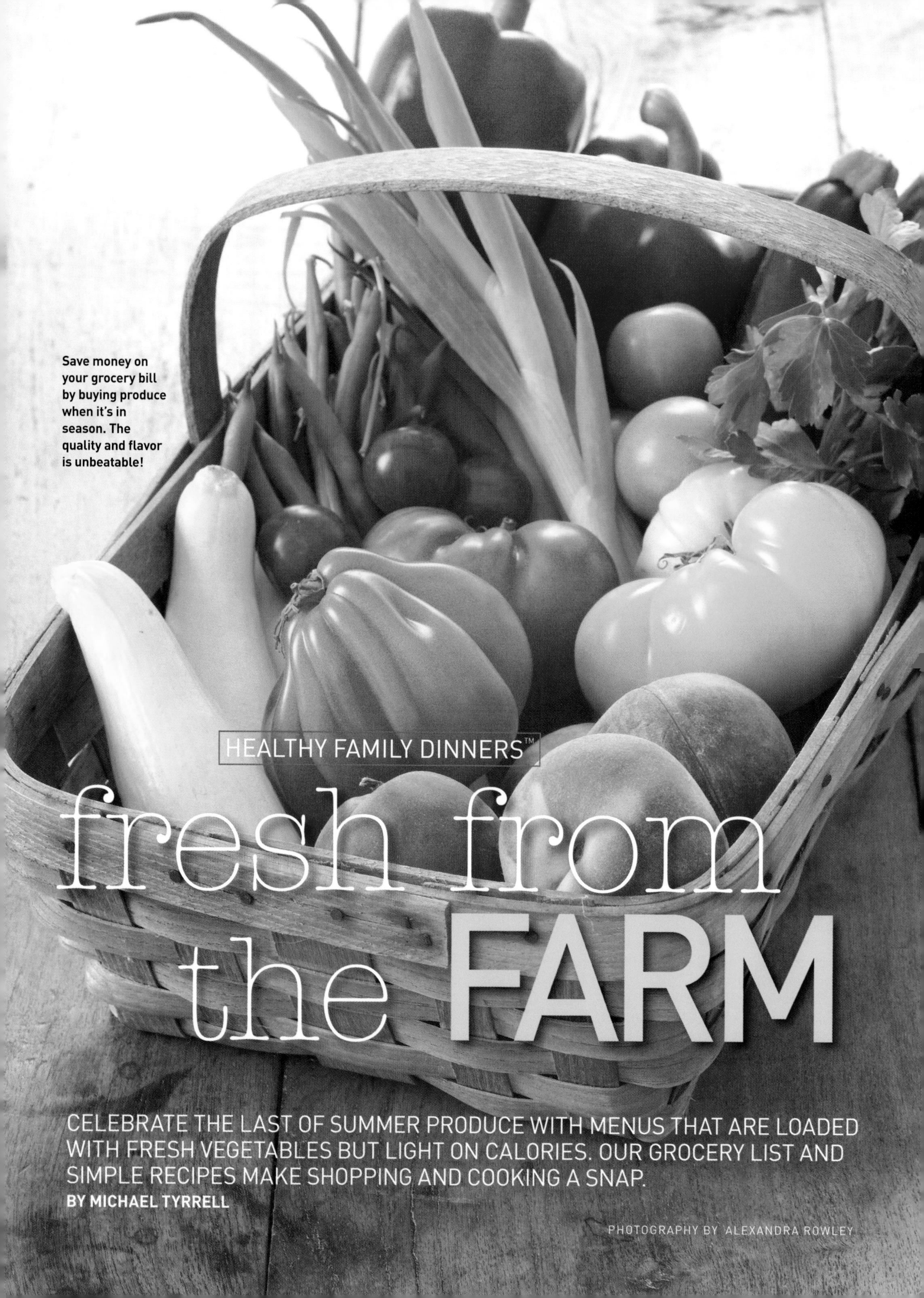

Save money on your grocery bill by buying produce when it's in season. The quality and flavor is unbeatable!

HEALTHY FAMILY DINNERS™

fresh from the FARM

CELEBRATE THE LAST OF SUMMER PRODUCE WITH MENUS THAT ARE LOADED WITH FRESH VEGETABLES BUT LIGHT ON CALORIES. OUR GROCERY LIST AND SIMPLE RECIPES MAKE SHOPPING AND COOKING A SNAP.

BY MICHAEL TYRRELL

PHOTOGRAPHY BY ALEXANDRA ROWLEY

five-spice tuna and sautéed vegetables

MAKES: 4 servings. **PREP:** 16 minutes. **MARINATE:** 1 hour. **COOK:** 12 minutes. **GRILL OR BROIL:** on high for 8 minutes.

- 3 tablespoons reduced-sodium soy sauce
- ½ teaspoon Chinese five-spice powder
- ¼ teaspoon red pepper flakes
- 4 tuna steaks, 6 ounces each, about 1 inch thick
- 2 tablespoons olive oil
- ¾ pound baby carrots
- ¾ pound green beans
- 3 cloves garlic, minced
- ⅓ cup cashews, toasted
  Lemon wedges

1. In a shallow dish, mix together soy sauce, Chinese five-spice and pepper flakes. Add tuna, turning to coat. Marinate, covered, in refrigerator for 1 hour.
2. Grill or broil tuna steaks on high for 3 to 4 minutes per side for medium, reserving marinade. Set aside; keep warm.
3. Meanwhile, heat oil in a large nonstick skillet. Add carrots; cook, stirring occasionally, for 5 minutes. Add green beans and garlic; cook, stirring occasionally, for 5 minutes. Stir in reserved marinade. Cook an additional 2 minutes. Add nuts.
4. Serve tuna over vegetables. Serve lemon on the side.

PER SERVING: 409 calories; 14 g fat (3 g sat.); 54 g protein; 14 g carbohydrate; 3 g fiber; 674 mg sodium; 99 mg cholesterol.

stuffed curry peppers

MAKES: 6 servings. **PREP:** 15 minutes. **MICROWAVE:** 5 minutes. **STAND:** 5 minutes.

3 sweet red peppers, halved and seeded
1 package (5.7 ounces) Mediterranean curry couscous mix (such as Near East)
2 teaspoons olive oil
½ pound cooked small shrimp, chopped
2 scallions, thinly sliced
6 tablespoons slivered almonds, toasted
    Fresh chopped parsley (optional)
1 jar (6 ounces) mango chutney

1. Place peppers, cut-side up, in a large microwave-safe baking dish. Add ¼ cup water to dish and cover with plastic wrap, venting one corner. Microwave on HIGH for 5 minutes, until peppers are softened.

2. Prepare couscous mix following package directions using oil. Stir in shrimp and scallions and allow to stand 5 minutes, until shrimp is heated through.

3. Fill each pepper with a generous ½ cup of the couscous mixture. Top with almonds and sprinkle with parsley (if using). Serve chutney on the side.

PER SERVING: 287 calories; 9 g fat (1 g sat.); 12 g protein; 42 g carbohydrate; 4 g fiber; 700 mg sodium; 56 mg cholesterol.

grilled pork chops and peach-plum salsa

MAKES: 4 servings. **PREP:** 15 minutes. **REFRIGERATE:** 1 hour. **GRILL OR BROIL:** on high for 10 minutes.

2 peaches, about ¾ pound
3 plums, about ¾ pound
½ cup chopped red onion
2 medium jalapeños, seeded and chopped
½ cup cilantro, chopped
2 tablespoons lime juice
1 tablespoon olive oil
¼ teaspoon salt
4 rib pork chops, about 6 ounces each
⅛ teaspoon pepper
   Cooked white rice (optional)

1. Pit peaches and plums and finely chop. Place in a medium-size bowl. Add red onion, jalapeños, cilantro, lime juice, olive oil and ⅛ teaspoon of the salt. Stir to combine. Cover and refrigerate for at least 1 hour.

2. Heat grill or broiler. Season pork chops with remaining ⅛ teaspoon salt and the pepper. Grill or broil for 5 minutes. Turn and grill for an additional 4 to 5 minutes or until internal temperature registers 155° on an instant-read thermometer.

3. Serve the grilled pork chops with the salsa and cooked rice, if desired.

PER SERVING: 386 calories; 13 g fat (4 g sat.); 46 g protein; 21 g carbohydrate; 3 g fiber; 384 mg sodium; 130 mg cholesterol.

rigatoni alla siciliana

MAKES: 6 servings. **PREP:** 10 minutes. **COOK:** 22 minutes.

- 1 **eggplant, about 1½ pounds**
- 3 **cloves garlic, sliced**
- 3 **tablespoons olive oil**
- 1 **can (28 ounces) fire-roasted whole tomatoes**
- 1½ **teaspoons dried oregano**
- 1½ **teaspoons salt**
- ¼ **teaspoon red pepper flakes**
- 1 **pound mini rigatoni pasta**
- 1 **cup shredded smoked mozzarella cheese (about 4 ounces)**

1. Trim eggplant and cut into ½-inch pieces. In a large skillet, cook eggplant and garlic in oil for 7 minutes over medium-high heat, stirring occasionally.

2. Stir in tomatoes and break up with a wooden spoon. Add oregano, salt and red pepper flakes. Simmer for 15 minutes, stirring occasionally.

3. While sauce is simmering, cook pasta following package directions. Drain, reserving 1 cup of the cooking water.

4. Toss drained pasta with sauce. Add reserved pasta water, in ¼ cup increments, until desired consistency.

5. Stir in cheese, allow to melt slightly and serve.

PER SERVING: 451 calories; 13 g fat (3 g sat.); 16 g protein; 68 g carbohydrate; 6 g fiber; 996 mg sodium; 15 mg cholesterol.

tomato-zucchini tart

MAKES: 6 servings. **PREP:** 15 minutes. **BAKE:** at 400° for 12 minutes, then at 350° for 40 minutes.

1 refrigerated rolled piecrust
1 package (4.4 ounces) light herb cheese spread, such as Boursin
4 medium-size ripe tomatoes, about 1 pound total, thinly sliced, patted dry
2 medium zucchini, about 1 pound total, sliced into ¼-inch coins
⅛ teaspoon salt
⅛ teaspoon pepper
Fresh thyme

1. Heat oven to 400°. Coat a 9-inch tart pan with nonstick cooking spray.
2. Fit piecrust into tart pan and remove excess dough from around edge (see Cooking Tip, page 211). Prick bottom of crust all over with a fork. Bake at 400° for 12 minutes; cool. Reduce oven temperature to 350°.
3. Spread cheese evenly over bottom of crust. Alternately fan tomato and zucchini slices in a decorative fashion. Sprinkle with salt and pepper.
4. Bake tart at 350° for 40 minutes or until crust is nicely browned and zucchini slices are fork tender. Garnish with fresh thyme; cool slightly and serve.

PER SERVING: 269 calories; 19 g fat (10 g sat.); 4 g protein; 24 g carbohydrate; 2 g fiber; 318 mg sodium; 31 mg cholesterol.

skillet summer squash parmesan

MAKES: 6 servings. **PREP:** 15 minutes. **BAKE:** at 400° for 20 minutes. **COOK:** 25 minutes.

- 3 **large summer squash, about 2 pounds**
- ½ **teaspoon garlic salt**
- ½ **teaspoon black pepper**
- 4 **plum tomatoes, cored and thinly sliced**
- 1 **can (14½ ounces) Italian-flavored diced tomatoes**
- 2 **cups shredded reduced-fat Italian-blend cheese**
- ¼ **cup grated Parmesan**
- ½ **pound whole-wheat spaghetti**

1. Heat oven to 400°. Cut squash on the diagonal into ¼-inch slices. Season with ¼ teaspoon *each* of the garlic salt and pepper. Coat 2 baking sheets with cooking spray; place squash slices on pans. Bake at 400° for 20 minutes.

2. Season tomato slices with remaining ¼ teaspoon each garlic salt and pepper. Spoon ⅓ of diced tomatoes into the bottom of a large nonstick skillet. Layer with half the squash, half the tomato slices, ⅓ of the diced tomatoes and half the Italian-blend cheese. Repeat layering. Top with Parmesan.

3. Cover and simmer 25 minutes over low heat. Prepare pasta following package directions; serve on the side.

PER SERVING: 458 calories; 11 g fat (7 g sat.); 30 g protein; 60 g carbohydrate; 13 g fiber; 886 mg sodium; 34 mg cholesterol.

september

shopping list

This grocery list and the pantry items are all you need to cook up a week of hearty suppers.

PRODUCE
1 eggplant
3 sweet red peppers
1 bunch scallions
3 large summer squash
4 plum tomatoes
4 medium-size ripe tomatoes
2 medium zucchini
1 bunch fresh thyme
¾ pound green beans
¾ pound baby carrots
1 lemon
2 peaches
3 plums
1 small red onion
2 jalapeños
1 bunch cilantro
1 lime

DAIRY
1 package (8 ounces) shredded reduced-fat Italian blend cheese
1 ready-to-roll piecrust
1 package (4.4 ounces) light herb cheese spread, such as Boursin
1 package smoked mozzarella cheese

MEAT, FISH AND POULTRY
½ pound cooked small shrimp
4 tuna steaks, about 6 ounces each
4 rib pork chops, about 6 ounces each

DRY GOODS
1 can (28 ounces) fire-roasted whole tomatoes
1 pound mini rigatoni
1 package (5.7 ounces) Mediterranean curry couscous
1 small bag slivered almonds
1 jar mango chutney
1 can (14½ ounces) Italian-flavored diced tomatoes
1 pound whole-wheat spaghetti
1 small bag cashew nuts

pantry items

- olive oil
- dried oregano
- salt and pepper
- red pepper flakes
- garlic salt
- Parmesan cheese
- reduced-sodium soy sauce
- Chinese five-spice powder
- garlic bulb

cooking tip

Tomato-Zucchini Tart

1. Fit crust into pan. Trim any excess dough.

2. Prick bottom of crust all over with a fork.

3. Spread cheese evenly over bottom of crust.

4. Alternately fan out zucchini and tomato slices.

Shortcut Suppers

To make your weeknight
dinners a breeze, we've
assembled an alphabet of tips,
tricks and fast recipes.

by Julie Miltenberger

a is for apples

Apples are the ultimate snack food, but for a little variety, try tucking pieces into
salad for a sweet, crunchy surprise or serve slices as a side dish in place of veggies.

b is for beans

Inexpensive and filling, beans are great supper starters. Our quick chili packs
11 g of protein and 12 g of fiber per serving. (Recipe page 213)

c is for chicken

This perennial favorite is the best go-to dinner ingredient as it can star in
many different dishes.

d is for do-ahead

Pick a night to pre-prep a few meals—even if that means simply chopping peppers or slicing mushrooms and slipping them into resealable bags. That way you can go from fridge to table in minutes. Try this with our 3-bean chili; drain and rinse the beans in advance.

e is for eggs

Eggs are one of the least expensive and easiest ways to get your protein. Why not stir up an omelet? We love breakfast for dinner!

f is for frozen foods

Ever come home to discover your kid needs help with a history report due the next morning? If so, reach into your freezer for an all-in-one meal kit. Simply heat, stir and serve.

g is for greens

If the same old salad is the only way you eat greens, why not make something new? Try our one-dish dinner: Spinach and Swiss Quiche. (Recipe page 214)

h is for hummus

This spread, made from ground chickpeas, is also great as a meal anchor. Spread onto pita, then top with cooked chicken strips, chopped cucumber and a little feta cheese: Presto! Greek pizzas.

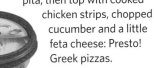

i is for instant-read thermometers

Not only for beef or poultry, these speedy temperature testers can be plunged into casseroles and leftovers to gauge warmth. Once the internal temperature registers at least 140°, the dish is hot enough to eat.

Use kidney, black and white beans for a hearty—and colorful—meal.

3-bean chili

MAKES: 8 cups. **PREP:** 10 minutes. **COOK:** 19 minutes.

- 1 tablespoon olive oil
- 1 medium-size onion, chopped
- 2 cloves garlic, peeled and chopped
- 3 tablespoons chili powder
- 2 sweet bell peppers, cored and diced
- 1 medium-size zucchini, diced
- 1 can (14½ ounces) diced tomatoes
- 1 can (8 ounces) no-salt-added tomato sauce
- ¼ cup ketchup
- ½ teaspoon dried oregano
- 1 can (15 ounces) black beans, drained and rinsed
- 1 can (15 ounces) small white beans, drained and rinsed
- 1 can (15 ounces) red kidney beans, drained and rinsed
- Grated cheddar cheese (optional)

1. Heat oil in a large nonstick pot over medium heat. Add onion, garlic and chili powder and cook 3 minutes.

2. Add peppers and zucchini; cook 5 minutes, stirring occasionally.

3. Stir in tomatoes, tomato sauce, ketchup and oregano. Cook 8 minutes.

4. Gently stir in the beans. Cover pot and continue to cook 3 minutes. Serve with grated cheese, if desired.

PER CUP: 203 calories; 4 g fat (0 g sat.); 11 g protein; 39 g carbohydrate; 12 g fiber; 678 mg sodium; 0 mg cholesterol.

spinach and swiss quiche

MAKES: 6 servings. **PREP:** 5 minutes. **BAKE:** at 375° for 15 minutes, then at 325° for 20 minutes.

- 1 refrigerated piecrust (from a 15-ounce package)
- 5 large eggs
- ¾ cup milk
- ½ teaspoon salt
- ¼ teaspoon black pepper
- ½ of a 10-ounce package frozen chopped spinach, thawed and squeezed dry (½ cup)
- 4 ounces Swiss cheese, shredded (1 cup)

1. Heat oven to 375°. Fit piecrust into a 9-inch pie plate, crimping edge.

2. In a medium-size bowl, whisk together eggs, milk, salt and pepper. Spread spinach into bottom of prepared piecrust. Pour egg mixture evenly over spinach, then sprinkle with the cheese.

3. Transfer quiche to 375° oven and bake 15 minutes. Reduce heat to 325° and continue to bake 20 minutes, until crust is puffed and browned (cover with foil if browning too quickly). Let stand 5 minutes before slicing and serving.

PER SERVING: 314 calories; 20 g fat (9 g sat.); 13 g protein; 21 g carbohydrate; 0 g fiber; 444 mg sodium; 203 mg cholesterol.

There's barely any cleanup with this one-bowl, one-dish spinach quiche.

j is for *juice it up*

Kids love juice drinks, but many brands sneak in high fructose corn syrup or other sweeteners. Look for Fizz Ed, brought to you by Apple & Eve, or Capri Sun 100% juice pouches, available nationwide in grocery stores.

k is for *ketchup*

Try something new on your burger or fries. Wholemato Organic Agave Ketchup is

made with sweet agave nectar, which is less likely than traditional sugars to raise blood sugar levels. Available at health food stores, or visit wholemato.com for retailers in your area.

l is for *leftovers*

Nothing's easier than reheating a meal, and what's better left over than lasagna! Why not prep two smaller ones (instead of one 13 x 9-inch) and pop one in the freezer for the future? Simply thaw overnight in the fridge before baking.

m is for *meal planning*

Finally answer "What's for dinner?" by writing up a weekly menu. Post it on the fridge, next to the school lunch list so your kids can check for themselves.

n is for *noodles*

This supper staple can be a quick snack too. On Sunday, cook some macaroni. Drain and toss with a little oil; spoon into bowls and refrigerate. Your kids can heat a serving topped with grated cheese or marinara.

pork with pear compote

MAKES: 4 servings. **PREP:** 5 minutes. **COOK:** 5 minutes.

- ¼ cup dried cranberries
- 1 pear, cored and diced (about 1 cup)
- ¼ cup chopped walnuts
  Pinch ground cinnamon
- 2 tablespoons unsalted butter
- 4 thin-cut boneless pork chops
- ¼ teaspoon salt
- ¼ teaspoon black pepper
- 1 teaspoon sugar

1. Soak cranberries in hot water for 5 minutes. Meanwhile, combine pear, walnuts and cinnamon in a small bowl. Drain cranberries and add to bowl.

2. Melt butter in a large skillet over medium-high heat. Season one side of the pork cutlets with ⅛ teaspoon *each* of the salt and pepper.

3. Place pork, seasoned-side down, in hot skillet and cook 2 minutes. Season with remaining ⅛ teaspoon *each* salt and pepper. Flip over pork and cook an additional 2 minutes. Remove to a plate or platter.

4. Add pear mixture and sugar to skillet and cook 1 minute. Remove skillet from heat, spoon pear compote over pork and serve.

PER SERVING: 376 calories; 25 g fat (9 g sat.); 24 g protein; 15 g carbohydrate; 2 g fiber; 189 mg sodium; 77 mg cholesterol.

This satisfying pork dish can be prepped and cooked in 10 minutes.

O is for *one pot*

For a dinner that's super easy to clean up, stir up our one-pot skillet supper: Fruity Chicken Stir-Fry. (Recipe page 217)

p is for *pantry*

Stock up on no-fuss side dishes—such as Knorr's Sides Plus Veggies—so when time is tight, you can focus on the main course.

q is for *quick-cook*

Think thin—pork, chicken, even turkey cutlets will take less than 5 minutes to prepare in a hot skillet. See our Pork with Pear Compote. (Recipe page 215)

r is for *rice*

Flavored versions of this versatile grain can be converted easily into a main event. Stir a little turkey sausage or some chicken pieces into quick-cooking Broccoli Rice au Gratin.

S is for *sausage links*

Need a quick meal? Reach for fully cooked Al Fresco Spinach & Feta sausages. A few minutes on the grill or in a skillet and they're ready to eat. Add a salad for a speedy supper.

t is for *tomatoes*

Whether canned or fresh, these end-of-summer staples are great in casseroles, stirred into salsa or cooked into sauce and spooned over linguine. See our Speedy Pasta Sauce. (Recipe at right)

u is for *use-by dates*

Always check the printed date on sauces and if necessary, rewrite on the top of the jar in permanent marker. Use tomato-based sauces within 1 week of opening and chicken, beef or vegetable broth within 2 weeks.

speedy pasta sauce

MAKES: 6 servings. **PREP:** 10 minutes. **COOK:** 13 minutes.

- 6 slices bacon, cut into pieces
- 1 can (28 ounces) tomatoes in juice
- 1 teaspoon sugar
- ½ teaspoon garlic powder
- ½ teaspoon Italian seasoning
- ½ teaspoon black pepper
- ½ teaspoon salt
- 1 cup frozen peas, thawed
- ¼ cup sour cream
- 12 ounces of your favorite pasta, cooked

1. Cook bacon in a medium-size saucepan over medium heat for 8 minutes, until cooked through but not crispy. Drain on paper towels and discard drippings, but do not wipe out pan.

2. Increase heat to medium-high. Add tomatoes and their juice, breaking apart tomatoes while stirring. Stir in sugar, garlic powder, Italian seasoning, pepper and salt. Cook 5 minutes (simmering vigorously), stirring every so often.

3. Remove pan from heat and add peas, sour cream and drained bacon. Serve over cooked pasta.

PER SERVING: 306 calories; 6 g fat (3 g sat.); 12 g protein; 52 g carbohydrate; 3 g fiber; 702 mg sodium; 13 mg cholesterol.

fruity chicken stir-fry

MAKES: 6 servings. **PREP:** 20 minutes.
COOK: 7 minutes.

- 1½ pounds chicken tenders, cut on the diagonal into ¼-inch slices
- 3 tablespoons hoisin sauce
- 1 tablespoon cornstarch
- 1½ teaspoons Chinese five-spice powder
- 2 cups canned pineapple slices, drained
- 2 tablespoons peanut oil
- 2 tablespoons minced fresh ginger
- 3 ribs celery, sliced
- 1 red pepper, cut in strips
- ½ cup chicken broth
- 2 teaspoons rice vinegar
  Fully cooked rice, heated (optional)

1. In a large bowl, combine chicken pieces, hoisin sauce, cornstarch and five-spice powder. Cut each pineapple slice into 8 wedges. Place in a small bowl.

2. Heat oil in large skillet over high heat. Add ginger, celery and red pepper; stir-fry 1 minute.

3. Add chicken mixture to skillet, stir-fry 4 to 5 minutes, or until chicken is no longer pink. Add pineapple, chicken broth and vinegar to skillet. Cook 1 minute, stirring, until sauce thickens and pineapple is just heated through. Serve with hot white rice on the side, if desired.

PER SERVING: 246 calories; 8 g fat (2 g sat.); 24 g protein; 19 g carbohydrate; 1 g fiber; 290 mg sodium; 63 mg cholesterol.

V is for vegetables

You know that veggies are good for you and microwaving is the perfect way to quickly cook them. Place 4 cups of vegetables in a glass bowl and add ¼ cup water. Cover with plastic wrap and microwave for 2 to 3 minutes.

W is for whole grains

Studies show that Americans want to add whole grains and fiber to their diets. Better-for-you versions of family favorites are popping up all over grocery shelves. Sneak in healthier crackers, bread— even breakfast cereals and waffles—whenever possible.

X is for xtra servings

When making dinner, increase the amount of meat or veggies called for in the recipe—that way you'll have extra for lunch the next day or an emergency late-night snack.

y is for yogurt

Not just for breakfast, yogurt can be added to dressings and dips for a tangy hit of calcium; look for brands with immune-system-boosting active cultures.

Z is for zip-top bags

Cut cleanup in half by marinating meat, prepping ingredients and even saving leftovers in resealable bags. Heavy-duty bags can be washed with soapy water and reused (except when raw meat is involved).

slow-cooker solutions

GREAT-TASTING RECIPES FOR EFFORTLESS MEALS. **BY CINDY HELLER**

Tangy Beef Stew
(Recipe page 219)

PHOTOGRAPHY BY JAMES BAIGRIE

tangy beef stew

MAKES: 4 servings. **PREP:** 10 minutes.
SLOW-COOK: 4 hours on HIGH or 6 hours on LOW.

- 1 large onion, cut into 1-inch pieces
- 1 pound boneless beef chuck, cut into 1-inch cubes
- 1 tablespoon ground ginger
- ¼ teaspoon salt
- 3 medium-size carrots, peeled and cut into 1-inch chunks
- 2 large celery stalks, cut into 1-inch slices
- 1 large beef bouillon cube
- 2 cups water
- 2 tablespoons red wine vinegar
- ¼ cup raisins
- ¼ teaspoon black pepper
- 2 tablespoons cornstarch
  Cooked egg noodles (optional)

1. Layer onions, beef, ginger, salt, carrots and celery in slow-cooker bowl. Add bouillon cube, water, vinegar and raisins. Cover and cook on HIGH for 4 hours or LOW for 6 hours or until beef is very tender.
2. Remove cover and stir in black pepper. Using a ladle, remove 3 tablespoons liquid from slow cooker and place in a small bowl. Whisk in cornstarch. Pour cornstarch mixture into slow cooker; whisk to combine. Stir until liquid has thickened. Serve with noodles, if desired.

PER SERVING: 250 calories; 5 g fat (2 g sat.); 27 g protein; 24 g carbohydrate; 3 g fiber; 653 mg sodium; 50 mg cholesterol.

pork chops with red cabbage

MAKES: 4 servings. **PREP:** 5 minutes. **SLOW-COOK:** 3½ hours on HIGH or 7 hours on LOW.

- 1 small head red cabbage, core removed and shredded (about 8 cups)
- 2 Fuji apples, peeled, cored and diced
- ½ cup red wine vinegar
- 2 tablespoons light brown sugar
- 2 teaspoons caraway seeds
- ½ teaspoon salt
- ½ teaspoon black pepper
- 4 bone-in pork loin chops (2 pounds)
- 2 tablespoons cornstarch

1. Place cabbage and apples in slow-cooker bowl. Stir in vinegar, sugar, caraway seeds and ¼ teaspoon *each* of the salt and pepper.
2. Place pork chops in slow cooker on top of the cabbage and sprinkle with remaining ¼ teaspoon pepper. Cover and cook on HIGH for 3½ hours or LOW for 7 hours or until cabbage is tender.
3. Remove pork from slow cooker; keep warm. Using a ladle, remove 2 tablespoons liquid from slow cooker; place in a small bowl. Whisk cornstarch into liquid. Move cabbage aside in slow cooker and whisk cornstarch mixture back into the liquid in the slow cooker. Using tongs, toss thickened liquid with cabbage; stir in remaining ¼ teaspoon salt. Spoon onto plates; top with pork.

PER SERVING: 335 calories; 8 g fat (3 g sat.); 32 g protein; 35 g carbohydrate; 6 g fiber; 412 mg sodium; 71 mg cholesterol.

Inexpensive cuts of meat like chuck and round steak are ideal for the slow cooker. Low temperatures, lots of liquid and a long cook time make these typically tougher cuts of beef tender and juicy.

chicken posole

MAKES: 8 servings. **PREP:** 10 minutes. **SLOW-COOK:** 3 hours on HIGH or 5 hours on LOW.

- 2 cloves garlic, finely chopped
- 1¼ pounds boneless, skinless chicken thighs, cut into 1-inch pieces
- 2 cans (15 ounces each) white hominy, drained and rinsed
- 1 medium-size onion, chopped
- 1 teaspoon dried oregano
- ½ teaspoon cumin
- ¼ teaspoon dried red pepper flakes
- 2 large chicken bouillon cubes
- 4 cups water
- 1 can (14.5 ounces) petite cut diced tomatoes with jalapeños (such as Del Monte), drained
- 1 tablespoon lime juice
- ¼ teaspoon salt
- ¼ teaspoon black pepper

1. Combine garlic, chicken, hominy, onion, oregano, cumin, red pepper flakes, bouillon cubes and water in slow cooker. Cover and cook on HIGH for 3 hours or LOW for 5 hours.
2. Remove cover and stir in tomatoes, lime juice, salt and pepper until warmed through. Serve immediately.

PER SERVING: 174 calories; 4 g fat (1 g sat.); 17 g protein; 22 g carbohydrate; 4 g fiber; 859 mg sodium; 69 mg cholesterol.

Hominy is more tender and creamy than regular corn, and can be served in many of the same ways as potatoes.

split pea soup with ham

MAKES: 10 servings. **PREP:** 10 minutes. **SLOW-COOK:** 4 hours on HIGH or 6 hours on LOW.

- 1 pound dried split green peas, picked over and rinsed
- 2 russet potatoes, peeled and diced
- 1 medium-size onion, chopped
- 2 garlic cloves, minced
- 2 ham hocks
- 3 large vegetable bouillon cubes
- 8 cups water
- 1 bay leaf
- ¼ teaspoon salt
- 3 small carrots, diced
- 3 ribs celery, sliced
- ½ teaspoon dried thyme
- ¼ teaspoon black pepper

1. Combine peas, potatoes, onion, garlic, ham hocks, bouillon cubes, water, bay leaf and salt in slow cooker, stirring to break up bouillon cubes. Cover and cook on HIGH for 2 hours or LOW for 3 hours.
2. Remove cover and stir in carrots, celery and thyme. Cover and cook about 2 hours on HIGH or 3 hours on LOW; peas and potatoes should be very tender.
3. Remove ham hocks and bay leaf from slow cooker; discard. Soup is very hot so puree carefully in batches in a blender until completely smooth. Stir in black pepper.

PER SERVING: 293 calories; 6 g fat (1 g sat.); 23 g protein; 40 g carbohydrate; 2 g fiber; 640 mg sodium; 20 mg cholesterol.

september

Slow cooking is good even for your energy bill. It costs about 2 cents per hour to use a slow cooker—just 18 cents for 8 hours! An oven costs about 50 cents per hour, or $4 for 8 hours.

red beans and rice

MAKES: 6 servings. **PREP:** 10 minutes.
COOK: 8 minutes. **SLOW-COOK:** 3½ hours on HIGH or 5 hours on LOW.

- 1 tablespoon olive oil
- 1 small onion, finely chopped
- 1 small green pepper, finely chopped
- 1 celery rib, thinly sliced
- 3 cloves garlic, minced
- 1½ teaspoons Cajun seasoning (such as McCormick)
- ½ teaspoon dried oregano
- ½ teaspoon dried thyme
- ½ pound dried red kidney beans, rinsed and picked over
- 1 large chicken bouillon cube
- 3 cups water
- ½ pound light kielbasa, cut into ¼-inch half moons
- ¼ teaspoon black pepper
- 3 cups cooked white rice

1. Heat oil in a medium-size skillet over medium-high heat. Add onion, green pepper and celery. Cook, stirring, for 7 minutes. Add garlic; cook 1 minute.
2. Scrape contents of skillet into slow cooker. Add Cajun seasoning, oregano, thyme, beans, bouillon cube and water. Cook for 3½ hours on HIGH or 5 hours on LOW or until beans are soft.
3. Stir in kielbasa and black pepper. Cook until heated through. Serve over rice.

PER SERVING: 344 calories; 8 g fat (2 g sat.); 8 g protein; 48 g carbohydrate; 11 g fiber; 890 mg sodium; 24 mg cholesterol.

cooking school

HAVE YOU EVER WONDERED HOW YOUR FAVORITE RESTAURANT ACHIEVES THAT DELICIOUS GOLDEN CRUST ON MEAT? USE OUR STEP-BY-STEP INSTRUCTIONS AND TIPS FOR NO-FAIL SAUTÉING. **BY JULIE MILTENBERGER**

Our Quick Florentine Sauce pairs perfectly with sautéed chicken breasts.

PHOTOGRAPHY BY ALEXANDRA GRABLEWSKI

sauté secrets

THIS CLASSIC CHEF'S TECHNIQUE SEALS IN MOISTURE AND FLAVOR. FOR FOOLPROOF SAUTÉING OF CHICKEN, TURKEY, PORK OR EVEN BEEF CUTLETS, KEEP THESE TIPS IN MIND:

1 Use a well-balanced, heavy pan—it shouldn't rock back and forth when on the countertop. The heavier the pan, the more even the heat.

2 Be sure your pan is large enough to hold your cutlets without touching or overlapping each other. As a general rule, four average-size cutlets will fit in a 12-inch skillet. If you are cooking more, sauté them in batches.

3 Heat your pan on medium-high heat before you add the oil, butter or a combination of both. Test this by holding your hand over the pan. If you have to remove your hand after only a few seconds, then the pan is ready (see first illustration).

4 Add a quarter-size portion of oil and a small pat of butter. Tilt pan to coat; reduce heat slightly if butter browns immediately. Pat cutlets dry with paper towels so they don't spatter in skillet (see second illustration). Season as directed; add to pan. Cook, without moving cutlets, a few minutes.

5 Turn cutlets with a spatula or tongs—not a fork—so they don't lose juices. If properly seared, pieces should release easily (see third illustration). Transfer cooked cutlets to a plate, sprinkle with a little salt and pepper and keep warm.

QUICK FLORENTINE SAUCE: Once cutlets are sautéed, add ½ cup low-sodium chicken broth to the pan, stirring up any browned bits with a wooden spoon. Add 1 small onion, chopped, and cook 5 minutes over medium heat. Add one 6-ounce bag of baby spinach, ¼ teaspoon each salt and pepper. Cook until spinach is wilted, then stir in 1 tablespoon unsalted butter and a squeeze of fresh lemon juice. Spoon over cutlets and serve.

PER SERVING: 257 calories; 12 g fat (5 g sat.); 31 g protein; 8 g carbohydrate; 3 g fiber; 292 mg sodium; 93 mg cholesterol.

1 Heat the dry pan over medium-high heat. Test readiness by holding your hand over pan for a few seconds.

2 To avoid spattering, pat cutlets dry with paper towels before adding to pan.

3 Once browned on one side, flip cutlets with tongs. If pan was heated correctly, cutlets will release easily from pan.

october

Chicken and Sage-Mushroom Gravy
(Recipe page 230)

BUSY WEEKDAYS AND COOL WEATHER
CALL FOR SIMPLE BUT WARMING MEALS.
WHIP UP A FALL HARVEST DESSERT
AND GRAB YOUR DUTCH OVEN FOR
UNBEATABLE ONE-POT DINNERS.

Thai-Style Scallops
page 244

**Bittersweet Almond-
Chocolate Pudding**
page 248

Savory Apple Strata
page 251

Purchased pie crusts make this updated classic simple and quick to prepare.

TAKE ADVANTAGE OF FRESH, CRISP APPLES WITH THIS AUTUMN CLASSIC.
BY KAREN TACK

classic apple pie

MAKES: 10 servings. **PREP:** 30 minutes. **COOK:** 10 minutes.
BAKE: at 400° for 20 minutes, then at 350° for 25 minutes.

- 1 **package refrigerated rolled piecrusts (2 per package, 15 ounces)**
- ½ **cup plus 1 teaspoon granulated sugar**
- ½ **cup packed light-brown sugar**
- 3 **tablespoons cornstarch**
- ½ **teaspoon ground cinnamon**
- ¼ **teaspoon salt**
  Pinch ground cloves
- 2 **pounds Granny Smith apples, peeled and cored**
- 2 **pounds Fuji apples, peeled and cored**
- 2 **tablespoons unsalted butter**
- 2 **tablespoons lemon juice**
- 1 **large egg, beaten with 1 tablespoon water**

1. Heat oven to 400°. Unroll one piecrust onto a work surface. Roll out slightly with rolling pin to 12 inches. Fit into bottom and up side of a 9-inch deep-dish pie plate. Prick bottom of crust with a fork; refrigerate while assembling filling.

2. In a small bowl, blend ½ cup of the granulated sugar, the light-brown sugar, cornstarch, cinnamon, salt and cloves. Set aside.

3. Cut apples into ½-inch pieces. Melt butter in a large skillet over medium heat. Add apples, lemon juice and sugar mixture. Cook 10 minutes, stirring occasionally, until pan juices thicken. Cool on a rack for 25 minutes.

4. Pour cooled apple mixture into prepared crust-lined pie plate. Unroll second pie crust and roll out slightly to 12 inches. Cut 1-inch vent hole in center of dough. Transfer dough to pie, centering over filling. Crimp edge together and flute decoratively.

5. Brush pie with egg mixture; sprinkle with remaining 1 teaspoon granulated sugar. Bake at 400° for 20 minutes, then reduce temperature to 350° and bake an additional 25 minutes. Cover pie with foil if it browns too quickly. Cool at least 1 hour before slicing and serving.

PER SERVING: 395 calories; 14 g fat (6 g sat.); 2 g protein; 68 g carbohydrate; 4 g fiber; 228 mg sodium; 25 mg cholesterol.

Food styling: Karen Tack. Prop styling: Leslie Siegel.

PHOTOGRAPHY BY RITA MASS

While at the store, be sure to stock up on pasta, potatoes, rice and veggies, all of which are perfect for mixing and matching with Pork Piccata. (Recipe page 232)

PHOTOGRAPHY BY JAMES BAIGRIE

clubbing it

WHETHER YOU BELONG TO COSTCO, BJ'S OR SAM'S CLUB, BUYING IN BULK IS THE WAY TO GET MORE BANG FOR YOUR BUCK. OUR EASY RECIPES AND PORTIONING PLANS WILL HELP YOU COOK DINNER TONIGHT AND SET YOU UP WITH A FREEZER FULL OF FUTURE MEALS.

BY MICHAEL TYRRELL

what to do with...

6-7 pounds
boneless, skinless chicken breasts

3 pounds
salmon fillet

6 pounds
lean ground beef

10 pounds
boneless pork roast

Food styling: Toni Borgan. Prop styling: Megan Hedgpeth.

Save space in your freezer by wrapping single chicken breasts tightly in plastic wrap, then stacking them.

chicken and sage-mushroom gravy

MAKES: 4 servings. **PREP:** 10 minutes. **COOK:** 16 minutes.

1½ pounds thin-sliced boneless, skinless chicken breasts
¼ teaspoon salt
¼ teaspoon black pepper
3 tablespoons vegetable oil
10 ounces mushrooms, cleaned and trimmed
2 tablespoons all-purpose flour
1 can (14½ ounces) chicken broth
¼ teaspoon dried sage
⅛ teaspoon ground nutmeg
Noodles and green beans (optional)

1. Season chicken on both sides with ⅛ teaspoon each of the salt and black pepper.
2. Heat 2 tablespoons of the oil in a large skillet. Add chicken and sauté for 3 minutes. Turn and sauté for an additional 2 to 3 minutes or until chicken is cooked through. Remove to a plate.
3. Add remaining 1 tablespoon oil and the mushrooms to the skillet. Cook for 5 minutes, stirring occasionally, or until softened and lightly browned. Sprinkle flour over mushrooms; cook 1 minute. Gradually stir in broth. Add dried sage, nutmeg and remaining ⅛ teaspoon each salt and pepper. Simmer for 2 minutes. Add chicken; simmer for 1 to 2 minutes or until heated through.
4. Serve with noodles and steamed green beans, if desired.

PER SERVING: 310 calories; 13 g fat (2 g sat.); 42 g protein; 6 g carbohydrate; 1 g fiber; 482 mg sodium; 99 mg cholesterol.

how to

To stretch your dollar even more, slice large chicken breasts in half.

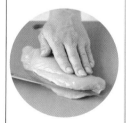

Simply place one piece on a cutting board and begin to cut, as if you were opening it up like a book. Then continue slicing apart.

spicy hoisin salmon

MAKES: 4 servings. **PREP:** 10 minutes.
ROAST: at 450° for 15 minutes.

- ¼ cup hoisin sauce
- 2 tablespoons reduced-sodium soy sauce
- 2 teaspoons rice vinegar
- ½ teaspoon ground ginger
- ¼ teaspoon red pepper flakes
- 4 pieces of salmon fillet, about 6 ounces each
- 2 scallions, trimmed and thinly sliced
  White rice and broccoli, and lemon wedges (optional)

1. Heat oven to 450°. Coat a baking dish with nonstick cooking spray.

2. In a small dish, stir together the hoisin, soy sauce, vinegar, ginger and red pepper flakes. Place salmon in prepared dish and spread top of each fillet with half of the hoisin mixture.

3. Roast at 450° for 10 minutes. Spread remaining hoisin mixture over the salmon and top with the scallions. Roast for an additional 5 minutes.

4. Serve with rice and broccoli, and lemon wedges for garnish, if desired.

PER SERVING: 308 calories; 12 g fat (2 g sat.); 39 g protein; 8 g carbohydrate; 0 g fiber; 795 mg sodium; 107 mg cholesterol.

SALMON FILLET

3-pound package: $15

2 meals

* Cut half into 4 servings. Wrap well in aluminum foil and freeze.
* Use remaining 4 servings in **Spicy Hoisin Salmon.**

Use a paring knife to check for doneness—insert in center of fillet to peek inside. Fish should look opaque and flaky but still be juicy.

When trimming pork roast, leave the thin layer of fat—it helps keep the meat moist and flavorful when cooking.

BONELESS PORK ROAST

10-pound package: $20

4 meals

* Cut off 4-pound roast; freeze for future. (see "how to" below)

* Cut eight 8-ounce chops; freeze separately for two future meals.

* Cut remaining 2 pounds into thin cutlets for **Pork Piccata**.

how to

Turn a 10-pound roast into 4 easy-to-freeze meals.

Step 1 • Cut off a 4-pound roast, about 10 inches long.

Step 2 • Cut another 4 pounds into eight 8-ounce chops.

Step 3 • Cut remaining 2 pounds into thin cutlets.

pork piccata

MAKES: 4 servings. **PREP:** 10 minutes. **COOK:** 8 minutes.

- 8 **thin boneless pork cutlets (about 1½ to 2 pounds total)**
- ¼ **teaspoon salt**
- ¼ **teaspoon black pepper**
- ⅓ **cup all-purpose flour**
- 2 **tablespoons olive oil**
- 1 **cup chicken broth**
- 3 **tablespoons capers**
- 2 **tablespoons lemon juice**
- 1 **tablespoon butter**
  Mashed potatoes, peas, lemon wedges and chopped parsley (optional)

1. Season both sides of pork with salt and pepper. Dredge in flour and shake off excess. Discard remaining flour.

2. Heat oil in a large skillet over medium-high heat. Add pork and sauté for 2 minutes per side. Remove pork to a plate and keep warm.

3. Add broth and simmer 2 minutes, scraping up any browned bits from bottom of skillet. Stir in the capers and lemon juice. Return the pork to the skillet and simmer gently for about 1 to 2 minutes, until pork is heated through. Whisk in the butter.

4. Serve with mashed potatoes and peas, and garnish with lemon and parsley, if desired.

PER SERVING: 366 calories; 21 g fat (7 g sat.); 35 g protein; 7 g carbohydrate; 0 g fiber; 582 mg sodium; 101 mg cholesterol.

basic meat sauce

MAKES: 16 cups. **PREP:** 10 minutes. **COOK:** 65 minutes.

- 4 pounds lean ground beef
- ¼ cup olive oil
- 2 large onions, peeled and chopped
- 4 medium carrots, peeled and chopped
- 6 cloves garlic, peeled and coarsely chopped
- 1 cup dry red wine
- 3 cans (28 ounces) whole tomatoes in juice, broken up
- 1 can (6 ounces) tomato paste
- 2 teaspoons Italian seasoning
- 2 teaspoons sugar
- 1½ teaspoons salt
- 1 teaspoon black pepper

1. Crumble ground beef into a large nonstick pot. Cook over medium-high heat for 12 minutes, stirring occasionally. Pour off accumulated liquid.
2. Add oil, onions, carrots and garlic. Cook for 7 minutes, stirring. Add wine; cook 1 minute. Add tomatoes, tomato paste, Italian seasoning, sugar, salt and pepper. Simmer, partially covered, for 45 minutes, stirring occasionally.
3. Divide 12 cups of sauce among three containers. Cool to room temperature, then cover and freeze for up to 2 months. Use remaining 4 cups for ziti recipe.

PER 1 CUP SAUCE: 263 calories; 9 g fat (3 g sat.); 27 g protein; 16 g carbohydrate; 4 g fiber; 587 mg sodium; 70 mg cholesterol.

baked ziti

MAKES: 4 servings.

Cook ½ **pound ziti,** following package directions. Toss with **4 cups meat sauce** and **1 cup shredded mozzarella cheese.** Spoon into a foil baking pan. Cool to room temperature. Cover tightly with foil and freeze for up to 1 month. To serve, thaw in refrigerator for 2 days. Bake at 350° for 35 to 40 minutes or until internal temperature registers 140°.

PER SERVING:
556 calories; 16 g fat (7 g sat.); 40 g protein; 57 g carbohydrate; 5 g fiber; 763 mg sodium; 92 mg cholesterol.

10/1/08 MEAT SAUCE

LEAN GROUND BEEF

6-pound package: $15

5 meals

* Form 2 pounds into burgers and freeze.

* With remaining 4 pounds make **Basic Meat Sauce** (3 servings).

* Use 4 cups **Basic Meat Sauce** in **Baked Ziti.**

Pair meat sauce with a short tubular pasta, like penne, which holds the small chunks of beef.

simple SUPPERS

IF YOU NEED AN EASY MEAL
(AND WHO DOESN'T?)
ONE-POT IS THE WAY TO GO.
WE'VE STIRRED UP SIX
DELICIOUS DINNERS THAT ARE
FILLING, FLAVOR-PACKED AND
FAST. OUR FAVORITE PART?
CLEANUP IS A BREEZE.

BY CINDY HELLER

PHOTOGRAPHY BY ANN STRATTON

turkey tetrazzini

MAKES: 6 servings. **PREP:** 15 minutes. **COOK:** 20 minutes.

- 1 teaspoon olive oil
- 10 ounces white mushrooms, sliced
- 1 small onion, chopped
- ½ teaspoon each salt and black pepper
- 2 tablespoons flour
- 6 ounces egg noodles
- 1 can (14.5 ounces) low-sodium chicken broth
- ¾ cup light cream
- 1 package (10 ounces) cooked turkey breast strips
- 1 package (10 ounces) frozen peas

1. Heat olive oil in a Dutch oven over medium heat. Add mushrooms and onion. Sprinkle with ¼ teaspoon each salt and pepper. Cook, stirring, for 7 minutes or until tender.

2. Stir in flour and cook 1 minute. Remove mushroom mixture from pot and set aside.

3. Return pot to medium-high heat and add noodles, broth, light cream and 2¼ cups water. Cover and cook, stirring occasionally, for about 12 minutes or until tender.

4. Stir in mushroom mixture, remaining ¼ teaspoon each salt and pepper, the turkey and peas. Heat through; serve.

PER SERVING: 339 calories; 10 g fat (4 g sat.); 28 g protein; 33 g carbohydrate; 4 g fiber; 497 mg sodium; 84 mg cholesterol.

white bean stew and greens

MAKES: 4 servings. **PREP:** 10 minutes. **COOK:** 17 minutes.

- 4 slices bacon, cut crosswise into ½-inch pieces
- 1 small onion, chopped
- 2 cans (15.5 ounces each) cannellini beans, drained and rinsed
- 1 teaspoon fresh, chopped rosemary
- 1 cup low-sodium chicken broth
- 1 bunch kale, rinsed, trimmed and cut into 1-inch pieces (about 7 cups)
- ⅛ teaspoon each salt and black pepper

1. Cook bacon in a Dutch oven over medium heat for 6 minutes or until crisp; remove with a slotted spoon and set aside.

2. Add onion to pot and cook for 5 minutes or until softened. Stir in beans and rosemary and cook 1 minute. Add broth to pot; bring to simmer.

3. Stir kale into beans in pot and cover; cook 5 minutes. Remove cover and stir kale until wilted. Stir in reserved bacon, salt and pepper. Serve immediately.

PER SERVING: 348 calories; 12 g fat (4 g sat.); 16 g protein; 45 g carbohydrate; 11 g fiber; 847 mg sodium; 17 mg cholesterol.

creamy pasta and chickpeas

MAKES: 6 servings. **PREP:** 10 minutes. **COOK:** 18 minutes.

1 pound asparagus, cut into 1-inch pieces
1 red pepper, chopped
½ teaspoon each salt and black pepper
8 ounces fiber-enriched penne pasta (such as Barilla Plus)
1 can (15.5 ounces) chickpeas, drained and rinsed
1 package (4.4 ounces) light, spreadable herb cheese (such as Boursin)
  Pinch nutmeg

1. Generously coat a medium-size nonstick saucepan with nonstick cooking spray; heat over medium-high heat. Add asparagus, red pepper and ¼ teaspoon each salt and pepper to pan. Cook, stirring, for 6 minutes. Remove and keep warm.

2. Cook penne in boiling salted water for 12 minutes. Drain; reserving 1 cup pasta water.

3. Return pasta to pot. Over medium heat, stir in asparagus mixture, remaining ¼ teaspoon each salt and pepper, chickpeas, cheese and nutmeg, adding reserved pasta water as needed to thin sauce. Serve immediately.

PER SERVING: 280 calories; 4 g fat (1 g sat.); 15 g protein; 47 g carbohydrate; 8 g fiber; 553 mg sodium; 6 mg cholesterol.

lemony chicken and orzo

MAKES: 4 servings. **PREP:** 5 minutes. **COOK:** 24 minutes.

- 4 boneless, skinless chicken breast halves
- ½ teaspoon each salt and black pepper
- 1 can (14.5 ounces) low-sodium chicken broth
- ⅓ cup lemon juice
- 2 teaspoons honey
- 2½ tablespoons low-fat sour cream
- ¾ cup orzo
- 8 ounces green beans, cut into 1-inch pieces

1. Cut chicken into 1-inch cubes. Sprinkle with ¼ teaspoon each of the salt and pepper.

2. Pour broth and lemon juice into a Dutch oven. Bring to boil and add chicken. Cover and reduce heat to medium. Cook for 9 minutes or until chicken is cooked through.

3. Remove chicken from pot; set aside. Increase heat to high and cook sauce for 5 minutes. Stir in remaining ¼ teaspoon

each salt and pepper; whisk in honey and sour cream.

4. Add **2 cups water** to pot; bring to a boil. Add orzo; cook for 10 minutes or until pasta is tender and most of the liquid has been absorbed. Add green beans to pot for final 4 minutes of cook time. Stir chicken back into pot and serve.

PER SERVING: 384 calories; 4 g fat (1 g sat.); 47 g protein; 39 g carbohydrate; 3 g fiber; 685 mg sodium; 106 mg cholesterol.

gingered tilapia and swiss chard

MAKES: 4 servings. **PREP:** 10 minutes. **COOK:** 10 minutes.

- 4 tilapia fillets, about 6 ounces each
- 1½ tablespoons grated fresh ginger
- ½ teaspoon each salt and black pepper
- 1½ tablespoons olive oil
- 1 small onion, chopped
- 2 bunches Swiss chard, stems removed and leaves roughly chopped (about 6 cups)
- ¼ cup low-sodium chicken broth
- ¼ cup white wine

1. Sprinkle tilapia with ¾ tablespoon of the ginger and ¼ teaspoon each of the salt and pepper. Heat 1 tablespoon of the oil in a large nonstick skillet over medium-high heat. Cook tilapia 2 to 3 minutes per side or until fish flakes easily. Remove from skillet; keep warm.
2. Heat remaining ½ tablespoon oil in skillet; cook onion and remaining ¾ tablespoon ginger for 1 minute.

3. Increase heat to high. Add Swiss chard, remaining ¼ teaspoon each salt and pepper, chicken broth and wine to skillet. Cook 3 minutes, stirring, until chard is wilted.

PER SERVING: 233 calories; 8 g fat (2 g sat.); 35 g protein; 3 g carbohydrate; 1 g fiber; 533 mg sodium; 85 mg cholesterol.

apple chicken and couscous

MAKES: 4 servings. **PREP:** 5 minutes. **COOK:** 17 minutes.

1 **cup unprepared whole-wheat couscous**
1 **cup baby spinach, chopped**
1 **cup frozen apple juice concentrate, thawed**
2 **pounds boneless, skinless chicken thighs**
½ **teaspoon each salt and black pepper**
1 **tablespoon honey**
3 **tablespoons Dijon mustard**

1. Place couscous and spinach in bowl. Heat ⅓ cup of the apple concentrate and ⅔ cup water to boiling over high heat in large nonstick skillet. Pour apple liquid into couscous. Stir and cover tightly with foil; set aside.

2. Sprinkle chicken with salt and pepper. Over medium-high heat, cook chicken 7 minutes per side or until cooked through. Fluff couscous with fork. Place chicken on top; cover.

3. Whisk together remaining ⅔ cup apple concentrate, honey and mustard. Add apple concentrate mixture to skillet; cook 3 minutes over high heat. Drizzle chicken and couscous with sauce; serve with additional sauce on the side.

PER SERVING: 533 calories; 13 g fat (3 g sat.); 49 g protein; 59 g carbohydrate; 4 g fiber; 749 mg sodium; 221 mg cholesterol.

shopping list

This grocery list and the pantry items are all you need to cook up a week of hearty suppers.

PRODUCE

10 ounces mushrooms
1 bunch fresh rosemary
1 bunch kale
1 pound asparagus
1 sweet red pepper
1 cup baby spinach
1 piece ginger
2 bunches Swiss chard
8 ounces green beans
3 small onions

DAIRY AND FROZEN

1 pint light cream
1 package (4.4 ounces) light, spreadable herb cheese
8 ounces low-fat sour cream
1 package frozen peas
1 can frozen apple juice concentrate

MEAT, FISH AND POULTRY

1 package (10 ounces) cooked turkey breast strips
4 slices bacon
4 boneless, skinless chicken breasts
2 pounds boneless, skinless chicken thighs
4 tilapia fillets, about 6 ounces each

DRY GOODS

1 bag (12 ounces) egg noodles
3 cans low-sodium chicken broth
2 cans cannellini beans
1 box orzo
1 box whole-wheat couscous
1 box fiber-enriched penne pasta

pantry items

- olive oil
- flour
- salt and pepper
- honey
- lemon juice
- Dijon mustard
- nutmeg
- white wine
- chickpeas

cooking tip

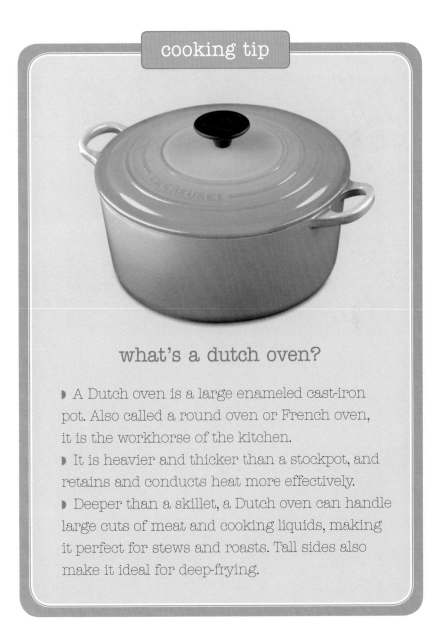

what's a dutch oven?

- A Dutch oven is a large enameled cast-iron pot. Also called a round oven or French oven, it is the workhorse of the kitchen.
- It is heavier and thicker than a stockpot, and retains and conducts heat more effectively.
- Deeper than a skillet, a Dutch oven can handle large cuts of meat and cooking liquids, making it perfect for stews and roasts. Tall sides also make it ideal for deep-frying.

Scallops—and most other
kinds of seafood—stay
moist and tender when
cooked in the microwave.
(Recipe page 244)

QUICK & EASY™

Meals in Minutes

THINK YOUR MICROWAVE
CAN'T MANAGE MORE THAN
REHEATING LEFTOVERS?
THINK AGAIN.
OUR **6** SUPERFAST
RECIPES WILL
HAVE YOU FALLING IN
LOVE WITH THAT LITTLE OVEN
ALL OVER AGAIN.

BY MICHAEL TYRRELL

thai-style scallops

MAKES: 4 servings. **PREP:** 10 minutes.
MICROWAVE: on HIGH for 5 minutes.
STAND: 5 minutes.

- ¼ cup unseasoned bread crumbs
- ¼ cup salted peanuts, finely chopped
- ¼ teaspoon red pepper flakes
- ¼ teaspoon garlic powder
- ¼ teaspoon ground ginger
- 1 tablespoon olive oil
- 1½ pounds sea scallops
  Green beans and red peppers
  (optional)

1. In a small bowl, mix together bread crumbs, peanuts, red pepper flakes, garlic powder and ginger. Set aside.
2. Spray a microwave-safe 9-inch glass pie dish with nonstick cooking spray. Place scallops in the dish and brush with the olive oil. Spoon peanut mixture over the scallops.
3. Loosely cover the pie dish with microwave-safe plastic wrap and vent slightly on one side. Microwave on HIGH 5 minutes. Let stand, covered, 5 minutes.
4. Serve with steamed green beans and red peppers, if desired.

PER SERVING: 290 calories; 12 g fat (2 g sat.); 33 g protein; 12 g carbohydrate; 2 g fiber; 439 mg sodium; 56 mg cholesterol.

perfect veggies

1 > **Cut vegetables into equal-size pieces.**

2 > **Check halfway through cooking time; stir.**

3 > **Season with salt just before serving.**

microwave-steaming vegetables

Trying to eat more vegetables but don't know how to cook them? Follow our quick and easy guidelines and you won't have any more excuses. (Studies show veggies retain more nutrients when cooked this way!)

▶ Place vegetables in a microwave-safe bowl with a small amount of water and cover with microwave-safe plastic wrap. Vent slightly and microwave on HIGH. Cooking times vary, so check for doneness.

▶ Leafy vegetables, such as spinach or cabbage, require 1 to 2 tablespoons of water per pound and take about 5 minutes.

▶ Green vegetables such as green beans and broccoli require about 4 tablespoons of water per pound and take about 8 minutes.

▶ Dense vegetables such as carrots and diced potatoes require about 6 tablespoons of water per pound and take about 10 minutes.

Fresh basil adds a lively accent to this simple-to-make "risotto."

chicken and artichoke "risotto"

MAKES: 6 servings. **PREP:** 15 minutes. **MICROWAVE:** on HIGH for 24 minutes. **STAND:** 10 minutes.

- 1 **small onion, peeled and chopped**
- 2 **tablespoons olive oil**
- 1¼ **cups long-grain white rice**
- 4 **cups chicken broth**
- ¼ **teaspoon salt**
- ¼ **teaspoon ground nutmeg**
  Pinch cayenne pepper
- 1 **pound uncooked chicken tenders, cut into 1-inch pieces**
- 4 **ounces drained marinated artichokes, from a 12-ounce jar, very coarsely chopped**

- 2 **tablespoons unsalted butter**
- ½ **cup grated Parmesan cheese**
- ½ **cup fresh basil leaves, torn into bite-size pieces**

1. Place onion and olive oil into a deep 4-quart covered microwave-safe dish. Microwave on HIGH, uncovered, for 4 minutes. Stir in rice, chicken broth, salt, nutmeg and cayenne. Cover and microwave on HIGH for 10 minutes.

2. Stir in chicken tenders and microwave, covered, for an additional 10 minutes.

3. Stir in artichokes and let stand, covered, for 10 minutes. Stir in butter, cheese and basil. Serve.

PER SERVING: 379 calories; 13 g fat (5 g sat.); 25 g protein; 39 g carbohydrate; 2 g fiber; 942 mg sodium; 60 mg cholesterol.

turkey and spinach manicotti

MAKES: 14 pieces. **PREP:** 20 minutes. **MICROWAVE:** on HIGH for 28 minutes. **STAND:** 10 minutes.

1¼ **pounds ground turkey**
 1 **package (10 ounces) frozen chopped spinach, thawed, excess liquid squeezed out**
 ¼ **cup pine nuts**
 1 **teaspoon dried Italian seasoning**
 ½ **teaspoon salt**
 ¼ **teaspoon black pepper**
 1 **jar (26 ounces) chunky pasta sauce**
14 **manicotti shells (such as Ronzoni)**
 1 **can (14½ ounces) chicken broth**
 1 **cup reduced-fat shredded mozzarella cheese**
 Grated Parmesan cheese (optional)

1. In a large bowl, mix together the ground turkey, spinach, pine nuts, Italian seasoning, salt and pepper. Spread ½ cup of the pasta sauce in the bottom of a 10-inch square microwave-safe dish. Fill the uncooked manicotti shells with the meat mixture and place in the dish. (It will be tight but all 14 filled shells will fit.)

2. Pour broth and remaining pasta sauce evenly over manicotti. Gently press shells into liquid. Cover with microwave-safe plastic wrap; vent one corner. Microwave on HIGH for 25 minutes.

3. Sprinkle with mozzarella cheese and microwave on HIGH for 3 minutes, uncovered. Allow to stand for 10 minutes before serving. Garnish with grated Parmesan cheese, if desired.

Make-Ahead Tip Prepare recipe up to Step 2. Cover and refrigerate overnight.

PER PIECE: 236 calories; 9 g fat (2 g sat.); 14 g protein; 24 g carbohydrate; 2 g fiber; 579 mg sodium; 37 mg cholesterol.

Pine nuts add a pleasant crunch to the turkey and spinach filling.

Try this quick and tangy tomato sauce over tilapia or even cod too.

here's the dish...

Most glass and ceramic dishes are safe for the microwave, but if you have any doubts, here's a quick way to test:

▶ Place 1 cup of water in the dish. Place in the microwave and cook on HIGH for 1 minute. If the water gets hot and the dish remains cool, that means the dish is safe to use in the microwave.

▶ If the dish gets hot, then it's not safe—it may contain lead or other metallic substances.

flounder with spicy cherry tomato sauce

MAKES: 4 servings. **PREP:** 10 minutes. **MICROWAVE:** on HIGH for 12 minutes. **STAND:** 10 minutes.

- 2 **cups cherry tomatoes, cut in half (about 12 ounces)**
- 1 **can (8 ounces) tomato sauce**
- ½ **teaspoon garlic salt**
- ½ **teaspoon dried oregano**
- ¼ **teaspoon red pepper flakes**
- ¼ **cup pimento-stuffed green olives, cut in half**
- 4 **flounder fillets, 5 to 6 ounces each Mashed potatoes and salad (optional)**

1. Place tomatoes, tomato sauce, garlic salt, oregano and red pepper flakes in an 11 x 7 x 2-inch microwave-safe dish. Cover with microwave-safe plastic wrap and vent at one corner. Microwave on HIGH for 5 minutes.

2. Uncover and stir in olives. Fold flounder fillets in half and tuck into sauce. Spoon sauce over fillets. Cover and vent. Microwave for 5 minutes. Stir sauce and spoon over fillets. Microwave an additional 2 minutes. Let stand for 10 minutes, covered.

3. Serve warm, with mashed potatoes and a green salad, if desired.

PER SERVING: 196 calories; 3 g fat (1 g sat.); 34 g protein; 7 g carbohydrate; 2 g fiber; 750 mg sodium; 82 mg cholesterol.

Lean ground beef or chicken can easily substitute for veal in these meatballs.

sweet and sour meatballs

MAKES: 36 meatballs. **PREP:** 15 minutes. **MICROWAVE:** Sauce on HIGH for 5 minutes; Meatballs on HIGH for 10 minutes. **STAND:** 10 minutes.

Sauce:
- 1   can (8 ounces) crushed pineapple in juice
- 1   can (8 ounces) tomato sauce
- 2   tablespoons cider vinegar
- 1   tablespoon sugar

Meatballs:
- 1½   pounds ground veal
- ⅓   cup unseasoned bread crumbs
- 2   eggs, lightly beaten
- 1   teaspoon chili powder
- ¼   teaspoon ground cumin
- ¼   teaspoon salt

1. Prepare **Sauce:** Place pineapple, tomato sauce, vinegar and sugar in an 11 x 7 x 2-inch microwave-safe dish; stir. Cover with microwave-safe plastic wrap and vent at one corner. Microwave on HIGH for 5 minutes. Set aside.

2. Prepare **Meatballs:** In a large bowl, mix together the veal, bread crumbs, eggs, chili powder, cumin and salt. Roll 1 tablespoon of the veal mixture into a small meatball. Repeat, for a total of 36.

3. Spray a second 11 x 7-inch microwave-safe dish with nonstick cooking spray. Place half of the meatballs in dish, cover with plastic wrap and vent. Microwave on HIGH for 3 minutes. Transfer meatballs to dish containing sauce. Recoat second dish with nonstick spray; microwave remaining uncooked meatballs for 3 minutes. Add to sauce.

4. Cover sauce and meatballs with plastic wrap and vent. Microwave on HIGH for 4 minutes. Stir; re-cover and let stand for 10 minutes.

5. Serve meatballs as an appetizer, or spoon over cooked noodles as a main course, if desired.

PER MEATBALL: 42 calories; 2 g fat (1 g sat.); 4 g protein; 2 g carbohydrate; 0 g fiber; 73 mg sodium; 27 mg cholesterol.

bittersweet almond-chocolate pudding

MAKES: 4 servings. **PREP:** 5 minutes.
MICROWAVE: on HIGH for 8½ minutes.
REFRIGERATE: 4 hours or overnight.

- 2   cups milk
- ⅓   cup sugar
- 2   eggs
- 2   tablespoons cornstarch
       Pinch salt
- 3   ounces bittersweet chocolate, chopped
- ½   teaspoon almond extract
- ¼   cup sliced almonds
- ¼   teaspoon olive oil
- ½   cup frozen whipped topping, thawed

1. In a large microwave-safe bowl, combine milk, sugar, eggs, cornstarch and salt. Whisk until well blended.

2. Microwave, uncovered, on HIGH for 5 minutes. Whisk until smooth.

3. In second bowl, melt chocolate on HIGH for 1 minute. Stir. Microwave on HIGH another 30 seconds. Stir until smooth. Whisk chocolate and almond extract into milk mixture until smooth.

4. Spoon into four serving dishes, cover and refrigerate for at least 4 hours.

5. Just before serving, toast almonds: Place nuts in a glass pie plate. Toss with olive oil. Microwave, uncovered, for 1 minute on HIGH. Stir. Microwave an additional minute or until lightly toasted. Garnish puddings with whipped topping, then sprinkle with toasted nuts.

PER SERVING: 358 calories; 20 g fat (9 g sat.); 10 g protein; 40 g carbohydrate; 2 g fiber; 84 mg sodium; 118 mg cholesterol.

Toasted sliced
almonds add a
pleasant crunch
to this velvety
pudding.

cooking **school**

IF YOU'RE A FAN OF FOODS THAT ARE BOTH SWEET AND SAVORY, CHECK OUT THIS EASY-TO-MAKE STRATA RECIPE—PLUS A CRASH COURSE ON THE MOST USEFUL CUTLERY FOR ANY COOK'S KITCHEN. **BY JULIE MILTENBERGER**

PHOTOGRAPHY BY ALEXANDRA GRABLEWSKI

Use your chef's knife to cut apples into equal-size pieces (each about 1 inch); that way the fruit will cook more evenly.

savory apple strata

MAKES: 8 servings. **PREP:** 15 minutes.
COOK: 5 minutes. **BAKE:** at 375° for 40 minutes.

- 8 ounces turkey kielbasa (½ package), cut into half-moons
- 2 Granny Smith apples, peeled, cored and chopped
- 1 medium-size onion, chopped
- 6 eggs
- 1½ cups milk
- 2 tablespoons honey mustard
- ½ teaspoon dried sage
- ¼ teaspoon black pepper (or more, if desired)
- 1 loaf (about 12 ounces) Italian bread, cut into 1-inch cubes
- 1 cup shredded cheddar cheese

1. Coat a 13 x 9-inch baking pan with nonstick cooking spray. In a 10-inch nonstick skillet, sauté kielbasa, apples and onion for 5 minutes over medium heat. If sticking to skillet, add 1 tablespoon water. Cool slightly.
2. In medium-size bowl, whisk together eggs, milk, honey mustard, sage and pepper. Set aside. Place bread cubes in a large bowl. Gently stir in kielbasa mixture and ½ cup of the shredded cheese. Spoon into prepared baking dish and then pour egg mixture evenly over it. Compress lightly with hands until all ingredients are moistened. Sprinkle with remaining ½ cup shredded cheese.
3. Cover with foil and bake at 375° for 20 minutes. Uncover and bake an additional 20 minutes. Cool slightly before serving.

PER SERVING: 325 calories; 13 g fat (6 g sat.); 18 g protein; 35 g carbohydrate; 3 g fiber; 692 mg sodium; 194 mg cholesterol.

knife primer

EVERY GOOD COOK NEEDS A FEW GOOD-QUALITY KNIVES ON HAND FOR PEELING, SLICING AND DICING. HERE ARE FOUR THAT ARE ALWAYS GOOD TO HAVE AROUND—WHETHER YOU'RE A NOVICE COOK OR AN EXPERIENCED CHEF.

CHEF'S KNIFE Available in 7-, 8- or 10-inch options, this will be your go-to knife for chopping fruit and vegetables, and for dicing pieces of meat and poultry. Hold firmly with your thumb running parallel to the handle for control. Rock knife up and down, keeping the tip on your work surface and using your opposite hand to guide the motion.

UTILITY KNIFE With a length of 5 to 8 inches, this is more thin and flexible than a chef's knife. Best for small, precise jobs, such as slicing steak and trimming fat from chicken thighs. Also called a sandwich knife.

SERRATED KNIFE Usually 10 inches long (sometimes offset for ease), this knife is handy for cutting through crusty bread (see strata recipe) or slicing soft-fleshed fruit and vegetables—such as tomatoes—without bruising. Look for one with evenly spaced pointed teeth. Run knife back and forth, using a sawing motion.

PARING KNIFE A small, multi-purpose knife whose size can vary from 3 to 4½ inches long. Perfect for peeling apples, coring fruit or slicing garlic and other small foods.

november

Bulgur-Stuffed Squash
(Recipe page 275)

AS COOLER WEATHER ARRIVES AND THE
HOLIDAYS NEAR, EMBRACE THE SEASON
WITH HEARTY FAMILY DINNERS AND
SPECIAL-OCCASION DESSERTS.

Mahogany Roast Turkey
page 260

plus

Chocolate-Crunch Cheesecake
page 269

Holiday Sunrise
page 279

CELEBRATE THE SEASON'S COLORFUL HARVEST WITH THESE PUMPKIN PATCH SWEETS.

pumpkin cupcakes

MAKES: 30 cupcakes. **PREP:** 15 minutes. **BAKE:** at 350° for 26 minutes.

Cupcakes:
- 3 cups all-purpose flour
- 1 tablespoon pumpkin pie spice
- 2½ teaspoons baking soda
- 1 teaspoon baking powder
- ¾ teaspoon salt
- 1½ cups granulated sugar
- ¾ cup vegetable oil
- ½ cup buttermilk
- 1 can (15 ounces) pumpkin puree
- 4 eggs

Frosting:
- 1 package (8 ounces) cream cheese, softened
- ¾ cup (1½ sticks) unsalted butter, softened
- 1 box (16 ounces) confectioners' sugar
- 1 teaspoon vanilla extract
- 2 tablespoons milk, plus more if needed
  Orange food coloring
  Fine and coarse orange decorating sugar
  Pretzel sticks or rods

1. Heat oven to 350°. Line 12 mini cupcake pan indents, 12 regular indents and 6 jumbo cupcake indents with foil or paper liners.

2. Prepare **Cupcakes:** In a medium-size bowl, whisk together flour, pumpkin pie spice, baking soda, baking powder and salt; set aside.

3. Beat sugar, vegetable oil, buttermilk, pumpkin puree and eggs in a large bowl on low speed for 2 minutes or until combined. Add flour mixture and beat for 2 minutes or until just combined. Divide batter among liners, filling each ⅔ full.

4. Bake at 350° for about 12 minutes for the minis, 18 minutes for the regulars and 26 minutes for the jumbos, or until a toothpick inserted in the center comes out clean. Transfer to a wire rack and cool completely.

5. Prepare **Frosting:** Beat cream cheese and butter in a large bowl on high for 3 minutes or until light and fluffy. Gradually add the confectioners' sugar, vanilla and milk and beat until smooth and of a spreading consistency, 2 minutes. Add an additional tablespoon milk if mixture is too thick.

6. Divide the frosting into two bowls and tint to different shades of orange with food coloring. Mound the frosting on top of cupcakes and spread until rounded. Roll the entire cupcake in the sugar to coat, or roll just edges in sugar, alternating between fine and coarse sugars as desired. To make indentations, press a wooden skewer on top of the sugared cupcake. Add pretzel sticks or rods as stems.

PER SERVING: 699 calories; 34 g fat (14 g sat.); 8 g protein; 93 g carbohydrate; 2 g fiber; 557 mg sodium; 122 mg cholesterol.

cupcake chemistry
USE THESE GUIDELINES WHEN BAKING FROM SCRATCH.

▶ A tall, light and tender cupcake requires a little patience. Beating together butter and sugar—a process called creaming—is key and shouldn't be rushed. Creaming takes time to create volume-producing air bubbles in the batter. If you are using a mixer, beat up to 5 minutes; beating by hand will give you a 10-minute arm workout.

▶ Be sure to have all ingredients at room temperature before blending together—otherwise, when adding cold milk or eggs to other ingredients, your batter may appear curdled.

▶ Most cupcakes use a leavening agent—baking powder or baking soda—in addition to eggs. The general proportion is 1 to 1½ teaspoons baking powder or ¼ teaspoon baking soda for every cup of flour. Cupcakes featuring heavy add-ins such as nuts, raisins or shredded carrots usually require slightly more leavening, and those extras should be stirred in last.

▶ If your cupcakes don't rise, the problem most likely isn't that you haven't spooned in enough baking powder or soda—in fact, you probably used too much. Excess leavening will cause your cupcake to rise too fast and then collapse.

▶ Use an oven thermometer to make sure your oven temperature is correctly calibrated.

PHOTOGRAPHY BY MIKI DUISTERHOF

THIS SUMPTUOUS WHITE CONFECTION IS WORTHY OF ANY CELEBRATION.

coconut cake

MAKES: 16 servings. **PREP:** 30 minutes. **BAKE:** at 350° for 40 minutes.

Cake:
- 3 cups cake flour (not self-rising)
- 2 teaspoons baking powder
- ½ teaspoon salt
- 1 cup (2 sticks) unsalted butter, softened
- 1½ cups sugar
- 3 eggs
- ½ teaspoon vanilla extract
- ½ teaspoon coconut extract
- 1 can (13½ ounces) coconut milk
- 1 cup sweetened flake coconut, chopped

Frosting and Filling:
- 1 package (8 ounces) reduced-fat cream cheese, softened
- 4 tablespoons unsalted butter, softened
- 1 teaspoon vanilla extract
- 1 box (16 ounces) confectioners' sugar
- ½ cup strawberry preserves
- 1½ cup sweetened flake coconut

1. Heat oven to 350°. Coat two 8-inch round cake pans with nonstick cooking spray. Line bottoms of pans with waxed paper and spray paper.

2. Cake: In a large bowl, whisk together flour, baking powder and salt. Set aside.

3. In another large bowl, beat butter and sugar on medium speed until light and fluffy. Beat in eggs, one at a time, beating well after each addition. Add vanilla and coconut extracts; beat until combined.

4. On low speed, beat in flour mixture in 3 additions, alternating with coconut milk. Beat well after each addition. Fold in chopped coconut. Divide batter equally between prepared pans.

5. Bake at 350° for 40 minutes or until wooden pick inserted in center comes out clean. Cool in pans on wire rack for 15 minutes. Remove cake layers from pans and cool completely.

6. Prepare **Frosting:** In large bowl, beat cream cheese and butter until smooth. Beat in vanilla. On low speed, beat in confectioners' sugar until smooth.

7. Trim cake layers level if crowned. Place one cake layer on a cake stand. Spread top with strawberry preserves. Place remaining cake layer on top. (See how-to for securing with skewers to hold layers in place.) Spread top and side of cake with a generous amount of frosting. Gently press shredded coconut onto side of cake. Refrigerate 1 hour before serving.

PER SERVING: 550 calories; 29 g fat (20 g sat.); 5 g protein; 72 g carbohydrate; 1 g fiber; 240 mg sodium; 87 mg cholesterol.

PHOTOGRAPHY BY RITA MAAS

The Menu

Chicken and Shrimp
Coconut Curry

Mahogany Roast Turkey

Sausage Stuffing

Broccoli-Cheddar Casserole

Cranberry Salad

Pumpkin Chiffon Pie

PHOTOGRAPHY BY LUCY SCHAEFFER

Giving Thanks

Make your Thanksgiving deliciously stress-free with our food editors' favorite home recipes—from turkey to cranberry sauce to a quick-fix dessert.

Regina Ragone
FOOD DIRECTOR

"Mom's stuffing is the star at our family's dinner."

sausage stuffing

MAKES: 8 servings. **PREP:** 10 minutes.
BAKE: at 350° for 1 hour.

- 1 pound sweet Italian sausage
- 2 tablespoons butter
- 12 ounces mushrooms, cleaned and quartered
- 2 celery stalks, chopped
- 1 large onion, chopped
- ½ cup golden raisins
- ¼ cup chopped fresh parsley
- ¾ teaspoon dried sage
- 12 cups cubed stale Italian bread
- 1 can (14½ ounces) chicken broth

1. Heat oven to 350°. Coat a 13 x 9 x 2-inch baking pan with nonstick cooking spray; set aside.
2. Place a large nonstick skillet over medium-high heat. Remove sausage casings and crumble sausage into skillet. Cook 7 minutes or until no longer pink. Remove sausage from skillet using a slotted spoon.
3. Add 1 tablespoon of the butter to skillet. When melted, add mushrooms to pan and cook 7 minutes or until lightly browned. Remove to a large bowl.
4. Melt remaining butter in pan. Add celery and onion; cook for 5 minutes or until softened. Stir in raisins, parsley and sage and cool for 2 minutes. Transfer to the bowl with mushrooms. Add sausage, celery mixture, cubed bread and chicken broth, stirring well.
5. Pour mixture into prepared pan and cover with foil. Bake at 350° for 50 minutes. Remove foil and bake another 10 minutes or until lightly browned on top.

PER SERVING: 170 calories; 7 g fat (3 g sat.); 10 g protein; 19 g carbohydrate; 1 g fiber; 507 mg sodium; 20 mg cholesterol.

Michael Tyrrell
ASSOCIATE FOOD EDITOR
Maple syrup and
soy sauce seal in
the juicy flavors
of this turkey.

mahogany roast turkey

MAKES: 14 servings. **PREP:** 15 minutes.
ROAST: at 450° for 30 minutes, then at 350° for 1½ hours.

Turkey:
- 1 16-pound turkey
- ½ teaspoon salt
- ½ teaspoon black pepper
- 1 onion, chopped
- 2 carrots, peeled and halved crosswise
- 2 celery ribs, halved crosswise
- ¼ cup low-sodium soy sauce
- ¼ cup maple syrup
- ¼ cup (½ stick) unsalted butter, melted

Gravy:
- 4 cups chicken broth
- ½ cup white wine
- 6 tablespoons flour

1. Prepare **Turkey:** Heat oven to 450°.
2. Season turkey cavity with salt and pepper. Stuff with onion, carrots and celery. Tie up legs or tuck them into flap of skin. Place turkey in a large deep roasting pan; roast at 450° for 30 minutes.
3. Whisk soy, maple syrup and butter in a bowl.
4. Reduce oven temperature to 350°. Roast turkey at 350° for 1½ hours or until instant-read thermometer inserted in thickest part of thigh registers 180°, basting every 15 minutes with soy sauce mixture. Remove from oven; tent with foil.
5. Prepare **Gravy:** Scrape pan drippings into a fat separator. Pour de-fatted liquid into a medium-size saucepan. Add chicken broth and wine. Whisk in flour and cook for 5 minutes, or until thickened.

PER SERVING: 775 calories; 26 g fat (8 g sat.); 117 g protein; 9 g carbohydrate; 1 g fiber; 776 mg sodium; 428 mg cholesterol.

chicken and shrimp coconut curry

MAKES: 12 appetizers or 6 main dish servings.
PREP: 15 minutes. **COOK:** 14 minutes.

- 2 tablespoons flour
- 1 can (14 ounces) coconut milk
- 1 can (14 ounces) vegetable broth
- 2 tablespoons minced fresh ginger
- 1 tablespoon lemon juice
- 2 teaspoons curry powder
- ½ teaspoon black pepper
- ½ teaspoon garlic powder
- ¼ teaspoon salt
- 1 pound boneless, skinless chicken breast, cut into 1-inch cubes
- 1 pound shrimp

1. In a small bowl, stir together flour and 1 tablespoon water; set aside.
2. In a medium-size saucepan, whisk together coconut milk, vegetable broth, ginger, lemon juice, curry powder, black pepper, garlic powder and salt. Bring to a boil over medium-high heat and cook for 10 minutes until reduced.
3. Add chicken to saucepan and cook 2 minutes. Stir flour mixture and shrimp into pot and cook for 2 minutes or until shrimp is cooked through and liquid has thickened. Serve warm.

PER SERVING: 157 calories; 8 g fat (7 g sat.); 17 g protein; 3 g carbohydrate; 1 g fiber; 291 mg sodium; 79 mg cholesterol.

Althea Needham
TEST KITCHEN ASSOCIATE
"My friends love this rich combination of coconut and curry."

Julie
Miltenberger
SENIOR FOOD
EDITOR
"We adapted
this recipe from
our church's
cookbook."

broccoli-cheddar casserole

MAKES: 12 servings. **PREP:** 10 minutes.
BAKE: at 350° for 1 hour.

- 2 **bags (16 ounces each) frozen chopped broccoli, warmed (in microwave, then drained in colander)**
- 3 **large eggs, beaten**
- 1½ **cans (10¾ ounces each) reduced-fat, low sodium condensed cream of mushroom soup (such as Campbell's Healthy Request)**
- ⅔ **cup light mayonnaise**
- 1 **medium yellow onion, grated**
- 1½ **cups shredded sharp cheddar cheese**
- 1½ **cups square cheese crackers, crushed (such as Cheeze-Its)**

1. Heat oven to 350°. Spray a 12-cup casserole dish with nonstick cooking spray.
2. In a large mixing bowl, whisk eggs. Add soup, mayonnaise and onion, and whisk together. Fold in broccoli, cheese and ½ cup of the crushed crackers. Put into prepared casserole dish. Top with remaining 1 cup crushed crackers.
3. Bake at 350° for 1 hour, then open oven and check casserole—when shaken, it should be set except for the very center. Cook 5 minutes longer, if necessary. Let stand 10 minutes before serving.

PER SERVING: 231 calories; 15 g fat (5 g sat.);
9 g protein; 17 g carbohydrate; 3 g fiber;
745 mg sodium; 76 mg cholesterol.

cranberry salad

MAKES: 8 servings.
PREP: 10 minutes. **REFRIGERATE:** overnight.

- 1 **package (3 ounces) raspberry flavored gelatin (such as Jell-o)**
- 1 **can (16 ounces) whole berry cranberry sauce**
- 1 **Granny Smith apple, diced**
- 1 **large orange, peeled and sections cut into ½-inch pieces**
- ¾ **cup chopped walnuts**
- ⅛ **teaspoon cinnamon**
  Dash ground cloves

Cindy Heller
ASSOCIATE FOOD EDITOR
My mom's go-to
recipe for a sweet
autumn salad.

1. Prepare gelatin according to package directions in an 8 x 8 x 2-inch baking dish.
2. Stir in cranberries, apple, orange, walnuts, cinnamon and cloves into gelatin mixture.
3. Refrigerate overnight, or until firm.

PER SERVING: 220 calories; 7 g fat (0 g sat.);
4 g protein; 39 g carbohydrate; 3 g fiber;
63 mg sodium; 0 mg cholesterol.

Perfect Ending
Impress guests with this
twist on pumpkin pie.

pumpkin chiffon pie

MAKES: 12 servings. **PREP:** 15 minutes. **BAKE:** at 325° for 15 minutes. **COOK:** 12 minutes. **REFRIGERATE:** overnight.

Crust:
- 12 graham cracker boards
- 6 tablespoons unsalted butter, melted
- 2 tablespoons granulated sugar

Filling:
- 3 tablespoons apple juice
- 1 teaspoon vanilla extract
- 1 envelope unflavored gelatin
- 1 can (15 ounces) pumpkin puree (not pumpkin pie filling)
- 1 can (12 ounces) evaporated milk
- 1 cup packed light brown sugar
- 4 egg yolks
- 2 teaspoons pumpkin pie spice
- ¼ teaspoon salt
- 1 cup heavy cream
  Whipped cream (optional)

1. Crust: Heat oven to 325°. Finely crush graham crackers. Add butter and sugar and mix until all crumbs are moist. Press into bottom and up side of a 9-inch round springform pan.

2. Bake crust at 325° for 15 minutes or until lightly browned around edges. Place on wire rack and cool completely.

3. Prepare **Filling:** In a small bowl, stir together apple juice and vanilla. Sprinkle gelatin over top and let stand 5 minutes.

4. In a heavy bottomed medium-size saucepan, whisk together pumpkin puree, evaporated milk, brown sugar, egg yolks, pumpkin pie spice and salt until smooth. Cook over medium heat, whisking, for 9 minutes or until temperature registers 140° on an instant-read thermometer. Continue stirring over low heat for 3 minutes, maintaining 140°.

5. Microwave gelatin mixture for 10 seconds until melted. Whisk into pumpkin mixture and remove from heat.

6. Pour filling into a large bowl. Set into a larger bowl of ice water; cool for 12 minutes, stirring occasionally.

7. With electric mixer, whip cream on medium-high speed until stiff peaks form. Gently fold into cooled pumpkin mixture. Pour filling into cooled crust. Cover and refrigerate overnight.

8. When ready to serve, run a thin knife between pan and pie. Remove side of pan; slice. Garnish with whipped cream, if desired.

PER SLICE: 340 calories; 19 g fat (11 g sat.); 5 g protein; 39 g carbohydrate; 2 g fiber; 152 mg sodium; 119 mg cholesterol.

GRAND
Finale

Bake up a memorable
ending to your holiday meal.
Our 6 sensational cakes,
pies and tarts are desserts
everyone will applaud.

BY MICHAEL TYRRELL

PHOTOGRAPHY BY ALISON MIKSCH

mini chocolate cakes

MAKES: 12 servings. **PREP:** 25 minutes.
BAKE: at 350° for 25 minutes.

Cakes:

  2 cups all-purpose flour
  ⅔ cup cocoa powder
1½ teaspoon allspice
  1 teaspoon baking powder
  ¾ teaspoon baking soda
  ¼ teaspoon salt
  ¾ cup (1½ sticks) unsalted
      butter, softened
1½ cups light brown sugar
  3 eggs
  2 teaspoons vanilla
      extract
  1 cup sour cream
  4 ounces bittersweet
      chocolate, chopped

Ganache:

  1 cup heavy cream
  8 ounces bittersweet chocolate,
      chopped
      Assorted holiday decorations

1. Heat oven to 350°. Coat two jumbo-size muffin pans with nonstick cooking spray.
2. Prepare **Cakes:** Whisk together flour, cocoa, allspice, baking powder, baking soda and salt; set aside.
3. Beat butter 2 minutes. Add sugar; beat until fluffy. Add eggs, one at a time, beating well after each. Beat in vanilla. Beat in flour mixture in 3 additions, alternating with sour cream. Beat 2 minutes more. Fold in chopped chocolate. Fill prepared muffin cups half full.
4. Bake at 350° for 25 minutes or until tops spring back when touched. Cool cakes for 10 minutes in pan on rack. Turn cakes onto rack; cool completely.
5. Prepare **Ganache:** Bring cream to a boil in a small saucepan. Place chocolate in a medium-size bowl; pour hot cream over top. Stir until smooth.
6. Place a rack over a jelly-roll pan. Place cakes, flat-side down, on rack. Pour 2 to 3 tablespoons ganache over each cake, smoothing with spatula. Refrigerate 1 hour or until set and decorate, if desired. If using silver dragées (as pictured) remove before eating.

PER SERVING: 563 calories; 37 g fat (21 g sat.); 8 g protein; 61 g carbohydrate; 4 g fiber; 210 mg sodium; 119 mg cholesterol.

peanut butter-and-jelly linzer torte

MAKES: 30 servings. **PREP:** 25 minutes.
BAKE: at 400° for 15 minutes, at 350° for 35 minutes.

3¼ cups all-purpose flour
  ½ teaspoon salt
  1 cup (2 sticks) cold butter,
      cut into pieces
  ½ cup peanut butter
1½ cups sugar
  1 egg
  1 egg yolk
  1 jar (12 ounces) salted peanuts,
      finely ground
  2 jars (12 ounces each) seedless
      raspberry jam
  1 egg yolk beaten with 1 tablespoon
      water
  ⅓ cup coarsely chopped peanuts

1. Heat oven to 400°. Coat a 15½ x 10½ x 1-inch jelly roll pan with nonstick cooking spray.
2. Blend flour and salt. Cut in butter with pastry blender until mixture resembles coarse crumbs. Add peanut butter; quickly work into mixture. Stir in sugar, egg and egg yolk. Add peanuts; mix well. Divide dough in half; form into two discs.
3. Press half of the dough evenly into bottom and up sides of prepared pan. Bake at 400° for 15 minutes.
4. Roll remaining dough between two sheets of waxed paper to a ¼-inch thickness. Place on a baking sheet; freeze for 15 minutes.
5. Reduce oven temperature to 350°. Spread jam over baked dough. Remove top piece of waxed paper from dough; cut into 1-inch strips. Arrange in lattice pattern on top of jam. Press ends of strips to edge.
6. Brush egg wash over pastry. Sprinkle nuts around edge. Bake at 350° for 35 minutes. Cool on rack.

PER PIECE: 298 calories; 15 g fat (5 g sat.); 6 g protein; 39 g carbohydrate; 2 g fiber; 155 mg sodium; 37 mg cholesterol.

Food styling: Megan Schlow. Prop styling: Megan Hedgpeth.

banana cream fruit tart

MAKES: 12 servings. **PREP:** 20 minutes.
BAKE: at 425° for 17 minutes.

- 1 package (17.3 ounces) frozen puff pastry sheets, thawed
- 1 egg beaten with 1 tablespoon water
- 1 package (3.4 ounces) instant banana cream pudding
- 1¾ cups half and half
- 4 cups assorted sliced fruit, such as bananas, raspberries, kiwi, figs
- 2 tablespoons red currant jelly

1. Heat oven to 425°. Coat a large baking sheet with nonstick cooking spray.
2. Place one thawed pastry sheet on a lightly floured work surface. Cut a 1-inch strip from each long side. Brush pastry with egg wash and place strips over each long edge to form a border. Brush top of border with egg wash. Prick bottom of pastry with a fork (see photo below). Transfer to a baking sheet. Repeat with remaining pastry sheet.
3. Bake at 425° for 17 minutes. Transfer to wire rack to cool. Gently press down centers if puffed.
4. Prepare pudding following package directions using half and half instead of milk.
5. Spread half of the pudding over each cooled pastry. Arrange a row of each type of fruit between the two pudding-topped sheets of pastry.
6. Heat jelly until melted. Brush over fruit on both tarts. Refrigerate for at least 1 hour before serving.

PER SERVING: 315 calories; 16 g fat (6 g sat.); 5 g protein; 39 g carbohydrate; 3 g fiber; 336 mg sodium; 31 mg cholesterol.

pumpkin spice bundt

MAKES: 16 servings. **PREP:** 20 minutes. **BAKE:** at 350° for 55 minutes.

- 2¾ cups cake flour (not self-rising)
- 2 teaspoons pumpkin pie spice
- 1½ teaspoons baking powder
- ½ teaspoon baking soda
- ½ teaspoon salt
- 1 cup (2 sticks) unsalted butter, softened
- 1½ cups sugar
- 3 eggs
- 1 cup solid pack pumpkin puree
- 1 teaspoon vanilla extract
- 1 cup milk
- 1 cup sweetened dried cranberries, coarsely chopped

Glaze:
- 1½ cups confectioners' sugar
- 1 tablespoon light corn syrup
- 6 to 7 teaspoons lemon juice
  Lemon peel and pumpkin pie spice (optional)

1. Heat oven to 350°. Butter and flour a 12-cup bundt pan. Set aside.
2. In a large bowl, whisk together flour, pumpkin pie spice, baking powder, baking soda and salt. Set aside.
3. Beat butter until smooth. Add sugar; beat until fluffy. Beat in eggs, one at a time, beating well after each addition. Add pumpkin and vanilla. Beat until combined.
4. On low speed, beat flour mixture into butter mixture in three additions, alternating with milk. Beat 2 minutes on medium-high. Fold in cranberries. Spoon into prepared pan.
5. Bake at 350° for 55 minutes or until a toothpick inserted in the center of the cake comes out clean. Cool in pan on wire rack for 20 minutes. Run a knife around edge of the pan. Turn out; cool completely.
6. Prepare **Glaze:** In a small bowl mix together confectioners' sugar, corn syrup and lemon juice until smooth. Drizzle over top of cake and allow to drip down the sides. Garnish with lemon peel and pumpkin pie spice, if desired.

PER SLICE: 361 calories; 13 g fat (8 g sat.); 4 g protein; 58 g carbohydrate; 1 g fiber; 172 mg sodium; 72 mg cholesterol.

PERFECT PUFF CRUSTS Always prick puff pastry with a fork before baking. This allows steam to escape so the layers remain flat and compressed, creating a crisp and flaky crust.

chocolate-crunch cheesecake

MAKES: 16 servings. **PREP:** 25 minutes.
BAKE: at 350° for 90 minutes.
REFRIGERATE: overnight.

- 1 box (10 ounces) shortbread cookies (such as Lorna Doone), finely crushed
- 4 tablespoons butter, melted
- 3 packages (8 ounces each) reduced-fat cream cheese, softened
- 1 cup sugar
- 2 tablespoons cornstarch
- 4 eggs
- 1 cup sour cream
- 2 tablespoons coffee liqueur (such as Kahlúa)
- 1 teaspoon vanilla extract
- 1 large Nestlé Crunch candy bar (5 ounces), chopped
- 1 cup heavy cream
- 1 tablespoon granulated sugar
  Chopped Nestlé Crunch bar (optional)

1. Heat oven to 350°.
2. Mix together the crumbs and butter. Press over bottom and partially up side of a 9-inch springform pan (see photo). Refrigerate while making filling.
3. Beat cream cheese 1 minute. Add sugar and cornstarch; beat for 3 minutes. Beat in eggs, one at a time. Add sour cream, liqueur and vanilla; beat until smooth. Fold in chopped candy bar. Pour into crust.
4. Bake at 350° for 90 minutes until just set. Run a knife around edge of cake to separate from pan. Cool in pan on rack. Cover; refrigerate overnight.
5. Remove side of pan. Whip cream and sugar to stiff peaks. Spread onto cake; garnish with candy bar, if desired.

PER SERVING: 358 calories; 23 g fat (13 g sat.); 8 g protein; 28 g carbohydrate; 0 g fiber; 289 mg sodium; 114 mg cholesterol.

CRUMB CRUSTS SIMPLIFIED For a crust with an even thickness use the bottom of a glass or measuring cup to press crumbs down into the pie plate.

coconut croissant bread pudding

MAKES: 12 servings. **PREP:** 20 minutes. **STAND:** 30 minutes. **BAKE:** at 350° for 90 minutes.

- 8 egg yolks
- 4 whole eggs
- 2½ cups milk
- 1 can (13½ ounces) coconut milk
- 1 cup sugar
- 1 teaspoon coconut extract
- 1 teaspoon vanilla extract
- ½ teaspoon salt
- 5 large croissant pastries
- 1 cup semisweet chocolate chips
- 1 cup sweetened flake coconut
- 1 tablespoon confectioners' sugar, for dusting (optional)

1. Whisk together egg yolks, eggs, milk, coconut milk, sugar, coconut extract, vanilla extract and salt.
2. Coat a 2½-quart baking dish with nonstick cooking spray. Cut croissants in half horizontally. Place bottom halves, cut side up, in prepared pan. Sprinkle with chocolate chips and coconut. Cover with top halves of croissants, cut side down.

Pour egg mixture over top. Top with baking sheet weighed down with cans so croissants get pressed down and submerged in liquid. Let stand 30 minutes.
3. Heat oven to 350°. Remove baking sheet used as weight.
4. Cover pudding loosely with foil. Place pudding pan in a larger pan on oven rack. Pour hot water into larger pan to reach depth of one inch.
5. Bake at 350° for 1 hour. Remove foil; bake an additional 30 minutes or until temperature registers 160° on an instant-read thermometer. Carefully remove dish to wire rack; cool slightly. Dust with confectioners' sugar before serving, if desired.

PER SERVING: 398 calories; 27 g fat (15 g sat.); 10 g protein; 31 g carbohydrate; 2 g fiber; 466 mg sodium; 212 mg cholesterol.

amazing GRAINS

WHOLE GRAINS OFFER THE COMPLETE PACKAGE—THEY'RE EASY TO PREPARE, DELICIOUS AND NUTRITIOUS. TRY A HOMEMADE VERSION OF PORK FRIED RICE OR A NEW TWIST ON CHICKEN SALAD. YOUR FAMILY WILL NEVER GUESS THEY'RE GOOD FOR THEM. BY JULIE MILTENBERGER

Chicken and Barley Salad (Recipe page 274)

PHOTOGRAPHY BY YUNHEE KIM

steak skewers and couscous

MAKES: 4 servings. **PREP:** 10 minutes. **BROIL:** 8 minutes.

- 1 **pound sirloin steak, about 1½ inches thick, trimmed**
- 1 **sweet red pepper, cored and cut into 1-inch pieces**
- ¼ **teaspoon curry powder**
- ¼ **plus ⅛ teaspoon salt**
- ⅛ **teaspoon pumpkin pie spice**
- ⅛ **teaspoon black pepper**
- 1 **large chicken bouillon cube**
- 1 **box (7.6 ounces) whole-wheat couscous**
- 3 **scallions, chopped**
- ⅓ **cup apricots, chopped**
- ⅓ **cup pistachios, chopped**

1. Heat broiler. Cut steak into 1-inch cubes. Thread onto four metal skewers, dividing equally and alternating with pepper pieces. Stir together curry powder, ¼ teaspoon of the salt, the pumpkin pie spice and pepper. Sprinkle over skewers (all sides). Place on a broiler pan and set aside.

2. Bring 1½ cups water, bouillon and remaining ⅛ teaspoon salt to a boil in a saucepan. Stir in couscous, scallions and apricots. Turn off heat and cover. Let stand 5 minutes.

3. Broil skewers, 2 inches from heat, 8 minutes. Turn once. Fluff couscous and stir in pistachios. Spoon onto platter; top with skewers and serve.

PER SERVING: 430 calories; 10 g fat (2 g sat.); 33 g protein; 54 g carbohydrate; 9 g fiber; 268 mg sodium; 42 mg cholesterol.

turkey quinoa alfredo

MAKES: 4 servings. **PREP:** 5 minutes. **BAKE:** at 350° for 50 minutes.

1 **cup quinoa**
1 **cup jarred reduced-fat Alfredo sauce**
1 **box (10 ounces) frozen Brussels sprouts, thawed and halved**
1 **package turkey cutlets (about 1 pound)**
¼ **cup grated Parmesan cheese**
 Freshly ground black pepper
 Chopped fresh parsley

1. Heat oven to 350°. Coat a 2½-quart baking dish with nonstick cooking spray. Set aside.

2. In a large bowl, stir together quinoa, 1 cup water, Alfredo sauce and Brussels sprouts. Pour into prepared dish.

3. Top quinoa mixture with turkey cutlets, spacing them slightly apart so they do not touch. Sprinkle with grated Parmesan and pepper.

4. Cover with nonstick foil and bake at 350° for 35 minutes. Carefully remove foil and continue to bake an additional 15 minutes. Cool for 10 minutes; sprinkle with chopped parsley before serving.

PER SERVING: 442 calories; 15 g fat (6 g sat.); 40 g protein; 39 g carbohydrate; 6 g fiber; 698 mg sodium; 97 mg cholesterol.

pork fried rice

MAKES: 4 servings. **PREP:** 10 minutes. **COOK:** 6½ minutes.

- 1 **egg, lightly beaten**
- 1 **pound boneless, center-cut pork chops, fat trimmed and cut into ¼-inch strips**
- 2 **scallions, trimmed and sliced**
- 2 **packages (8.8 ounces each) fully cooked brown rice**
- 1 **cup frozen peas, thawed**
- ¼ **cup low-sodium soy sauce**
- 2 **teaspoons sesame oil**

1. Coat a 12-inch nonstick skillet with nonstick cooking spray and heat over medium heat. Add beaten egg and let cook, undisturbed, for 1 minute. Use a large silicone spatula to flip over egg and cook an additional 30 seconds, until cooked through. Transfer to a cutting board and cut into 2 x ½-inch strips.

2. Increase heat under skillet to medium-high and add pork. Cook 3 minutes, until no longer pink, then add scallions, brown rice and peas. Cover with a sheet of foil and cook an additional 2 minutes. Stir in egg, soy sauce and sesame oil and heat through. Serve warm.

PER SERVING: 442 calories; 11 g fat (2 g sat.); 33 g protein; 42 g carbohydrate; 4 g fiber; 493 mg sodium; 123 mg cholesterol.

chicken and barley salad

MAKES: 4 servings. **PREP:** 5 minutes. **COOK:** 10 minutes.

- 1 **cup quick-cooking barley**
- 2 **cups broccoli florets**
- ½ **cup sweetened dried cranberries**
- 1 **package fully cooked grilled chicken strips (such as Perdue)**
- ½ **cup walnuts, chopped**
- ⅛ **teaspoon salt**
- ¾ **cup raspberry vinaigrette dressing (such as Wish-Bone Bountifuls)**

1. Bring 3 cups water to boiling in a medium-size saucepan.

2. Stir in barley, reduce heat to medium-high and cook 6 minutes. Add broccoli, and continue to cook for 3 minutes. Stir in cranberries, cook 1 minute, then drain.

3. Transfer barley mixture to a serving bowl, and stir in chicken pieces, walnuts and salt. Pour vinaigrette over salad and gently stir to combine. Serve slightly warm or at room temperature.

PER SERVING: 423 calories; 13 g fat (1 g sat.); 23 g protein; 57 g carbohydrate; 7 g fiber; 907 mg sodium; 40 mg cholesterol.

bulgur-stuffed squash

MAKES: 6 servings. **PREP:** 5 minutes. **COOK:** 5 minutes. **BAKE:** at 400° for 45 minutes.

- 3 **small acorn squash, halved and seeded**
- ¾ **cup bulgur wheat**
- 2 **hot Italian sausages, casings removed**
- ½ **teaspoon garlic powder**
- 1 **small sweet red pepper, seeded and diced**
- 2 **tablespoons chili sauce**
- ¼ **teaspoon salt**
- 2 **tablespoons maple syrup**

1. Heat oven to 400°. Place squash halves, cut-side down, on a 15 x 10 x 1-inch baking pan. Add 2 cups water, and transfer to oven. Bake at 400° for 35 minutes.

2. Meanwhile, put bulgur in a bowl. Pour ¾ cup boiling water over bulgur; cover with plastic wrap. Let stand 30 minutes.

3. Once bulgur is softened, heat a nonstick skillet over medium-high heat. Add sausage; cook 2 minutes. Stir in garlic powder and red pepper; cook 3 minutes. Remove from heat. Stir in bulgur, chili sauce and ⅛ teaspoon of the salt. Remove squash from oven; pour off water. Flip over squash; brush with maple syrup. Season with remaining ⅛ teaspoon salt. Spoon filling into squash; return to oven. Bake 10 minutes.

PER SERVING: 274 calories; 7 g fat (2 g sat.); 9 g protein; 50 g carbohydrate; 12 g fiber; 455 mg sodium; 13 mg cholesterol.

polenta with cauliflower

MAKES: 6 servings. PREP: 5 minutes. COOK: 5 minutes. BAKE: at 375° for 50 minutes.

- 1⅓ **cups instant polenta**
- ¼ **cup grated Parmesan cheese**
- ½ **teaspoon salt**
- ¼ **teaspoon black pepper**
- 1 **2-pound head cauliflower**
- 1 **jar (28 ounces) marinara sauce**
- ¼ **cup dry bread crumbs**
- 2 **cups shredded mozzarella cheese**

1. Heat oven to 375°. Coat a 13 x 9 x 2-inch baking dish with nonstick cooking spray. Set aside.

2. Bring 2 cups water to a boil in a medium-size saucepan. In small bowl, combine polenta and 2 cups cool water. Stir in 2 tablespoons of the Parmesan, the salt and pepper. Stir polenta into boiling water. Reduce heat to medium-high; cook 5 minutes, stirring. Spread in prepared dish.

3. Cut cauliflower into equal-size florets. Spread half over polenta. Top with 1½ cups marinara sauce. Sprinkle with half

the bread crumbs and half of the mozzarella. Repeat layering, ending with mozzarella. Cover with foil. Bake at 375° for 40 minutes. Uncover, top with remaining 2 tablespoons Parmesan and bake 10 more minutes. Let rest 15 minutes.

PER SERVING: 348 calories; 8 g fat (4 g sat.); 17 g protein; 52 g carbohydrate; 7 g fiber; 945 mg sodium; 27 mg cholesterol.

cooking grains

Use these guidelines to prepare the grain varieties in these recipes. These grains also make great side dishes or stand-ins for pasta or white rice in your favorite recipes.

barley
Bring 1¾ cups broth or water to a boil. Add 1 cup barley; reduce heat to low. Simmer, covered, for 10-12 minutes. Yields: 2 cups

brown rice
Bring 2 cups water or broth to a boil and add 1 cup of rice. Reduce heat and cover. Cook for 40 to 50 minutes. Let stand 5 minutes; fluff with a fork. Yields: 3 cups

quinoa
Rinse in cold water before cooking. Bring 1 cup quinoa and 2 cups broth or water to a boil. Reduce heat and simmer 15-20 minutes or until liquid is absorbed. Yields: 3 cups

bulgur
Add 2½ cups boiling water to 1 cup bulgur. Reduce heat to low, cover and simmer for 10-15 minutes or until liquid is absorbed. Yields: 2½ cups

whole-wheat couscous
Bring 1½ cups broth or water to boiling; stir in 1 cup couscous. Cover and let stand for 5 minutes. Fluff with a fork. Yields: 3 cups

polenta
Bring 4 cups water to a boil. Stir while adding 1⅓ cups polenta in a steady stream, continuing to stir to prevent lumps. Add more water as needed. Cook for 5 minutes or more. Yields: 4 cups

grain facts

BROWN RICE
• rice that is stripped of its inedible outer husk but retains its vitamin-rich bran layer • has a nutty flavor and a chewy texture • takes longer to cook than white rice but is available parboiled or precooked

BULGUR
• made from wheat kernels that have been steamed, dried and crushed • has a tender, chewy texture • versatile • cooks quickly

WHOLE-WHEAT COUSCOUS
• made of granular semolina flour • staple of North African cuisine • cooks in 5 minutes • can be made to be sweet or savory as it has a mild flavor

QUINOA
• more protein per serving than any other grain • considered "complete" because it contains all eight essential amino acids • can be easily added to soups, salads and baked goods

BARLEY
• chewy, mild taste • protein-rich and contains a type of fiber called beta-glucan, which helps to lower cholesterol

POLENTA
• made from ground yellow or white cornmeal • traditionally a slow-cooked grain • high starch content makes it smooth and creamy when cooked

Ready set

Celebrate!

Let us take the stress out of party planning. Our festive menu is deliciously easy, fast and hassle-free—a guaranteed crowd-pleaser.

Drinks

holiday sunrise

MAKES: 2 cocktails. **PREP:** 5 minutes.

- 3 ounces orange-flavored vodka
- 4 ounces cranberry juice blend
- 1 ounce grenadine liqueur or syrup
- 1 ounce orange juice
- 2 teaspoons freshly squeezed lemon or lime juice

1. In a medium-size pitcher, blend together vodka, cranberry juice, grenadine, orange juice and lemon juice.
2. Add about 1 cup ice and stir to chill. Strain into two 8-ounce martini glasses. Garnish with lemon or lime peel and serve immediately. This recipe can easily be doubled or tripled.

PER SERVING: 194 calories; 0 g fat; 0 g protein; 26 g carbohydrate; 0 g fiber; 11 mg sodium; 0 mg cholesterol.

caramel apple cocktail

MAKES: 8 servings. **PREP:** 5 minutes.

- 1 tablespoon cinnamon sugar
- 1 wedge lemon
- 1½ cups apple cider
- 6 tablespoons butterscotch schnapps or apple brandy (such as Calvados)
- 1 bottle (750 ml) sparkling wine, chilled
- 8 stemless maraschino cherries

1. Spread cinnamon sugar on a small plate or saucer. Run the lemon wedge along the rim of eight champagne glasses, then dip rims into cinnamon sugar. Shake off excess.
2. Combine apple cider and schnapps (or brandy) in a measuring cup. Divide evenly among prepared glasses.
3. Pour sparkling wine evenly among glasses. Garnish each with a cherry.

PER SERVING: 181 calories; 0 g fat; 0 g protein; 15 g carbohydrate; 0 g fiber; 13 mg sodium; 0 mg cholesterol.

Appetizers

Photo: Mark Ferri. Photo, above: Ann Stratton.

skewer savvy
To prevent burning, soak toothpicks in water for 15 minutes before broiling or grilling.

bacon-wrapped shrimp

MAKES: 24 pieces. **PREP:** 20 minutes. **MARINATE:** 15 minutes. **MICROWAVE:** 1 minute. **BROIL:** 5 minutes.

24 medium-size shrimp (about 1 pound), shelled and deveined
⅓ cup prepared balsamic vinaigrette
12 slices bacon
24 pickled jalapeño slices
24 wood toothpicks
½ cup mayonnaise
1 tablespoon chili sauce
1 tablespoon sweet pickle relish
1 tablespoon minced sweet red pepper

1. Place shrimp and vinaigrette into a large resealable plastic bag; refrigerate for 15 minutes.
2. Microwave bacon for 1 minute on HIGH. Cut slices in half crosswise (for a total of 24 pieces) and let cool.
3. Heat broiler. Coat a large broiler pan with nonstick cooking spray.
4. Remove shrimp from marinade, reserving marinade. Put one piece of bacon on work surface. Place a shrimp at one end; tuck a jalapeño slice into curl of shrimp. Roll bacon up tightly to enclose filling, securing with toothpick. Repeat using all bacon, shrimp and jalapeños.
5. Stir together mayonnaise, chili sauce, pickle relish, red pepper and 1 tablespoon water in small bowl.
6. Place shrimp rolls on prepared pan. Brush with reserved marinade. Broil 3 minutes. Turn, brush with marinade and broil 2 minutes more. Serve with sauce for dipping.

PER PIECE: 120 calories; 12 g fat (3 g sat.); 2 g protein; 1 g carbohydrate; 0 g fiber; 182 mg sodium; 20 mg cholesterol.

spinach-soufflé-stuffed mushrooms

MAKES: about 2½ dozen stuffed mushrooms. **PREP:** 5 minutes. **BAKE:** at 375° for 25 minutes.

1 package (10 ounces) frozen chopped spinach, thawed and squeezed dry
½ pound Havarti cheese, cut into ½-inch cubes
⅓ cup grated Parmesan cheese
3 eggs
2 tablespoons milk
1 teaspoon garlic powder
1 teaspoon dried oregano
½ teaspoon black pepper
½ teaspoon ground nutmeg

2 pounds medium-size white mushrooms (about 30), stems removed and caps cleaned
½ teaspoon salt

1. Heat oven to 375°. Put spinach, Havarti, Parmesan, eggs, milk, garlic powder, oregano, pepper and nutmeg in processor. Pulse until cheese is finely chopped.
2. Place mushroom caps on 11 x 15 x ½-inch baking pan. Coat mushrooms with cooking spray; sprinkle with salt. Fill each cap with 1 level tablespoon spinach mixture. (Filling can be made one day ahead; refrigerate, tightly covered.)
3. Bake at 375° for 25 minutes or until the mushrooms are tender and the filling is set.

PER MUSHROOM: 51 calories; 3 g fat (2 g sat.); 4 g protein; 2 g carbohydrate; 0 g fiber; 115 mg sodium; 29 mg cholesterol.

On the Side

classic biscuits

MAKES: 8 biscuits. **PREP:** 10 minutes.
BAKE: at 400° for 14 minutes.

- 2 cups all-purpose flour
- 1 tablespoon baking powder
- 2 teaspoons sugar
- ¾ teaspoon salt
- ⅓ cup solid vegetable shortening
- ¾ cup milk
- 1 tablespoon melted butter

1. Heat oven to 400°. In a large bowl, whisk together flour, baking powder, sugar and salt.

2. Add shortening with a pastry blender or potato masher, cutting until shortening is in very small pieces. Stir in milk.

3. Gather dough together, kneading slightly if dry. Pat out to ½-inch thickness, and cut out as many biscuits as possible with a 2¾-inch round biscuit cutter. Gently gather scraps together and repeat patting and cutting, for a total of 8 biscuits. Transfer to an ungreased baking sheet. Brush biscuits with butter.

4. Bake biscuits at 400° for 14 minutes, until risen and golden on top. Cool slightly before serving.

PER SERVING: 219 calories; 11 g fat (4 g sat.); 4 g protein; 26 g carbohydrate; 1 g fiber; 380 mg sodium; 7 mg cholesterol.

whipped-potato casserole

MAKES: 12 servings. **PREP:** 15 minutes. **COOK:** 20 minutes.
BAKE: at 350° for 45 minutes. **STAND:** 15 minutes.

- 5 pounds all-purpose potatoes, peeled and quartered
- ½ cup (1 stick) unsalted butter, softened
- 1¼ cups half-and-half
- 1 tub (8 ounces) whipped cream cheese with chives (or 1 tub plain mixed with 2 tablespoons chopped fresh chives)
- 1 teaspoon garlic salt
- ¼ teaspoon ground nutmeg
- 1 cup sliced almonds
  Fresh chives (optional)

1. Heat oven to 350°. Coat 13 x 9 x 2-inch glass baking dish with nonstick cooking spray.

2. Place potatoes in a large pot with enough water to cover. Lightly salt and bring to a boil. Lower to simmering; cook for 15 to 20 minutes or until fork-tender. Drain.

3. In large bowl, mash potatoes with hand mixer. Add butter, half-and-half, cream cheese, garlic salt and nutmeg. With mixer, beat potatoes on medium-high speed until very smooth. Spoon into prepared dish.

4. Bake at 350°, uncovered, for 30 minutes. Sprinkle sliced almonds over casserole; bake an additional 15 minutes, uncovered, until lightly browned.

5. Let stand 15 minutes before serving. Garnish with chopped chives, if desired.

To make ahead: Proceed through Step 3 and allow to cool. Cover with plastic wrap and refrigerate for up to two days. When ready to serve, unwrap and allow to stand at room temperature for at least 30 minutes. Begin with step 4 and bake until internal temperature registers 140° on an instant-read thermometer.

PER SERVING: 364 calories; 21 g fat (11 g sat.); 8 g protein; 37 g carbohydrate; 4 g fiber; 232 mg sodium; 54 mg cholesterol.

Main Event

orange-glazed spiral ham

MAKES: 24 servings. **PREP** 10 minutes.
HEAT: at 375° for 1 hour and 30 minutes, covered, and 30 minutes, uncovered. **STAND:** 10 minutes.

1 fully cooked spiral-cut ham
  (about 8 pounds)
1 cup packed dark-brown sugar
¼ cup orange juice
1 cup orange marmalade (12-ounce jar)
¼ cup Dijon mustard
  Sliced oranges (optional)

1. Heat oven to 375°.
2. Place ham, cut-side down, on a rack in large roasting pan. Pour 2 cups of water into roasting pan. Cover ham with aluminum foil.
3. Heat at 375° for 1 hour 30 minutes.

4. While ham is heating, whisk together brown sugar, orange juice, marmalade and mustard. Set aside.
5. Remove foil and brush ham liberally with about ¾ cup of the orange glaze. Heat uncovered for 30 minutes or until ham is nicely colored and internal temperature registers 140° on an instant-read thermometer.
6. Let ham stand 10 minutes before slicing. To slice, cut around center bone with a knife, freeing as many slices as you wish. Cut along the natural seams of the ham to remove slices separated from the bone. Serve with remaining glaze on the side. Garnish with orange slices, if desired.

PER SERVING: 186 calories; 4 g fat (1 g sat.); 18 g protein; 19 g carbohydrate; 0 g fiber; 1,384 mg sodium; 52 mg cholesterol.

slow-cooker solutions
EASY NEW WAYS TO MAKE ITALIAN FAVORITES.

Food styling: Sara Neumeier. Prop styling: Lynda White.

chicken cacciatore

MAKES: 6 servings. **PREP:** 15 minutes. **COOK:** 18 minutes. **SLOW-COOK:** 3½ hours on HIGH or 5 hours on LOW.

1 package chicken pieces (about 4½ pounds), skin removed, trimmed of excess fat
¼ cup flour
1 tablespoon olive oil
2 cups thinly sliced mushrooms
1 large green pepper, seeded and chopped
1 large onion, chopped
1 carrot, peeled and chopped
2 cups canned diced tomatoes, drained
½ cup white wine

1 teaspoon Italian seasoning
2 tablespoons chopped fresh basil
½ teaspoon black pepper
¼ teaspoon salt

1. Pat chicken dry with paper towels. Place flour on a plate. Coat chicken in flour, shaking off excess. Heat oil in a large nonstick skillet over medium-high heat. Cook chicken for 12 minutes or until browned, turning halfway.
2. Remove chicken from skillet and place in slow cooker bowl. Place

mushrooms in skillet; cook over medium-high heat for 6 minutes.
3. Place mushrooms in slow cooker, and add green pepper, onion, carrot, tomatoes, wine and Italian seasoning. Cook on HIGH for 3½ hours or LOW for 5 hours. Stir in basil, pepper and salt and serve immediately.

PER SERVING: 392 calories; 10 g fat (2 g sat.); 55 g protein; 13 g carbohydrate; 2 g fiber; 493 mg sodium; 172 mg cholesterol.

PHOTOGRAPHY BY ALEXANDRA GRABLEWSKI

italian wedding soup

MAKES: 8 servings. **PREP:** 15 minutes.
SLOW-COOK: 6 hours on LOW.

- 1 egg, lightly beaten
- ¾ pound lean ground beef
- ½ cup finely chopped onion
- 3 tablespoons plain bread crumbs
- 3 tablespoons grated Parmesan cheese
- 2 tablespoons chopped fresh parsley
- ¾ teaspoon salt
- ½ teaspoon black pepper
- 8 cups low-sodium chicken broth
- 3 large carrots, chopped
- 1 small head escarole (8 ounces), washed, trimmed and cut into ½-inch strips
- 1½ teaspoons dried oregano
- 1¼ cups acini di pepe pasta (such as Ronzoni)

1. In a large bowl, stir together egg, beef, onion, bread crumbs, 1 tablespoon Parmesan, 1 tablespoon parsley and ¼ teaspoon each of the salt and pepper. Form into 1-inch meatballs (about 45) and place on baking sheet; refrigerate while preparing soup.
2. Combine broth, carrots, escarole and oregano in slow cooker. Gently add meatballs. Cover and cook on LOW for 6 hours. Stir in pasta for last 20 minutes of cook time. Stir in remaining ½ teaspoon salt and ¼ teaspoon black pepper. Sprinkle each serving with remaining parsley and Parmesan cheese and serve.

PER SERVING: 175 calories; 3 g fat (1 g sat.); 12 g protein; 25 g carbohydrate; 3 g fiber; 681 mg sodium; 41 mg cholesterol.

eggplant caponata

MAKES: 20 servings. **PREP:** 15 minutes. **SLOW-COOK:** 4 hours on HIGH or 6 hours on LOW.

- 2 plum tomatoes, seeded and chopped
- 1 small eggplant (about 12 ounces), cut into ½-inch pieces
- 1 medium-size zucchini, cut into ½-inch pieces
- 1 celery rib, chopped
- 1 small onion, chopped
- ¾ cup tomato puree
- 3 tablespoons red wine vinegar
- 1 tablespoon sugar
- 2 tablespoons chopped fresh parsley
- 1½ teaspoons dried basil
- ⅓ cup chopped green olives
- 1 tablespoon capers, rinsed and drained
- 1 large loaf Italian bread, cut into ½-inch slices (about 18-20) and lightly toasted

1. Stir together tomatoes, eggplant, zucchini, celery, onion, tomato puree, vinegar, sugar, parsley and basil in a slow cooker. Cover and cook on HIGH for 4 hours or LOW for 6 hours.
2. Stir in olives and capers. Serve warm, at room temperature, or chill overnight. Spoon about ¼ cup onto each toasted bread slice.

PER SLICE: 46 calories; 1 g fat (0 g sat.); 2 g protein; 9 g carbohydrate; 1 g fiber; 151 mg sodium; 0 mg cholesterol.

Slow-cookers lend themselves well to many old-world Italian dishes: Long cooking times at low temperatures coax amazing flavors from simple ingredients.

cooking school

EVER MADE MUFFINS THAT TURNED OUT DRY, DENSE, OR BLAND? TRY OUR SIMPLE RECIPE, ALONG WITH STEP-BY-STEP INSTRUCTIONS, FOR MOIST AND DELICIOUS CARROT-RAISIN BRAN MUFFINS. **BY JULIE MILTENBERGER**

carrot-raisin bran muffins

MAKES: 12 muffins. **PREP:** 10 minutes. **BAKE:** at 375° for 18 minutes.

- 1¼ cups unprocessed wheat bran or oat bran cereal
- ¾ cup whole-wheat flour
- ¾ cup all-purpose flour
- 1½ teaspoons baking powder
- 1½ teaspoons baking soda
- ½ teaspoon salt
- ½ teaspoon cinnamon
- ⅔ cup skim milk
- 2 large eggs
- ½ cup packed light-brown sugar
- ⅓ cup vegetable oil
- ¾ cup finely grated carrots (about 2 medium-size carrots)
- ¾ cup raisins

1. Heat oven to 375°. Coat 12 indents of standard-size muffin tin(s) with nonstick cooking spray. Set aside.

2. In a large bowl, whisk together bran cereal, both types of flour, the baking powder, baking soda, salt and cinnamon. Make a well in the center of the mixture.

3. In a small bowl, whisk together the milk, eggs, sugar and oil. Stir in the grated carrots and raisins. Pour into well of dry ingredients and fold together until all ingredients are moistened. Divide batter among prepared muffin indentations, a scant ⅓ cup in each. Let rest 5 minutes at room temperature.

4. Bake muffins at 375° for 16 to 18 minutes or until crowned and toothpick comes out clean when inserted in center of muffin. Cool on a wire rack before serving.

Variations: Substitute golden raisins for the regular raisins and stir in ¼ cup chopped walnuts. Or soak sweetened dried cranberries in boiling water for 5 minutes and use in place of raisins. Stir a little dried ginger into batter before baking.

PER MUFFIN: 204 calories; 7 g fat (1 g sat.); 5 g protein; 33 g carbohydrate; 4 g fiber; 332 mg sodium; 36 mg cholesterol.

Mix together the dry ingredients, then make a well in the center.

Pour egg mixture into well in dry ingredients, then fold together.

Spoon batter into prepared pans; let rest at least 5 minutes before baking.

december

Gingerbread Family
(Recipe page 301)

WHEN WINTER WEATHER KEEPS YOU
INDOORS, HEAD INTO THE KITCHEN.
WARMING DINNERS AND HOME-BAKED
CHRISTMAS COOKIES ARE PERFECT WAYS
TO SPREAD HOLIDAY CHEER.

Citrus Snowflakes
page 295

Asian Beef and Noodles
page 303

**Chocolate Swirl
Cookie Mix**
page 311

Very Merry Cookies

Make the holidays extra sweet with recipes that give a twist to traditional favorites—and ensure a creative and especially delicious season.

By Julie Miltenberger

This festive display of cookies is sure to delight your holiday guests. (Recipes opposite page)

PHOTOGRAPHY BY ANN STRATTON

december

holiday trees

MAKES: 2½ dozen.
PREP: 20 minutes.
REFRIGERATE: 2 hours.
BAKE: at 325° for 15 minutes.

- 2 cups all-purpose flour
- ½ teaspoon salt
- ¾ cup (1½ sticks) unsalted butter, softened
- ¾ cup granulated sugar
- 2 large egg yolks
- 1 egg white
- 1 teaspoon vanilla extract
- 6 drops green food coloring
- 6 ounces white chocolate, melted with 1 teaspoon canola oil

1. Blend flour and salt in a small bowl. In a large bowl, beat butter and sugar. Beat in yolks, vanilla and food coloring. Stir in flour mixture until dough comes together. Divide in half; flatten into disks. Wrap in plastic and refrigerate 2 hours.

2. Heat oven to 325°. Roll dough ¼ inch thick on floured surface. Cut out trees; reroll scraps. Transfer to baking sheets.

3. Bake at 325° for 10 minutes. Remove cookies from oven and brush with egg white. Return to oven; bake 4 to 5 minutes more, until shiny but not brown. Transfer cookies to rack to cool. Dip edges in white chocolate. Let dry on waxed paper.

PER COOKIE: 128 calories; 7 g fat (4 g sat.); 2 g protein; 15 g carbohydrate; 0 g fiber; 48 mg sodium; 27 mg cholesterol.

Food styling: Sara Neumeier. Prop styling: Denise Canter.

coconut snowballs

MAKES: 2 dozen. **PREP:** 10 minutes. **BAKE:** at 350° for 15 minutes.

- 1 cup sweetened flake coconut
- 1 cup all-purpose flour
- 1¼ cups confectioners' sugar
  Pinch salt
- 6 tablespoons (¾ stick) unsalted butter, softened
- 1 teaspoon vanilla extract
- 4 teaspoons milk

1. Grind ½ cup of the coconut in food processor. Chop remaining coconut and set aside. Add flour, ¼ cup of the confectioners' sugar and the salt. Pulse to blend. Add butter and vanilla; pulse until dough comes together.

2. Heat oven to 350°. Roll dough into 1-inch balls. Place dough balls 1 inch apart on an ungreased baking sheet.

3. Bake cookies until firm but tender, about 15 minutes. Remove to rack; let cool completely.

4. In small bowl, stir together remaining 1 cup confectioners' sugar and enough milk until thick but smooth. Dip cookies in glaze (about ½ teaspoon for each), letting glaze drip down sides. Dip in chopped coconut and set aside to dry.

PER COOKIE: 89 calories; 4 g fat (3 g sat.); 1 g protein; 12 g carbohydrate; 0 g fiber; 11 mg sodium; 8 mg cholesterol.

mint meringues

MAKES: 4½ dozen. **PREP:** 15 minutes. **BAKE:** at 200° for 2 hours.

- 4 large egg whites, at room temperature
- ½ teaspoon cream of tartar
- ¾ cup sugar
  Red and green food coloring
- ¼ teaspoon mint extract or imitation peppermint extract
- 2 candy canes, finely crushed

1. Heat oven to 200°. Line 2 large baking sheets with nonstick foil. In a bowl, combine egg whites and cream of tartar. Beat on high speed with whisk attachment until whites become foamy. Gradually add sugar, until thick, then add mint extract.

2. Divide batter in half; with red food coloring, tint one half pink. With green food coloring, tint second half green. Transfer to two large resealable bags (or pastry bags fitted with large round tips). Snip a ½-inch corner off bags. Squeeze meringue batter onto foil-lined sheets, about 26 per sheet. Sprinkle each with crushed candy cane pieces.

3. Bake meringues at 200° for 2 hours, then turn oven off and let cookies sit in oven for 30 minutes. Remove cookies from pans and transfer to a wire rack. Cool completely.

PER COOKIE: 14 calories; 0 g fat (0 g sat.); 0 g protein; 3 g carbohydrate; 0 g fiber; 4 mg sodium; 0 mg cholesterol.

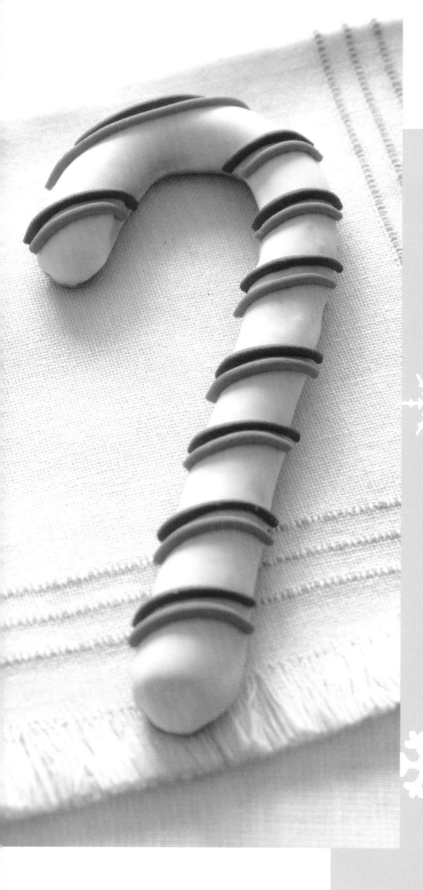

candy canes

MAKES: 2½ dozen. **PREP:** 10 minutes.
BAKE: at 350° for 12 minutes.
REFRIGERATE: 1 hour. **DECORATE:** 1½ hours.

- 1⅔ cups all-purpose flour
  Pinch salt
- 1 stick (½ cup) butter, softened
- ½ cup sugar
- 1 egg yolk
- 1 teaspoon vanilla extract
  Royal Icing (recipe follows)
  Red and green food coloring

1. Heat oven to 350°. In small bowl, combine flour and salt. In large bowl, beat butter, sugar and egg yolk until smooth. Beat in vanilla; stir in flour mixture. Flatten dough into a disk; refrigerate 1 hour.
2. Roll 2 teaspoons dough into 6-inch rope. Transfer to nonstick baking sheet; curve into candy cane shape. Repeat with remaining dough. Bake at 350° for 12 minutes. Cool on pan 1 minute, then carefully transfer to rack.
3. Prepare Royal Icing. Remove ½ cup thicker icing to a small bowl and tint red; remove ½ cup thicker icing to a small bowl and tint green. Use a small clean brush to "paint" thinned white icing over cookies; let dry. Transfer colored icings to two pastry bags fitted with small round tips. Pipe lines on cookies; let dry.

PER COOKIE: 97 calories; 3 g fat (2 g sat.); 1 g protein; 16 g carbohydrate; 0 g fiber; 5 mg sodium; 15 mg cholesterol.

royal icing

MAKES: 3 cups. **PREP:** 5 minutes.

- 1 box (16 ounces) confectioners' sugar
- 3 tablespoons powdered egg whites
- 6 tablespoons orange juice or water

1. Beat sugar, powdered egg whites and juice or water for 5 minutes. Divide in half; stir 2 tablespoons water into one half. Use thinned icing for coating and thicker icing for piping.

PER SERVING: 37 calories; 0 g fat; 1 g protein; 9 g carbohydrate; 0 g fiber; 0 mg sodium; 0 mg cholesterol.

cherry-pistachio biscotti

MAKES: about 3 dozen. **PREP:** 15 minutes.
REFRIGERATE: 2 hours. **BAKE:** at 375° for
23 minutes and at 325° for 20 minutes.

- 2¼ cups all-purpose flour
- 1½ teaspoons baking powder
  Pinch salt
- ½ cup (1 stick) unsalted butter, softened
- ½ cup light-brown sugar
- 2 eggs
- 1 teaspoon vanilla extract
- ½ cup dried cherries, chopped
- ½ cup pistachios, chopped
- 3 ounces milk chocolate, melted

1. Heat oven to 375°. Mix flour,
baking powder and salt in a bowl. Beat
butter and sugar in second bowl until
creamy. Beat in eggs, one at a time.
Add vanilla. Stir in flour mixture.
Add cherries and nuts. Gather dough
into a ball; divide in half.
2. With floured hands, roll dough into
two 12-inch logs. Place on a large baking
sheet. Flatten logs slightly so each is 2 to
3 inches wide.
3. Bake at 375° for 23 minutes or until
lightly browned. Remove to rack to cool.
4. Lower oven temperature to 325°.
Cut loaves into ¾-inch-thick slices (about
18 per log). Place, cut side down, on
sheet. Bake 10 minutes. Turn over; bake
an additional 10 minutes. Cool on rack.
Dip one end in melted chocolate; let dry
on waxed paper.

PER COOKIE: 95 calories; 4 g fat (2 g sat.);
2 g protein; 13 g carbohydrate; 1 g fiber;
24 mg sodium; 19 mg cholesterol.

almond meltaways

MAKES: 3 dozen crescents. **PREP:** 10 minutes. **REFRIGERATE:** 2 hours.
BAKE: at 325° for 18 minutes.

- ½ cup (1 stick) unsalted butter, softened
- 1 cup confectioners' sugar
- ½ teaspoon almond extract
- 1 cup all-purpose flour
- ½ cup finely ground blanched
  slivered almonds

1. Beat together butter and ½ cup of the
confectioners' sugar in bowl until smooth
and creamy. Beat in almond extract. On
low speed, beat in flour and nuts. Wrap
dough in plastic wrap; refrigerate until
firm, 2 hours.
2. Heat oven to 325°. Pinch off pieces of
dough in heaping teaspoonfuls. Roll into
logs. Taper ends; bend into crescents.
Place on ungreased baking sheets.
3. Bake in 325° oven for 16 to 18 minutes
until lightly browned.
4. Remove cookies to wire rack. While
warm, dust with a generous layer of
about ½ cup confectioners' sugar. Cool
completely. Sprinkle again with any
remaining confectioners' sugar.

PER COOKIE: 61 calories; 4 g fat (2 g sat.);
1 g protein; 6 g carbohydrate; 0 g fiber;
1 mg sodium; 7 mg cholesterol.

Tangy lemon-flavored cookies filled with raspberry jam and decadent chocolate thumbprint cookies are sure to be stars at any holiday party. (Recipes opposite page)

lemon-berry sandwiches

MAKES: 2½ dozen. **PREP:** 15 minutes. **REFRIGERATE:** 1 hour. **BAKE:** at 350° for 13 minutes.

- 2¼ cups all-purpose flour
- ¼ teaspoon baking powder
- ¼ teaspoon salt
- ½ cup (1 stick) unsalted butter, softened
- ¾ cup sugar
- 1 large egg
- 1 tablespoon lemon juice
- ½ teaspoon grated lemon zest
- ½ cup seedless raspberry jam
- 2 tablespoons confectioners' sugar, for dusting

1. Mix flour, baking powder and salt. Beat butter, sugar, egg, lemon juice and zest in large bowl. Beat in flour mixture. Divide in half and flatten. Wrap in plastic; refrigerate 1 hour.

2. Heat oven to 350°. Line baking sheet with nonstick foil. Roll half of dough on floured surface ⅛ inch thick. Cut out 24 cookies with 2¼-inch round cutter. Repeat with remaining dough to make 48 cookies. Transfer to baking sheets. Cut a 1-inch hole in center of 24 of the cookies. Remove centers and reroll for a total of 30 rounds and 30 cutouts. Bake at 350° for 13 minutes, until brown around edges. Cool on rack.

3. Spread ½ teaspoon jam on each cookie round. Dust cutouts with confectioners' sugar. Place on jam-covered cookies.

PER COOKIE: 98 calories; 3 g fat (2 g sat.); 1 g protein; 16 g carbohydrate; 0 g fiber; 26 mg sodium; 15 mg cholesterol.

thumbprints

MAKES: 3 dozen. **PREP:** 15 minutes. **REFRIGERATE:** 2 hours. **BAKE:** at 350° for 14 minutes.

- 2 cups all-purpose flour
- ¼ cup cocoa powder
- ¼ teaspoon salt
- 1 cup granulated sugar
- ½ cup (1 stick) butter, softened
- 1 large egg
- 1½ cups confectioners' sugar
- 4 ounces cream cheese, softened
- 4 squares (1 ounce each) semisweet chocolate, melted

1. Heat oven to 350°. In bowl, mix flour, cocoa and salt.

2. In a large bowl, beat sugar, butter and egg until creamy. Stir in flour mixture. Shape 2 teaspoons dough into a ball and repeat. Place balls 1 inch apart on ungreased baking sheets. Make indentation in center of each with thumb.

3. Bake at 350° for 14 minutes, until set. Cool on wire racks.

4. In bowl, stir 1 cup of the confectioners' sugar with 3½ teaspoons water. Transfer to a plastic bag and snip a small corner from bag. Drizzle over cooled cookies; let dry.

5. Beat remaining ½ cup confectioners' sugar and cream cheese until smooth. Beat in chocolate. Transfer to a plastic bag. Snip off corner of bag; fill centers of cookies.

PER COOKIE: 119 calories; 5 g fat (3 g sat.); 1 g protein; 18 g carbohydrate; 1 g fiber; 28 mg sodium; 16 mg cholesterol.

citrus snowflakes

MAKES: 1½ dozen.
PREP: 5 minutes.
BAKE: at 350° for 14 minutes.
DECORATE: 1 hour.

- 1 tube (16 ounces) refrigerated sugar cookie dough
- ¼ cup orange juice
- 1 tablespoon orange zest
- 1¼ cups all-purpose flour
  Royal Icing (recipe page 292)

1. Heat oven to 350°. Beat cookie dough, orange juice and zest. Stir in flour (dough will be soft). Generously sprinkle flour on countertop.

2. Divide dough in half, then roll one half to ¼-inch thickness. Cut out shapes with snowflake cutter. Transfer to baking sheets. Repeat with remaining dough, dusting with flour as needed.

3. Bake at 350° for 14 minutes. Cool on racks.

4. Prepare Royal Icing. Spread thinned icing over cookies. Let dry. Place thicker icing into a decorating bag fitted with a small round tip. Pipe lines and dots decoratively on all cookies; let dry.

PER COOKIE: 209 calories; 6 g fat (2 g sat.); 3 g protein; 37 g carbohydrate; 0 g fiber; 125 mg sodium; 8 mg cholesterol.

Gingerbread Family
(Recipe page 301)

Sugar & Spice

It's never been easier to bake up a delicious assortment of holiday cookies—and just one recipe is all you need. Sweet!

BY **MICHAEL TYRRELL**

PHOTOGRAPHY BY JAMES BAIGRIE

Food styling: Sara Neumeier. Prop styling: Loren Simons.

chocolate-chip shortbread

MAKES: 16 cookies.
PREP: 5 minutes.
REFRIGERATE: 2 hours.
BAKE: at 350° for 27 to 30 minutes.

To **basic sugar cookie dough** (recipe page 299), mix in **½ cup mini semisweet chocolate chips.** Form into one disk and refrigerate for 2 hours. Press into a 9-inch round fluted nonstick tart pan. Score into 16 pie-shaped wedges without cutting completely through dough. Bake at 350° for 27 to 30 minutes. Cool and remove side of pan. Just before serving, melt **3 tablespoons seedless raspberry preserves** and drizzle over top of tart. Cut into 16 wedges.

PER COOKIE: 179 calories; 8 g fat (5 g sat.); 2 g protein; 25 g carbohydrate; 1 g fiber; 36 mg sodium; 28 mg cholesterol.

jumbo cherry-chunk cookies

MAKES: 15 jumbo cookies.
PREP: 15 minutes. **REFRIGERATE:** 2 hours.
BAKE: at 350° for 18 minutes.

To **basic sugar cookie dough** (recipe below left), add **¼ cup cocoa powder** to flour mixture. Add **½ cup (1 stick) unsalted butter**, and add **½ teaspoon cherry extract** when adding the vanilla. Stir in **6 ounces semisweet chocolate chunks, ½ cup cherry-flavored sweetened dried cranberries and ½ cup chopped walnuts.** Refrigerate for 2 hours. With a measuring cup or ice cream scoop, spoon ¼-cup mounds onto 2 ungreased baking sheets. Gently press down with palm of your hand into 3-inch disk. Bake at 350° for 18 minutes until set. Cool on sheet 3 minutes. Gently remove to cooling rack to cool completely. Wrap in cellophane bags and tie with holiday ribbon, if desired.

PER SERVING: 288 calories; 18 g fat (10 g sat.); 4 g protein; 32 g carbohydrate; 2 g fiber; 40 mg sodium; 46 mg cholesterol.

basic sugar cookie dough

MAKES: 3 dozen cookies. **PREP:** 15 minutes. **REFRIGERATE:** 4 hours.
BAKE: at 350° for 10 to 12 minutes.

- 1½   cups all-purpose flour
- ½   teaspoon baking powder
- ⅛   teaspoon salt
- ½   cup (1 stick) unsalted butter, softened
- ¾   cup sugar
- 1   egg
- ¾   teaspoon vanilla extract
  White nonpareils for decorating (optional)

1. In a medium-size bowl, whisk together the flour, baking powder and salt. Set aside.
2. In a large bowl, beat butter and sugar until smooth, about 2 minutes. Beat in the egg and vanilla. On low speed, beat in the flour mixture until just combined. Divide the dough in half and form each half into a disk. Wrap in plastic wrap and refrigerate 4 hours or overnight.

3. Heat oven to 350°. On a lightly floured surface, roll out one disk to ¼-inch thickness. Cut into bells using a 2-inch bell cookie cutter. Place on an ungreased baking sheet. Sprinkle with white nonpareils, gently pressing to adhere. Bake for 10 to 12 minutes until lightly golden around edges. Remove cookies to wire racks to cool completely.
4. Repeat with remaining half of dough. Gather scraps and refrigerate. Reroll and cut into additional bells. Bake and cool as directed. When completely cool, serve or store in airtight container up to 2 weeks.

PER COOKIE: 60 calories; 3 g fat (2 g sat.); 1 g protein; 8 g carbohydrate; 0 g fiber; 16 mg sodium; 13 mg cholesterol.

spice crackles

MAKES: 24 cookies. **PREP:** 15 minutes.
REFRIGERATE: 1 hour.
BAKE: at 350° for 14 minutes.

To **basic sugar cookie dough**
(recipe page 299), whisk
**2 teaspoons pumpkin pie spice,
2 teaspoons cocoa powder and
1¼ teaspoons baking soda** into
flour mixture. Refrigerate dough
1 hour. Shape tablespoonfuls
into 1-inch disks and place on
ungreased baking sheets.
Sprinkle each with about
**1 teaspoon colored sanding
sugar.** Bake at 350° for
14 minutes. Transfer cookies
to wire rack; cool.

PER SERVING: 106 calories;
4 g fat (3 g sat.); 1 g protein;
17 g carbohydrate; 0 g fiber;
90 mg sodium; 19 mg cholesterol.

orange sandwiches

MAKES: 16 sandwiches.
PREP: 10 minutes. **REFRIGERATE:** 4 hours.
BAKE: at 350° for 12 minutes.

To **basic sugar cookie dough** (recipe page 299), add **1 tablespoon grated orange zest** and **½ teaspoon orange extract.** Divide into 2 disks and refrigerate for at least 4 hours. On a lightly floured work surface roll out one disk to ³⁄₁₆-inch thickness. Cut into rounds using a 2-inch cutter. Place on ungreased baking sheet. Bake at 350° for 12 minutes until lightly golden around edges. Remove cookies to wire rack to cool completely. Repeat with remaining dough. Gather scraps and refrigerate. Reroll, cut into additional rounds and bake. Spread half of the rounds with **1 teaspoon orange marmalade** each. Place remaining rounds over marmalade to form a sandwich. Melt **1 cup semi-sweet chocolate chips.** Dip one side of sandwiches in chocolate; place on a waxed paper-lined baking sheet. Allow chocolate to set at room temperature.

PER SANDWICH: 223 calories; 10 g fat (6 g sat.); 2 g protein; 32 g carbohydrate; 1 g fiber; 40 mg sodium; 29 mg cholesterol.

gingerbread family

MAKES: 16 cookies. **PREP:** 15 minutes. **REFRIGERATE:** 4 hours.
BAKE: at 350° for 14 minutes.

To **basic sugar cookie dough** (recipe page 299), add **1 tablespoon ground ginger, 2 teaspoons cocoa powder and ½ teaspoon cinnamon** to flour mixture. Halve dough and form into 2 disks. Refrigerate 4 hours.

On a lightly floured work surface, roll out one disk to ¼ inch thickness. Using large gingerbread cookie cutters, cut into 2 figures. Place on ungreased baking sheet. Repeat with small cookie cutters and other half of dough. Gather scraps and refrigerate. Reroll to form total of 2 large cookies and 14 small cookies. Bake for 10 to 14 minutes until lightly golden around edges. Remove cookies to wire racks to cool completely. **Make royal icing** (recipe page 292). Decorate cookies as desired.

PER SERVING: 298 calories; 11 g fat (7 g sat.); 4 g protein; 47 g carbohydrate; 1 g fiber; 65 mg sodium; 50 mg cholesterol.

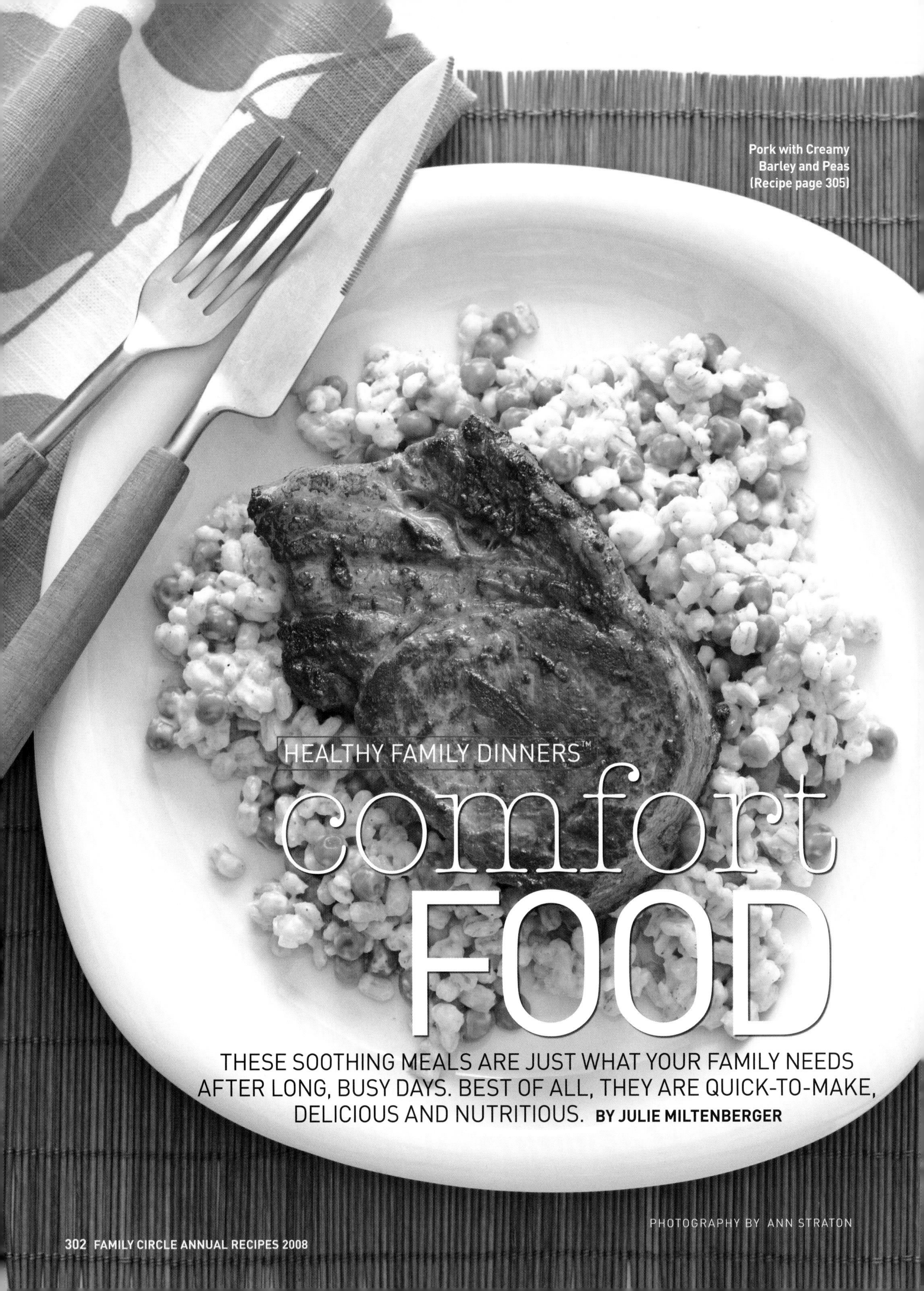

Pork with Creamy
Barley and Peas
(Recipe page 305)

HEALTHY FAMILY DINNERS™

comfort
FOOD

THESE SOOTHING MEALS ARE JUST WHAT YOUR FAMILY NEEDS
AFTER LONG, BUSY DAYS. BEST OF ALL, THEY ARE QUICK-TO-MAKE,
DELICIOUS AND NUTRITIOUS. **BY JULIE MILTENBERGER**

PHOTOGRAPHY BY ANN STRATON

asian beef and noodles

MAKES: 4 servings. **PREP:** 15 minutes. **COOK:** 12 minutes.

1 tablespoon vegetable oil
1 pound lean ground beef
1 small sweet green pepper, seeded and thinly sliced
4 scallions, trimmed and thinly sliced
2 tablespoons finely chopped ginger
1 clove garlic, finely chopped
¼ teaspoon red pepper flakes
1 teaspoon sugar
3 tablespoons stir-fry sauce
3 tablespoons lime juice

8 ounces fiber- and calcium-enriched thin spaghetti (such as Ronzoni Smart Taste)

1. Bring a large pot of lightly salted water to a boil.
2. In large skillet, heat oil over medium-high heat. Add beef to skillet and cook for 6 minutes or until no longer pink.
3. Add sweet pepper, scallions, ginger, garlic, red pepper and sugar to skillet; cook for 5 minutes, stirring occasionally.

Turn off heat and stir in stir-fry sauce and lime juice.
4. While beef is cooking, prepare spaghetti following package directions. Drain and add to skillet with beef mixture. Toss to combine.

PER SERVING: 404 calories; 10 g fat (3 g sat.); 32 g protein; 52 g carbohydrate; 7 g fiber; 481 mg sodium; 70 mg cholesterol.

Food styling: Liza Jernow. Prop styling: Leslie Siegel.

mushroom and broccoli omelet

MAKES: 4 servings. **PREP:** 10 minutes. **COOK:** 7 minutes.

4 **eggs**
8 **egg whites**
1 **package (3.5 ounces) crumbled reduced fat feta cheese**
2 **tablespoons half and half**
½ **teaspoon salt**
½ **teaspoon black pepper**
 Pinch nutmeg
1 **teaspoon vegetable oil**
1 **cup mushrooms, chopped**
1 **cup frozen chopped broccoli, thawed**
4 **cups salad greens**
3 **tablespoons reduced-fat red wine vinaigrette**

1. In a small bowl, whisk together eggs, egg whites, half and half, ¼ teaspoon each of the salt and pepper and the nutmeg; set aside.

2. Heat oil in a medium-size skillet over medium-high heat. Add mushrooms to skillet and sprinkle with remaining ¼ teaspoon each salt and pepper. Cook mushrooms for 2 minutes; stir in broccoli and cook another 2 minutes. Remove skillet from heat. Scrape mushroom mixture into a bowl and set side.

3. Place skillet back over medium heat and coat generously with nonstick cooking spray. When pan is hot, pour ⅔ cup of the egg mixture into skillet.

Sprinkle ¼ cup of the mushroom mixture and a quarter of the feta down the left side of the egg mixture. Cook for 2 minutes. Using a rubber spatula, fold right side of egg over mushroom and cheese filling. Cook for 1 more minute. Carefully slide onto plate and keep warm while preparing others. Repeat procedure for remaining three omelets.

4. In a medium-size bowl, mix salad greens with vinaigrette until well coated. Serve alongside omelets.

PER SERVING: 217 calories; 12 g fat (5 g sat.); 20 g protein; 8 g carbohydrate; 2 g fiber; 965 mg sodium; 223 mg cholesterol.

pork with creamy barley and peas

MAKES: 4 servings. **PREP:** 10 minutes. **COOK:** 14 minutes.

- ¼ cup plus 3 tablespoons light ranch salad dressing
- 4 boneless center cut pork chops (about 1½ pounds total)
- 1 cup quick-cooking barley
- 1 cup frozen peas, thawed
- ¼ teaspoon salt
- ¼ teaspoon black pepper
- ⅛ teaspoon cayenne pepper

1. Place ¼ cup dressing and pork in a resealable bag. Refrigerate at least 1 hour.

2. Remove pork from bag and discard marinade. Heat a large nonstick skillet over medium heat. Cook pork chops 7 minutes, then turn and cook an additional 7 minutes, or until internal temperature registers 150° on an instant-read thermometer.

3. Meanwhile, bring 3 cups water to a boil in a medium-size saucepan. Stir in barley, reduce heat to medium and cook for 8 minutes. Add peas and continue to cook for 2 minutes, then drain and return to pot. Stir in remaining 3 tablespoons ranch dressing, salt, pepper and cayenne. Serve with pork.

PER SERVING: 469 calories; 17 g fat (4 g sat.); 42 g protein; 37 g carbohydrate; 6 g fiber; 526 mg sodium; 115 mg cholesterol.

seafood chowder

MAKES: 6 servings. **PREP:** 15 minutes. **COOK:** 38 minutes.

- 1 tablespoon olive oil
- 1 large onion, chopped
- 1 cup white mushrooms, chopped
- ¼ teaspoon salt
- ½ teaspoon black pepper
- 2½ cups clam juice
- 2 cups low sodium chicken broth
- 1 medium-size Yukon Gold potato, (about 8 ounces) peeled and cubed
- 2 cups cooked shrimp, tails removed
- 1 cup chopped imitation crab
- ⅔ cup light whipping cream
- 3 cups baby spinach

1. Heat oil in a medium-size nonstick saucepan over medium-high heat. Add onion, mushrooms and ¼ teaspoon each of the salt and pepper to pot; cook, stirring occasionally, for 8 minutes or until softened.

2. Stir in clam juice, broth and potato and bring to a boil. Reduce heat to medium-low and simmer for 20 minutes or until potato is tender.

3. Puree soup in a blender in batches until smooth. Return to pot and stir in remaining ¼ teaspoon pepper, shrimp, crab, light cream and spinach; simmer for 10 minutes. Serve warm.

PER SERVING: 184 calories; 8 g fat (4 g sat.); 15 g protein; 14 g carbohydrate; 2 g fiber; 944 mg sodium; 102 mg cholesterol.

december

sausage and pepper calzones

MAKES: 6 servings. **PREP:** 15 minutes. **COOK:** 9 minutes. **BAKE:** at 450° for 15 minutes.

¾ pound sweet Italian turkey sausage, casings removed
1 medium-size sweet red pepper, seeded and chopped
1 large onion, thinly sliced
1½ teaspoons Italian seasoning
¼ teaspoon black pepper
1¼ cups part-skim shredded mozzarella cheese
¼ cup tomato sauce
2 pounds fresh pizza dough
1½ cups marinara sauce (optional)

1. Heat oven to 450°. Coat a large baking sheet with nonstick cooking spray; set aside.
2. Heat a large nonstick skillet over medium-high heat. Crumble sausage into skillet and add red pepper and onion. Sprinkle with Italian seasoning and black pepper; cook for 9 minutes.
3. Remove skillet from heat; drain off any fat. Stir in tomato sauce and cheese.
4 . Divide dough into 6 pieces, each about 5¼ ounces. On a floured surface, roll each piece into a 7-inch circle. Place a heaping ⅔ cup filling onto one half of each circle. Fold dough over filling; press edges together firmly to seal. Cut a slit through tops and place calzones on prepared baking sheets. Bake at 450° for 15 minutes. Cool slightly before serving. Serve with marinara sauce, if desired.

PER SERVING: 551 calories; 12 g fat (4 g sat.); 28 g protein; 81 g carbohydrate; 4 g fiber; 997 mg sodium; 52 mg cholesterol.

grilled chicken salad wraps

MAKES: 4 servings. **PREP:** 15 minutes. **COOK:** 4 minutes.

½ **cup light mayonnaise**
¼ **cup chopped cilantro**
4 **scallions, trimmed and thinly sliced**
1 **small red pepper, seeded and finely chopped**
2 **tablespoons light sour cream**
1 **package (9 ounces) grilled chicken strips (such as Perdue Short Cuts)**
½ **cup reduced-fat shredded Mexican cheese blend**
4 **8-inch whole wheat tortillas**

1. In a large bowl, whisk together mayonnaise, cilantro, scallions, red pepper, and sour cream. Cut the chicken into ½-inch pieces and stir into mayonnaise mixture.

2. Sprinkle tortillas with 2 tablespoons cheese slightly off center of tortilla. Spread heaping ½ cup chicken mixture over cheese; roll up tightly like an envelope (see steps 1 through 4 on page 309).

3. Heat a large nonstick skillet over medium-high heat. Coat wraps with nonstick cooking spray. Place wraps in skillet, seam side down, and cook for 2 minutes or until crisp. Turn over; cook another 2 minutes. Repeat with remaining wraps.

PER BURRITO: 353 calories; 16 g fat (3 g sat.); 20 g protein; 29 g carbohydrate; 3 g fiber; 903 mg sodium; 52 mg cholesterol.

december

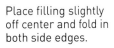

Place filling slightly off center and fold in both side edges.

Fold bottom edge up and over side edges and filling.

Make sure filling stays in place while continuing to roll up burrito.

Continue to roll until burrito is sealed.

cooking **school**

THIS CHRISTMAS, RATHER THAN BAKING DOZENS OF COOKIES FOR FRIENDS, FAMILY AND CO-WORKERS, GIVE THEM A HOMEMADE MIX. IT'S LESS WORK AND MORE ECONOMICAL—BUT JUST AS THOUGHTFUL. **BY JULIE MILTENBERGER**

Chocolate Swirl Cookies: In large bowl, combine ⅔ cup (1½ sticks) melted and cooled butter with 3 eggs and 1 teaspoon vanilla extract. Stir in contents of jar. Drop dough by rounded tablespoons onto baking sheets. Bake at 350° for 13 to 14 minutes. Cool on sheets 1 minute; transfer to rack.

chocolate swirl cookie mix

MAKES: 1 mix in a jar; about 3 dozen cookies. **PREP:** 15 minutes.

2½ cups all-purpose flour
1 teaspoon baking powder
½ teaspoon baking soda
¼ teaspoon salt
½ cup unsweetened cocoa powder
¼ teaspoon ground cinnamon
¾ cup granulated sugar
¾ cup brownulated sugar*
¾ cup swirled chocolate chips

1. Clean and dry a 1-quart reusable plastic or glass canister.
2. In a medium-size bowl, stir together the flour, baking powder, baking soda and salt. For cocoa mixture, spoon 1 cup of the flour mixture into a second bowl and add cocoa powder and cinnamon. Whisk to thoroughly mix.

3. Begin packing jar for gift: Spoon about half the flour mixture into bottom of jar. Use a small spice jar to lightly compress (see illustration, below). Spoon in half the cocoa mixture; compress. Spoon in remaining flour mixture and cocoa mixture, compressing each layer.
4. Top second cocoa layer with granulated sugar and brownulated sugar, compressing slightly. Pour chips over sugar and seal jar.
5. Write baking instructions on a tag (or print out); secure to jar with ribbon.
***Note:** Brownulated sugar can be found in your grocery store's baking section.

PER BAKED COOKIE: 130 calories; 6 g fat
(3 g sat.); 2 g protein; 19 g carbohydrate;
1 g fiber; 53 mg sodium; 28 mg cholesterol.

Spoon half of the flour mixture into your container, then press down gently to flatten.

Use a spice jar to compress each level; don't press too hard or surface will be uneven.

After layering all the dry ingredients use a ribbon to tie baking directions onto the jar.

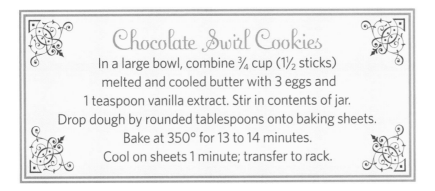

Chocolate Swirl Cookies

In a large bowl, combine ¾ cup (1½ sticks) melted and cooled butter with 3 eggs and 1 teaspoon vanilla extract. Stir in contents of jar. Drop dough by rounded tablespoons onto baking sheets. Bake at 350° for 13 to 14 minutes. Cool on sheets 1 minute; transfer to rack.

Alfredo Pizza
(Recipe page 314)

DURING 2008, WE RECEIVED MANY TASTY RECIPES FROM OUR READERS' HOME KITCHENS. AFTER COOKING, BAKING AND TASTING OUR WAY THROUGH THEM, HERE ARE SOME OF OUR FAVORITES.

sweet potato latkes

MAKES: 18 servings. **PREP:** 15 minutes. **COOK:** 6 minutes.

- 3 medium sweet potatoes, peeled, about 1 pound
- 1 large onion
- 1 tablespoon chili powder
- 2 eggs
- ½ teaspoon salt
- ⅛ teaspoon black pepper
- 3 heaping tablespoons potato starch
- ½ cup vegetable oil
  Sour cream (optional)

1. Fit food processor with shredding disc. Shred sweet potato and place in colander. Shred onion and toss with sweet potato. Drain for 10 minutes. Transfer to a large bowl.
2. Whisk together chili powder, eggs, salt and pepper. Stir into sweet potato-onion mixture. Sift potato starch into the mixture and mix well.
3. In a large nonstick skillet, heat oil over medium-high heat. Place 6 mounds of mixture (about ¼ cup each) into the skillet. Press down lightly. Cook until browned, about 2 to 3 minutes per side (cook in three batches). Drain on a baking sheet lined with paper towels. Sprinkle with salt to taste. Serve with sour cream, if desired.

PER SERVING: 94 calories; 7 g fat (1 g sat.); 1 g protein; 8 g carbohydrate; 1 g fiber; 89 mg sodium; 24 mg cholesterol.

DORRIE BERKOWITZ Whitestone, New York
"Every year I host a large family Hanukkah party. We keep it pretty simple. Cheese, crackers, dips, then the main event—a parade of latkes, including this sweet potato version."

nanny's meatballs

MAKES: 4 servings. **PREP:** 15 minutes. **COOK:** 40 minutes.

- 1¼ pounds lean ground beef
- ½ cup plain bread crumbs
- ¼ cup freshly grated Locatelli cheese
- 1 egg, lightly beaten
- 2 tablespoons dried parsley flakes
- 1 clove garlic, finely chopped
- ½ teaspoon salt
- ½ teaspoon black pepper
- ⅓ cup canola oil
- 1 jar (26 ounces) marinara sauce or 3 cups homemade sauce
- ½ pound of your favorite pasta, such as rigatoni, cooked
  Extra grated cheese (optional)

1. In a large bowl, mix together ground beef, bread crumbs, cheese, egg, parsley flakes, garlic, salt and pepper. Form into 12 meatballs (about ¼ cup mixture each).
2. In a large nonstick skillet, heat oil over medium heat until shimmering slightly. Add meatballs; brown on all sides, 8 to 10 minutes. Remove to a paper-towel-lined baking sheet.
3. Place sauce in a large pot and bring to a simmer over medium-high heat. Add meatballs and simmer, covered, on medium-low heat for 30 minutes. Stir occasionally.
4. Serve over pasta, with additional grated cheese, if desired.

PER SERVING: 932 calories; 49 g fat (13 g sat.); 43 g protein; 78 g carbohydrate; 7 g fiber; 1338 mg sodium; 157 mg cholesterol.

ANN MAZZANOBILE Commack, New York
"I use freshly grated cheese for these meatballs, which makes them even more flavorful."

sweet crispix mix

MAKES: 18 cups. **PREP:** 10 minutes. **COOK:** 5 minutes.
BAKE: at 300° for 15 minutes.

- 1 box (12 ounces) Crispix cereal
- ½ pound pecan halves
- ½ can (11 ounces) deluxe mixed nuts
- 1 cup small pretzels
- 1 cup cheese crackers (such as Cheez-Its)
- 1 cup (2 sticks) butter
- ½ cup light corn syrup
- 2 cups light-brown sugar
- ½ teaspoon baking soda
  Pinch cream of tartar

1. Heat oven to 300°. Spray two baking sheets with nonstick cooking spray.
2. In a large bowl, mix together the cereal, pecans, mixed nuts, pretzels and cheese crackers. Set aside.
3. In a medium-size saucepan, melt the butter over medium-low heat. Stir in the corn syrup and brown sugar. Cook mixture for 5 minutes, stirring continuously. Take off heat and stir in the baking soda and cream of tartar.
4. Carefully pour hot mixture over cereal, stirring with a wooden spoon to coat all of the ingredients. Divide the mixture evenly over both of the baking sheets. Bake at 300° for 15 minutes, stirring twice.
5. Let mixture cool on baking sheets and break apart. Store in plastic bags or sealed containers.

PER SERVING: 421 calories; 25 g fat (8 g sat.); 5 g protein;
67 g carbohydrate; 2 g fiber; 335 mg sodium; 27 mg cholesterol.

CAROL HAVILL Rockford, Ohio
"This recipe is from a former student, but I've made changes over the years. The cheese crackers are my favorite, and the pretzels are my husband's."

alfredo pizza

MAKES: 6 slices. **PREP:** 10 minutes. **BAKE:** at 450° for 15 minutes.

- 1 prepared regular or whole-wheat pizza crust (such as Boboli)
- 1 tablespoon olive oil
- ½ jar (16 ounces) roasted red pepper Alfredo sauce (such as Classico)
- 1 pound grilled chicken, cut into cubes
- 1 green pepper, cored, seeded and diced
- 1½ cups shredded Monterey Jack cheese
- ¼ teaspoon red pepper flakes

1. Heat oven to 450°.
2. Place crust on large baking sheet or pizza pan; brush with oil. Spread the Alfredo sauce over crust. Top with chicken and green pepper. Sprinkle with shredded cheese and red pepper flakes.
3. Bake at 450° for 15 minutes or until bubbly and crust has started to brown. Cool slightly before slicing into six pieces.

PER SERVING: 474 calories; 24 g fat (11 g sat.); 36 g protein;
28 g carbohydrate; 4 g fiber; 858 mg sodium; 137 mg cholesterol.

SUZI WEST Adrian, Michigan
"This is my family's favorite weekend meal. It's easy and goes great with a glass of white wine."

celery and olive salad

MAKES: 2½ cups. **PREP:** 10 minutes. **REFRIGERATE:** 4 hours.

- 2 cups chopped celery, including leaves
- ½ cup chopped pitted green olives
- 2 tablespoons olive oil
- 2 tablespoons white wine vinegar
- 1 teaspoon dried oregano
- 1 teaspoon garlic powder
- ½ teaspoon salt
- ¼ teaspoon black pepper

1. In a medium-size glass or plastic bowl, stir together celery, olives, olive oil, vinegar, oregano, garlic powder, salt and pepper until well combined. Cover and refrigerate for at least 4 hours or overnight.
2. Serve as an accompaniment to fish or meat.

PER SERVING: 38 calories; 4 g fat (0 g sat.); 0 g protein; 1 g carbohydrate; 0 g fiber; 295 mg sodium; 0 mg cholesterol.

ARLETTA SLOCUM Venice, Florida
"This is always served at our favorite Italian restaurant. They would not part with the recipe so I created my own."

orange streusel coffee cake

MAKES: 8 servings. **PREP:** 15 minutes.
BAKE: at 375° for 45 minutes.

- 2 cups all-purpose flour
- ½ cup sugar
- 2 teaspoons baking powder
- ½ teaspoon salt
- 1 tablespoon orange zest
- ½ cup milk
- ½ cup orange juice
- ⅓ cup corn oil
- 1 egg, lightly beaten
- ½ teaspoon vanilla extract
- ½ cup sugar
- ¼ cup all-purpose flour
- 2 tablespoons butter, cut into small pieces
  Confectioners' sugar for dusting, optional

1. Heat oven to 375°. Spray a 9-inch cake pan with nonstick cooking spray.
2. In a large bowl, whisk together flour, sugar, baking powder and salt. Stir in the orange zest. Make a well in the flour mixture. Pour in the milk, orange juice, corn oil, egg and vanilla. Stir until just combined and all dry ingredients are moistened. Turn into prepared pan.
3. In a small bowl, mix together sugar, flour and butter until the consistency of cornmeal. Sprinkle mixture evenly over the cake batter.
4. Bake at 375° for 40 to 45 minutes or until a toothpick inserted in the center comes out clean. Allow to cool completely in pan. Dust with confectioners' sugar, if desired, before slicing and serving.

PER SERVING: 357 calories; 13 g fat (3 g sat.); 5 g protein; 55 g carbohydrate; 1 g fiber; 272 mg sodium; 35 mg cholesterol.

MILDRED PETERS Pleasant Valley, New York
"My family loves this light citrus cake for breakfast, but it also makes a great quick dessert."

spinach artichoke dip

MAKES: 4 cups. **PREP:** 15 minutes. **COOK:** 9 minutes.
BAKE: at 350° for 10 minutes.

- 2 tablespoons unsalted butter
- 1 medium onion, peeled and chopped
- 6 cloves garlic, chopped
- 1 package (10 ounces) frozen chopped spinach, thawed and squeezed dry
- 1 jar (6 ounces) marinated artichokes, drained and chopped
- 1 package (8 ounces) cream cheese, cut into cubes
- ½ pint sour cream
- 1½ cups shredded sharp cheddar cheese
- ½ cup grated Parmesan cheese
- 1 teaspoon paprika
- 1 teaspoon black pepper
- ½ teaspoon salt
- ¼ teaspoon red pepper flakes
  Tortilla chips or crackers, for serving

1. Heat oven to 350°.
2. In a large skillet, melt butter over medium heat. Add onion and cook for about 8 minutes, stirring occasionally, until golden. Add garlic and cook for about 1 minute. Stir in spinach, artichokes, cream cheese, sour cream, 1 cup of the cheddar cheese, the Parmesan, paprika, pepper, salt and red pepper flakes. Stir well.
3. Place dip in an oven-proof 2-quart dish and top with remaining ½ cup of cheddar cheese. Bake at 350° for 10 minutes or until warmed through. Serve with chips or crackers on the side.

PER SERVING: 171 calories; 15 g fat (9 g sat.); 6 g protein; 4 g carbohydrate; 1 g fiber; 275 mg sodium; 38 mg cholesterol.

STACI MORRISSEY Whitehall, Pennsylvania
"This dip can easily be doubled for a crowd. I made it recently, and it was the hit of the party."

meal-in-one meatloaf

MAKES: 8 servings. **PREP:** 15 minutes. **BAKE:** at 375° for 1 hour.

- 1½ pounds ground beef
- 1 cup Saltine cracker crumbs
- 1 medium onion, peeled and diced
- 1 can (10¾ ounces) condensed tomato soup
- 1 egg
- ½ teaspoon salt
- ½ teaspoon ground black pepper
- 6 medium potatoes (about 1¾ pounds) peeled and cut into ⅛-inch slices
- 1 can (15¼ ounces) corn kernels, drained

1. Heat oven to 375°.
2. In a large bowl, combine ground beef, cracker crumbs, ½ of the onion, ⅔ cup of soup, the egg and ½ teaspoon *each* salt and pepper.
3. Lightly grease a 9 x 9-inch baking dish. Layer the potatoes and remaining onion, salt and pepper in two layers. Spoon the corn over the potatoes.
4. Evenly spread the meat loaf mixture over the corn. Top with the remaining tomato soup. Cover with foil and bake at 375° for 1 hour. Cool slightly before cutting.

PER SERVING: 403 calories; 19 g fat (7 g sat.); 20 g protein; 38 g carbohydrate; 3 g fiber; 664 mg sodium; 87 mg cholesterol.

MARY BASER Norfork, Arkansas
"I adapted this from my granny's recipe. Round it out with salad and rolls and you have an easy dinner."

cajun pasta

MAKES: 6 servings. **PREP:** 20 minutes. **COOK:** 35 minutes.

- 2 tablespoons olive oil
- ¾ pound boneless, skinless chicken breasts, cut into 1-inch pieces
- ½ pound spicy Italian sausage, sliced
- ½ pound asparagus, cut into 1-inch pieces
- 1 medium onion, cut into 1-inch pieces
- 1 medium bell pepper, cored and seeded, cut into 1-inch pieces
- 1 small zucchini or summer squash, cut into 1-inch pieces
- 2 cans (14½ ounces each) diced tomatoes with jalapeños
- 2 cloves garlic, peeled and chopped fine
- 1 teaspoon dried oregano
- ½ teaspoon paprika
- ½ teaspoon black pepper
- ½ pound linguine, cooked
  Grated Parmesan cheese (optional)

1. Heat olive oil in a large skillet. Add the chicken and the sausage; cook for about 5 minutes, turning once.
2. Add the asparagus, onion, bell pepper, zucchini, diced tomatoes, garlic, oregano, paprika and black pepper. Stir well.
3. Bring to a boil. Reduce heat to medium and simmer for about 30 minutes or until all the vegetables are tender. Stir occasionally.
4. Toss with cooked linguine. Serve with cheese, if desired.

PER SERVING: 430 calories; 17 g fat (6 g sat.); 28 g protein; 42 g carbohydrate; 5 g fiber; 794 mg sodium; 58 mg cholesterol.

CASEY VAN GHEEM Kansas City, Missouri
"If your family doesn't like spicy foods, use tomatoes without jalapeños and sweet sausage. Serve over whole-wheat pasta to make it even healthier."

chewy chocolate chip cookies

MAKES: 8 dozen cookies. **PREP:** 5 minutes. **STAND:** 1 hour.
BAKE: at 350° for 10 minutes per batch.

- 3 eggs
- 1 teaspoon vanilla extract
- 1 cup raisins
- 2½ cups all-purpose flour
- 2 teaspoons baking soda
- 1 teaspoon salt
- 1 teaspoon ground cinnamon
- 1 cup (2 sticks) margarine
- 1 cup granulated sugar
- 1 cup light-brown sugar
- 2 cups oatmeal, not quick cooking
- 1 cup semisweet chocolate chips

1. Heat oven to 350°.
2. In a medium bowl, whisk together the eggs, vanilla extract and raisins. Cover and allow to stand for 1 hour.
3. In a large bowl, whisk together the flour, baking soda, salt and cinnamon.
4. In another large bowl, beat the margarine and sugars together until completely combined. On low speed, gradually beat in the flour mixture. Add the egg mixture and mix until combined. Stir in the oatmeal and the chocolate chips.
5. Drop by heaping teaspoonfuls onto ungreased baking sheets. Bake at 350° for 8 to 10 minutes, until set but still slightly soft. Cool 2 minutes on the sheets and then remove to a wire rack to cool completely. Cool cookie sheets before repeating with remaining dough.

PER SERVING: 74 calories; 3 g fat (1 g sat.); 1 g protein; 11 g carbohydrate; 1 g fiber; 76 mg sodium; 7 mg cholesterol.

CYNDY WHITE Atikokan, Ontario
"My husband takes pails of these with him on hunting trips. Everyone loves them, but this is the first time I'm sharing the recipe."

index

S

In-a-Pinch Substitutions

It can happen to the best of us: Halfway through a recipe,
you find you're completely out of a key ingredient. Here's what to do:

Recipe Calls For:	You May Substitute:
1 square unsweetened chocolate	3 Tbs unsweetened cocoa powder + 1 Tbs butter/margarine
1 cup cake flour	1 cup less 2 Tbs all-purpose flour
2 Tbs flour (for thickening)	1 Tbs cornstarch
1 tsp baking powder	$\frac{1}{4}$ tsp baking soda + $\frac{1}{2}$ tsp cream of tartar + $\frac{1}{4}$ tsp cornstarch
1 cup corn syrup	1 cup sugar + $\frac{1}{4}$ cup additional liquid used in recipe
1 cup milk	$\frac{1}{2}$ cup evaporated milk + $\frac{1}{2}$ cup water
1 cup buttermilk or sour milk	1 Tbs vinegar or lemon juice + enough milk to make 1 cup
1 cup sour cream (for baking)	1 cup plain yogurt
1 cup firmly packed brown sugar	1 cup sugar + 2 Tbs molasses
1 tsp lemon juice	$\frac{1}{4}$ tsp vinegar (not balsamic)
$\frac{1}{4}$ cup chopped onion	1 Tbs instant minced
1 clove garlic	$\frac{1}{4}$ tsp garlic powder
2 cups tomato sauce	$\frac{3}{4}$ cup tomato paste + 1 cup water
1 Tbs prepared mustard	1 tsp dry mustard + 1 Tbs water

How to Know What You Need

Making a shopping list based on a recipe can be tricky if you don't know
how many tomatoes yields 3 cups chopped. Our handy translations:

When the Recipe Calls For:	You Need:
4 cups shredded cabbage	1 small cabbage
1 cup grated raw carrot	1 large carrot
2 1/2 cups sliced carrots	1 pound raw carrots
4 cups cooked cut fresh green beans	1 pound beans
1 cup chopped onion	1 large onion
4 cups sliced raw potatoes	4 medium-size potatoes
1 cup chopped sweet pepper	1 large pepper
1 cup chopped tomato	1 large tomato
2 cups canned tomatoes	16 oz can
4 cups sliced apples	4 medium-size apples
1 cup mashed banana	3 medium-size bananas
1 tsp grated lemon rind	1 medium-size lemon
2 Tbs lemon juice	1 medium-size lemon
4 tsp grated orange rind	1 medium-size orange
1 cup orange juice	3 medium-size oranges
4 cups sliced peaches	8 medium-size peaches
2 cups sliced strawberries	1 pint
1 cup soft bread crumbs	2 slices fresh bread
1 cup bread cubes	2 slices fresh bread
2 cups shredded Swiss or Cheddar cheese	8 oz cheese
1 cup egg whites	6 or 7 large eggs
1 egg white	2 tsp egg white powder + 2 Tbs water
4 cups chopped walnuts or pecans	1 pound shelled